PRINCIPLES OF BANKING: UTILITY AND ECONOMY

PRINCIPLES OF BANKING: UTILITY AND ECONOMY

Dataram Joshi

CYBER TECH PUBLICATIONS
4264/3, Ansari Road, Daryaganj, New Delhi-110002 (India)
Ph.: 011-23244078. Fax: 011-23280028
E-Mail: cyberpublicationsdelhi@yahoo.com

PRINCIPLES OF BANKING: UTILITY AND ECONOMY

Dataram Joshi

First Edition 2009

Published by :

G.S. Rawat for **Cyber Tech Publications**
4264/3, Ansari Road, Daryaganj, New Delhi-110002 (India)
Ph.: 011-23244078. Fax: 011-23280028
E-Mail: cyberpublicationsdelhi@yahoo.com

Printed at : **Amit Enterprises, Maujpur, Delhi, (9810878184)**

Preface

The abundance or scantiness of this supply too seems to depend more upon the former of those two circumstances than upon the latter. Among the savage nations of hunters and fishers, every individual who is able to work, is more or less employed in useful labour, and endeavours to provide, as well as he can, the necessaries and conveniencies of life, for himself, or such of his family or tribe as are either too old, or too young, or too infirm to go a hunting and fishing. Such nations, however, are so miserably poor, that from mere want, they are frequently reduced, or, at least, think themselves reduced, to the necessity sometimes of directly destroying, and sometimes of abandoning their infants, their old people, and those afflicted with lingering diseases, to perish with hunger, or to be devoured by wild beasts. Among civilized and thriving nations, on the contrary, though a great number of people do not labour at all, many of whom consume the produce of ten times, frequently of a hundred times more labour than the greater part of those who work; yet the produce of the whole labour of the society is so great, that all are often abundantly supplied, and a workman, even of the lowest and poorest order, if he is frugal and industrious, may enjoy a greater share of the necessaries and conveniencies of life than it is possible for any savage to acquire.

The causes- of this improvement, in the productive powers of labour, and the order, according to which its produce is naturally distributed- among the different ranks and conditions of men in the society, make the subject of the First Book of this Inquiry.

—*Author*

CONTENTS

1

Core Principles for Effective Banking Supervision

Weaknesses in the banking system of a country, whether developing or developed, can threaten financial stability both within that country and internationally. The need to improve the strength of financial systems has attracted growing international concern. The Communiqué issued at the close of the Lyon G-7 Summit in June 1996 called for action in this domain. Several official bodies, including the Basle Committee on Banking Supervision, the Bank for International Settlements, the International Monetary Fund and the World Bank, have recently been examining ways to strengthen financial stability throughout the world.

The Basle Committee on Banking Supervision has been working in this field for many years, both directly and through its many contacts with banking supervisors in every part of the world. In the last year and a half, it has been examining how best to expand its efforts aimed at strengthening prudential supervision in all countries by building on its relationships with countries outside the G-10 as well as on its earlier work to enhance prudential supervision in its member countries. In particular, the Committee has prepared two documents for release:

a comprehensive set of Core Principles for effective banking supervision (The Basle Core Principles) (attached); and,

a Compendium (to be updated periodically) of the existing Basle Committee recommendations, guidelines and standards most of which are cross-referenced in the Core Principles document.

Both documents have been endorsed by the G-10 central bank Governors. They were submitted to the G-7 and G-10 Finance Ministers in preparation for the June 1997 Denver Summit in the hope that they would provide a useful mechanism for strengthening financial stability in all countries.

In developing the Principles, the Basle Committee has worked closely with non-G-10 supervisory authorities. The document has been prepared in a group containing representatives from the Basle Committee and from Chile, China, the Czech Republic, Hong Kong, Mexico, Russia and Thailand. Nine other countries (Argentina, Brazil, Hungary, India, Indonesia, Korea, Malaysia, Poland and Singapore) were also closely associated with the work. The drafting of the Principles benefited moreover from broad consultation with a larger group of individual supervisors, both directly and through the regional supervisory groups.

The Basle Core Principles comprise twenty-five basic Principles that need to be in place for a supervisory system to be effective. The Principles relate to:

Preconditions for effective banking supervision-Principle 1

Licensing and structure-Principles 2 to 5

Prudential regulations and requirements-Principles 6 to 15

Methods of ongoing banking supervision-Principles 16 to 20

Information requirements-Principle 21

Formal powers of supervisors-Principle 22, and

Cross-border banking-Principles 23 to 25.

In addition to the Principles themselves, the document contains explanations of the various methods supervisors can use to implement them.

National agencies should apply the Principles in the supervision of all banking organisations within their jurisdictions. The Principles are minimum requirements and in many cases may need to be supplemented by other measures designed to address particular conditions and risks in the financial systems of individual countries.

The Basle Core Principles are intended to serve as a basic reference for supervisory and other public authorities in all countries and internationally. It will be for national supervisory authorities, many of which are actively seeking to strengthen their current supervisory regime, to use the attached document to review their existing supervisory arrangements and to initiate a programme designed to address any deficiencies as quickly as is practical within their legal authority.

The Principles have been designed to be verifiable by supervisors, regional supervisory groups, and the market at large. The Basle Committee will play a role, together with other interested organisations, in monitoring the progress made by individual countries in implementing the Principles. It is suggested that the IMF, the World Bank and other interested organisations use the Principles in assisting individual countries to strengthen their supervisory arrangements in connection with work aimed at promoting overall macroeconomic and financial stability. Implementation of the Principles will be reviewed at the International Conference of Banking Supervisors in October 1998 and biennially thereafter.

Supervisory authorities throughout the world are encouraged to endorse the Basle Core Principles. The members of the Basle Committee and the sixteen other supervisory agencies that have participated in their drafting all agree with the content of the document.

The chairpersons of the regional supervisory groups are supportive of the Basle Committee's efforts and are ready to promote the endorsement of the Core Principles among their membership. Discussions are in progress to define the role the regional groups can play in securing the endorsement of the Principles and in monitoring implementation by their members.

The Basle Committee believes that achieving consistency with the Core Principles by every country will be a significant step in the process of improving financial stability domestically and internationally. The speed with which this objective will be achieved will vary. In many countries, substantive changes in the legislative framework and in the powers of supervisors will be necessary because many supervisory authorities do not at present have the statutory authority to implement all of the Principles. In such cases, the Basle Committee believes it is essential that national legislators give urgent consideration to the changes necessary to ensure that the Principles can be applied in all material respects.

10. The Basle Committee will continue to pursue its standard-setting activities in key risk areas and in key elements of banking supervision as it has done in documents such as those reproduced in the Compendium. The Basle Core Principles will serve as a reference point for future work to be done by the Committee and, where appropriate, in cooperation with non-G-10 supervisors and their regional groups. The Committee stands ready to encourage work at the national level to implement the Principles in conjunction with other supervisory bodies and interested parties. Finally, the Committee is committed to strengthening its interaction with supervisors from non-G-10 countries and intensifying its considerable investment in technical assistance and training.

LIST OF CORE PRINCIPLES

Preconditions for Effective Banking Supervision

An effective system of banking supervision will have clear responsibilities and objectives for each agency involved in the supervision of banking organisations. Each such agency should possess operational independence and adequate resources. A suitable legal framework for banking supervision is also necessary, including provisions relating to authorisation of banking organisations and their ongoing supervision; powers to address compliance with laws as well as safety and soundness concerns; and legal protection for supervisors. Arrangements for sharing information between supervisors and protecting the confidentiality of such information should be in place.

Licensing and Structure

The permissible activities of institutions that are licensed and subject to supervision as banks must be clearly defined, and the use of the word "bank" in names should be controlled as far as possible.

The licensing authority must have the right to set criteria and reject applications for establishments that do not meet the standards set. The licensing process, at a minimum, should consist of an assessment of the banking organisation's ownership structure, directors and senior management, its operating plan and internal controls, and its projected financial condition, including its capital base; where the proposed owner or parent organisation is a foreign bank, the prior consent of its home country supervisor should be obtained.

Banking supervisors must have the authority to review and reject any proposals to transfer significant ownership or controlling interests in existing banks to other parties.

Banking supervisors must have the authority to establish criteria for reviewing major acquisitions or investments by a bank and ensuring that corporate affiliations or structures do not expose the bank to undue risks or hinder effective supervision.

Prudential Regulations and Requirements

Banking supervisors must set prudent and appropriate minimum capital adequacy requirements for all banks. Such requirements should reflect the risks that the banks undertake, and must define the components of capital, bearing in mind their ability to absorb losses. At least for internationally active banks, these requirements must not be less than those established in the Basle Capital Accord and its amendments.

An essential part of any supervisory system is the evaluation of a bank's policies, practices and procedures related to the granting of loans and making of investments and the ongoing management of the loan and investment portfolios.

Banking supervisors must be satisfied that banks establish and adhere to adequate policies, practices and procedures for evaluating the quality of assets and the adequacy of loan loss provisions and loan loss reserves.

Banking supervisors must be satisfied that banks have management information systems that enable management to identify concentrations within the portfolio and supervisors must set prudential limits to restrict bank exposures to single borrowers or groups of related borrowers.

In order to prevent abuses arising from connected lending, banking supervisors must have in place requirements that banks lend to related companies and individuals on an arm's-length basis, that such extensions of credit are effectively monitored, and that other appropriate steps are taken to control or mitigate the risks. Banking supervisors must be satisfied that banks have adequate policies and procedures for identifying, monitoring and controlling country risk and transfer risk in their international lending and investment activities, and for maintaining appropriate reserves against such risks.

Banking supervisors must be satisfied that banks have in place systems that accurately measure, monitor and adequately control market risks; supervisors should have powers to impose specific limits and/or a specific capital charge on market risk exposures, if warranted.

Banking supervisors must be satisfied that banks have in place a comprehensive risk management process (including appropriate board and senior management oversight) to identify, measure, monitor and control all other material risks and, where appropriate, to hold capital against these risks.

Banking supervisors must determine that banks have in place internal controls that are adequate for the nature and scale of their business. These should include clear arrangements for delegating authority and responsibility; separation of the functions that involve committing the bank, paying away its funds, and accounting for its assets and liabilities; reconciliation of these processes; safeguarding its assets; and appropriate independent internal or external audit and compliance functions to test adherence to these controls as well as applicable laws and regulations.

Banking supervisors must determine that banks have adequate policies, practices and procedures in place, including strict "know-your-customer" rules, that promote high ethical and professional standards in the financial sector and prevent the bank being used, intentionally or unintentionally, by criminal elements.

Methods of Ongoing Banking Supervision

An effective banking supervisory system should consist of some form of both on-site and off-site supervision.

Banking supervisors must have regular contact with bank management and thorough understanding of the institution's operations. Banking supervisors must have a means of collecting, reviewing and analysing prudential reports and statistical returns from banks on a solo and consolidated basis. Banking supervisors must have a means of independent validation of supervisory information either through on-site examinations or use of external auditors. An essential element of banking supervision is the ability of the supervisors to supervise the banking group on a consolidated basis.

Information Requirements

Banking supervisors must be satisfied that each bank maintains adequate records drawn up in accordance with consistent accounting policies and practices that enable the supervisor to obtain a true and fair view of the financial condition of the bank and the profitability of its business, and that the bank publishes on a regular basis financial statements that fairly reflect its condition.

Formal Powers of Supervisors

Banking supervisors must have at their disposal adequate supervisory measures to bring about timely corrective action when banks fail to meet prudential requirements (such as minimum capital adequacy ratios), when there are regulatory violations, or where depositors are threatened in any other way. In extreme circumstances, this should include the ability to revoke the banking licence or recommend its revocation.

Cross-border Banking

Banking supervisors must practise global consolidated supervision over their internationally-active banking organisations, adequately monitoring and applying appropriate prudential norms to all aspects of the business conducted by these banking organisations worldwide, primarily at their foreign branches, joint ventures and subsidiaries.

A key component of consolidated supervision is establishing contact and information exchange with the various other supervisors involved, primarily host country supervisory authorities. Banking supervisors must require the local operations of foreign banks to be conducted to the same high standards as are required of domestic institutions and must have powers to share information needed by the home country supervisors of those banks for the purpose of carrying out consolidated supervision.

INTRODUCTION

Effective supervision of banking organisations is an essential component of a strong economic environment in that the banking system plays a central role in making payments and mobilising and distributing savings. The task of supervision is to ensure that banks operate in a safe and sound manner and that they hold capital and reserves sufficient to support the risks that arise in their business. Strong and effective banking supervision provides a public good that may not be fully provided in the marketplace and, along with effective macroeconomic policy, is critical to financial stability in any country. While the cost of banking supervision is indeed high, the cost of poor supervision has proved to be even higher. In drawing up these core principles for effective banking supervision the following precepts are fundamental:

the key objective of supervision is to maintain stability and confidence in the financial system, thereby reducing the risk of loss to depositors and other creditors;

supervisors should encourage and pursue market discipline by encouraging good corporate governance (through an appropriate structure and set of responsibilities for a bank's board of directors and senior management) and enhancing market transparency and surveillance;

in order to carry out its tasks effectively, a supervisor must have operational independence, the means and powers to gather information both on and off site, and the authority to enforce its decisions;

supervisors must understand the nature of the business undertaken by banks and ensure to the extent possible that the risks incurred by banks are being adequately managed;

effective banking supervision requires that the risk profile of individual banks be assessed and supervisory resources allocated accordingly;

supervisors must ensure that banks have resources appropriate to undertake risks, including adequate capital, sound management, and effective control systems and accounting records; and close cooperation with other supervisors is essential, particularly where the operations of banking organisations cross national boundaries.

Banking supervision should foster an efficient and competitive banking system that is responsive to the public's need for good quality financial services at a reasonable cost. Generally, it should be recognised that there is a trade-off between the level of protection that supervision provides and the cost of financial intermediation. The lower the tolerance of risk to banks and the financial system, the more intrusive and costly supervision is likely to be, eventually having an adverse effect on innovation and resource allocation. Supervision cannot, and should not, provide an assurance that banks will not fail.

In a market economy, failures are a part of risk-taking. The way in which failures are handled, and their costs borne, is in large part a political matter involving decisions on whether, and the extent to which, public funds should be committed to supporting the banking system. Such matters cannot therefore always be entirely the responsibility of banking supervisors; however, supervisors should have in place adequate arrangements for resolving problem bank situations.

There are certain infrastructure elements that are required to support effective supervision. Where such elements do not exist, supervisors should seek to persuade government to put them in place (and may have a role in designing and developing them).

In some countries responsibility for licensing banks is separate from the process of ongoing supervision. It is clearly essential that, wherever the responsibility lies, the licensing process establishes the same high standards as the process of ongoing supervision which is the main focus of this paper. Section III therefore discusses some principles and issues that should be addressed in the licensing process.

The core principles of banking supervision set out above and expanded in Sections III-VI of this document will provide the foundation necessary to achieve a sound supervisory system. Local characteristics will need to be taken into account in the specific way in which these standards are implemented. These standards are necessary but may not be sufficient, on their own, in all situations. Supervisory systems should take into account the nature of and risks involved in the local banking market as well as more generally the local infrastructure. Each country should therefore consider to what extent it needs to supplement these standards with additional requirements to address particular risks and general conditions prevailing in its own market. Furthermore, banking supervision is a dynamic function that needs to respond to changes in the marketplace. Consequently supervisors must be prepared to reassess periodically their supervisory policies and practices in the light of new trends or developments. A sufficiently flexible legislative framework is necessary to enable them to do this.

PRECONDITIONS FOR EFFECTIVE BANKING SUPERVISION

Banking supervision is only part of wider arrangements that are needed to promote stability in financial markets. These arrangements include:

1. sound and sustainable macro-economic policies;
2. a well developed public infrastructure;
3. effective market discipline;
4. procedures for efficient resolution of problems in banks; and
5. mechanisms for providing an appropriate level of systemic protection (or public safety net).

Providing sound and sustainable macro-economic policies are not within the competence of banking supervisors. Supervisors, however, will need to react if they perceive that existing policies are undermining the safety and soundness of the banking system. In the absence of sound macro-economic policies, banking supervisors will be faced with a virtually impossible task. Therefore, sound macro-economic policies must be the foundation of a stable financial system.

A well developed public infrastructure needs to cover the following facilities, which, if not adequately provided, can significantly contribute to the destabilisation of financial systems:

a system of business laws including corporate, bankruptcy, contract, consumer protection and private property laws, that is consistently enforced and provides a mechanism for fair resolution of disputes;

comprehensive and well-defined accounting principles and rules that command wide international acceptance;

a system of independent audits for companies of significant size so that users of financial statements, including banks, have independent assurance that the accounts provide a true and fair view of the financial position of the company and are prepared according to established accounting principles, with auditors held accountable for their work;

effective banking supervision (as outlined in this document);

well-defined rules governing, and adequate supervision of, other financial markets and, where appropriate, their participants; and,

a secure and efficient payment and clearing system for the settlement of financial transactions where counterparty risks are controlled.

Effective market discipline depends on an adequate flow of information to market participants, appropriate financial incentives to reward well managed institutions and arrangements that ensure that investors are not insulated from the consequences of their decisions. Among the issues to be addressed are corporate governance and ensuring that accurate, meaningful, transparent and timely information is provided by borrowers to investors and creditors.

Market signals can be distorted and discipline undermined if governments seek to influence or override commercial decisions, particularly lending decisions, to achieve public policy objectives. In these circumstances, it is important that if guarantees are provided for such lending, they are disclosed and arrangements are made to compensate financial institutions when policy loans cease to perform.

Sufficiently flexible powers are necessary in order to effect an efficient resolution of problems in banks. Where problems are remediable, supervisors will normally seek to identify and implement solutions that fully address their concerns; where they are not, the prompt and orderly exit of institutions that are no longer able to meet supervisory requirements is a necessary part of an efficient financial system. Forebearance, whether or not the result of political pressure, normally leads to worsening problems and higher resolution costs. The supervisory agency should be responsible for, or assist in, the orderly exit of problem banks in order to ensure that depositors are repaid to the fullest extent possible from the resources of the bank (supplemented by any applicable deposit insurance) and ahead of shareholders, subordinated debt holders and other connected parties. In some cases, the best interests of depositors may be served by some form of restructuring, possibly takeover by a stronger institution or injection of new capital or shareholders. Supervisors may be able to facilitate such outcomes. It is essential that the end result fully meets all supervisory requirements, that it is realistically achievable in a short and determinate time frame, and that, in the interim, depositors are protected.

Deciding on the appropriate level of systemic protection is by and large a policy question to be taken by the relevant authorities (including the central bank), particularly where it may result in a commitment of public funds. Supervisors will also normally have a role to play because of their in-depth knowledge of the institutions involved. In order to preserve the operational independence of supervisors, it is important to draw a clear distinction between this systemic protection (or safety net) role and day-to-day supervision of solvent institutions. In handling systemic issues, it will be necessary to address, on the one hand, risks to confidence in the financial system and contagion to otherwise sound institutions, and, on the other hand, the need to minimise the distortion to market signals and discipline. Deposit insurance arrangements, where they exist, may also be triggered.

Principle 1: An effective system of banking supervision will have clear responsibilities and objectives for each agency involved in the supervision of banking organisations. Each such agency should possess operational independence and adequate resources. A suitable legal framework for banking supervision is also necessary, including provisions relating to authorisation of banking organisations and their ongoing supervision; powers to address compliance with laws as well as safety and soundness concerns; and legal protection for supervisors. Arrangements for sharing information between supervisors and protecting the confidentiality of such information should be in place.

This standard requires the following components to be in place:

a clear, achievable and consistent framework of responsibilities and objectives set by legislation for (each of) the supervisor(s) involved, but with operational independence to pursue them free from political pressure and with accountability for achieving them;

adequate resources (including staffing, funding and technology) to meet the objectives set, provided on terms that do not undermine the autonomy, integrity and independence of the supervisory agency;

a framework of banking law that sets out minimum standards that banks must meet; allows supervisors sufficient flexibility to set prudential rules administratively, where necessary, to achieve the objectives set as well as to utilise qualitative judgement; provides powers to gather and independently verify information; and, gives supervisors power to enforce a range of penalties that may be applied when prudential requirements are not being met (including powers to remove individuals, invoke sanctions and revoke licences);

protection (normally in law) from personal and institutional liability for supervisory actions taken in good faith in the course of performing supervisory duties; and,

a system of interagency cooperation and sharing of relevant information among the various official agencies, both domestic and foreign, responsible for the safety and soundness of the financial system; this cooperation should be supported by arrangements for protecting the confidentiality of supervisory information and ensuring that it is used only for purposes related to the effective supervision of the institutions concerned.

LICENSING PROCESS AND APPROVAL FOR CHANGES IN STRUCTURE

Principle 2. The permissible activities of institutions that are licensed and subject to supervision as banks must be clearly defined, and the use of the word "bank" in names should be controlled as far as possible.

Principle 3. The licensing authority must have the right to set criteria and reject applications for establishments that do not meet the standards set. The licensing process, at a minimum, should consist of an assessment of the banking organisation's ownership structure, directors and senior management, its operating plan and internal controls, and its projected financial condition, including its capital base; where the proposed owner or parent organisation is a foreign bank, the prior consent of its home country supervisor should be obtained.

In order to facilitate a healthy financial system, and to define precisely the population of institutions to be supervised, the arrangements for licensing banking organisations and the scope of activities governed by licences should be clearly defined. In particular, at a minimum, the activity of taking a proper bank deposit from the public would typically be reserved for institutions that are licensed and subject to supervision as banks. The term "bank" should be clearly defined and the use of the word "bank" in names should be controlled to the extent possible in those circumstances where the general public might be misled by unlicensed, unsupervised institutions implying otherwise by the use of "bank" in their titles.

By basing banking supervision on a system of licensing (or chartering) deposit-taking institutions (and, where appropriate, other types of financial institutions), the supervisors will have a means of identifying the population to be supervised and entry to the banking system will be controlled. The licensing authority should determine that new banking organisations have suitable shareholders, adequate financial strength, a legal structure in line with its operational structure, and management with sufficient expertise and integrity to operate the bank in a sound and prudent manner. It is important that the criteria for issuing licences are consistent with those applied in ongoing supervision so that they can provide one of the bases for withdrawing authorisation when an established institution no longer meets the criteria. Where the licensing and supervisory authorities are different, it is essential that they cooperate closely in the licensing process and that the supervisory authority has a legal right to have its views considered by the licensing authority. Clear and objective criteria also reduce the potential for political interference in the licensing process. Although the licensing process cannot guarantee that a bank will be well run after it opens, it can be an effective method for reducing the number of unstable institutions that enter the banking system.

Licensing regulations, as well as supervisory tools, should be designed to limit the number of bank failures and the amount of depositor losses without inhibiting the efficiency and competitiveness of the banking industry by blocking entry to it. Both elements are necessary to maintain public confidence in the banking system.

Having established strict criteria for reviewing a banking licence application, the licensing authority must have the right to reject applications if it cannot be satisfied that the criteria set are met. The licensing process, at a minimum, should consist of an assessment of the banking organisation's ownership structure, directors and senior management, its operating plan and internal controls, and its projected financial condition, including its capital adequacy; when the proposed owner is a foreign bank, prior consent of its home country supervisor should be obtained.

Ownership Structure

Supervisors must be able to assess the ownership structure of banking organisations. This assessment should include the bank's direct and indirect controlling and major direct or indirect shareholders. This assessment should review the controlling shareholders' past banking and non-banking business ventures and their integrity and standing in the business community, as well as the financial strength of all major shareholders and their ability to provide further financial support should it be needed. As part of the process of checking integrity and standing, the supervisor should determine the source of the initial capital to be invested.

Where a bank will be part of a larger organisation, licensing and supervisory authorities should determine that the ownership and organisational structure will not be a source of weakness and will minimise the risk to depositors of contagion from the activities conducted by other entities within the larger organisation. The other interests of the bank's major shareholders should be reviewed and the financial condition of these related entities assessed. The bank should not be used as a captive source of finance for its owners. When evaluating the corporate affiliations and structure of the proposed bank within a conglomerate, the licensing and supervisory authorities should determine that there will be sufficient transparency to permit them to identify the individuals responsible for the sound operations of the bank and to ensure that these individuals have the autonomy within the conglomerate structure to respond quickly to supervisory recommendations and requirements.

Finally, the licensing and supervisory authorities must have the authority to prevent corporate affiliations or structures that hinder the effective supervision of banks. These can include structures where material parts are in jurisdictions where secrecy laws or inadequate financial supervision are significant obstacles and structures where the same owners control banks with parallel structures which cannot be subjected to consolidated supervision because there is no common corporate link.

Operating Plan, Systems of Control and Internal Organisation

Another element to review during the licensing process is the operations and strategies proposed for the bank. The operating plan should describe and analyse the market area from which the bank expects to draw the majority of its business and establish a strategy for the bank's ongoing operations. The application should also describe how the bank will be organised and controlled internally. The licensing agency should determine if these arrangements are consistent with the proposed strategy and should also determine whether adequate internal policies and procedures have been developed and adequate resources deployed. This should include determining that appropriate corporate governance will be in place (a management structure with clear accountability, a board of directors with ability to provide an independent check on management, and independent audit and compliance functions) and that the "four eyes" principle (segregation of various functions, cross-checking, dual control of assets, double signatures, etc.) will be followed. It is essential to determine that the legal and operational structures will not inhibit supervision on either a solo or consolidated basis and that the supervisor will have adequate access to management and information. For this reason, supervisors should not grant a licence to a bank when the head office will be located outside its jurisdiction unless the supervisor is assured that it will have adequate access to management and information.

Fit and Proper Test for Directors and Senior Managers

A key aspect of the licensing process is an evaluation of the competence, integrity and qualifications of proposed management, including the board of directors. The licensing agency should obtain the necessary information about the proposed directors and senior managers to consider individually and collectively their banking experience, other business experience, personal integrity and relevant skill. This evaluation of management should involve background checks on whether previous activities, including regulatory or judicial judgements, raise doubts concerning their competence, sound judgement, or honesty. It is critical that the bank's proposed management team includes a substantial number of individuals with a proven track record in banking. Supervisors should have the authority to require notification of subsequent changes in directors and senior management and to prevent such appointments if they are deemed to be detrimental to the interests of depositors.

Financial Projections Including Capital

The licensing agency should review pro forma financial statements and projections for the proposed bank. The review should determine whether the bank will have sufficient capital to support its proposed strategic plan, especially in light of start-up costs and possible operational losses in the early stages. In addition, the licensing authority should assess whether the projections are consistent and realistic, and whether the proposed bank is likely to be viable. In most countries, licensing agencies have established a minimum initial capital amount. The licensing agency should also consider the ability of shareholders to supply additional support, if needed, once the bank has commenced activities. If there will be a corporate shareholder with a significant holding, an assessment of the financial condition of the corporate parent should be made, including its capital strength.

Prior Approval from the Home Country Supervisor When the Proposed Owner is a Foreign Bank

When a foreign bank, subsidiary of a foreign banking group, or a foreign non-banking financial institution (subject to a supervisory authority) proposes to establish a local bank or branch office, the licensing authority should consider whether the Basle Minimum Standards are met and in particular the licence should not normally be approved until the consent of the home country supervisor of the bank or banking group has been obtained. The host authority should also consider whether the home country supervisor capably performs its supervisory task on a consolidated basis. In assessing whether capable consolidated supervision is provided, the host licensing authority should consider not only the nature and scope of the home country supervisory regime but also whether the structure of the applicant or its group is such as to not inhibit effective supervision by the home and host country supervisory authorities.

Transfer of a Bank's Shares

Principle 4. Banking supervisors must have the authority to review and reject any proposals to transfer significant ownership or controlling interests in existing banks to other parties.

In addition to licensing new banks, banking supervisors should be notified of any future significant direct or indirect investment in the bank or any increases or other changes in ownership over a particular threshold and should have the power to block such investments or prevent the exercise of voting rights in respect of such investments if they do not meet criteria comparable to those used for approving new banks. Notifications are often required for ownership or voting control involving established percentages of a bank's outstanding shares.

The threshold for approval of significant ownership changes may be higher than that for notification.

Major Acquisitions or Investments by a Bank

Principle 5. Banking supervisors must have the authority to establish criteria for reviewing major acquisitions or investments by a bank and ensuring that corporate affiliations or structures do not expose the bank to undue risks or hinder effective supervision.

In many countries, once a bank has been licensed, it may conduct any activities normally permissible for banks or any range of activities specified in the banking licence. Consequently, certain acquisitions or investments may be automatically permissible if they comply with certain limits set by the supervisors or by banking law or regulation. In certain circumstances, supervisors require banks to provide notice or obtain explicit permission before making certain acquisitions or investments. In these instances, supervisors need to determine if the banking organisation has both the financial and managerial resources to make the acquisition and may need to consider also whether the investment is permissible under existing banking laws and regulations. The supervisor should clearly define what types and amounts of investments need prior approval and for what cases notification is sufficient. Notification after the fact is most appropriate in those instances where the activity is closely related to banking and the investment is small relative to the bank's total capital.

ARRANGEMENTS FOR ONGOING BANKING SUPERVISION

Risks in Banking

Banking, by its nature, entails taking a wide array of risks. Banking supervisors need to understand these risks and be satisfied that banks are adequately measuring and managing them. The key risks faced by banks are discussed below.

Credit Risk

The extension of loans is the primary activity of most banks. Lending activities require banks to make judgements related to the creditworthiness of borrowers. These judgements do not always prove to be accurate and the creditworthiness of a borrower may decline over time due to various factors. Consequently, a major risk that banks face is credit risk or the failure of a counterparty to perform according to a contractual arrangement. This risk applies not only to loans but to other on-and off-balance sheet exposures such as guarantees, acceptances and securities investments. Serious banking problems have arisen from the failure of banks to recognise impaired assets, to create reserves for writing off these assets, and to suspend recognition of interest income when appropriate. Large exposures to a single borrower, or to a group of related borrowers are a common cause of banking problems in that they represent a credit risk concentration. Large concentrations can also arise with respect to particular industries, economic sectors, or geographical regions or by having sets of loans with other characteristics that make them vulnerable to the same economic factors (e.g., highly-leveraged transactions).

Connected lending-the extension of credit to individuals or firms connected to the bank through ownership or through the ability to exert direct or indirect control-if not properly controlled, can lead to significant problems because determinations regarding the creditworthiness of the borrower are not always made objectively. Connected parties include a bank's parent organisation, major shareholders, subsidiaries, affiliated entities, directors, and executive officers. Firms are also connected when they are controlled by the same family or group. In these, or in similar, circumstances, the connection can lead to preferential treatment in lending and thus greater risk of loan losses.

Country and Transfer Risk

In addition to the counterparty credit risk inherent in lending, international lending also includes country risk, which refers to risks associated with the economic, social and political environments of the borrower's home country. Country risk may be most apparent when lending to foreign governments or their agencies, since such lending is typically unsecured, but is important to consider when making any foreign loan or investment, whether to public or private borrowers. There is also a component of country risk called "transfer risk" which arises when a borrower's obligation is not denominated in the local currency. The currency of the obligation may become unavailable to the borrower regardless of its particular financial condition.

Market Risk

Banks face a risk of losses in on-and off-balance sheet positions arising from movements in market prices. Established accounting principles cause these risks to be typically most visible in a bank's trading activities, whether they involve debt or equity instruments, or foreign exchange or commodity positions. One specific element of market risk is foreign exchange risk. Banks act as "market-makers" in foreign exchange by quoting rates to their customers and by taking open positions in currencies. The risks inherent in foreign exchange business, particularly in running open foreign exchange positions, are increased during periods of instability in exchange rates.

Interest Rate Risk

Interest rate risk refers to the exposure of a bank's financial condition to adverse movements in interest rates. This risk impacts both the earnings of a bank and the economic value of its assets, liabilities and off-balance sheet instruments. The primary forms of interest rate risk to which banks are typically exposed are: (1) repricing risk, which arises from timing differences in the maturity (for fixed rate) and repricing (for floating rate) of bank assets, liabilities and off-balance sheet positions; (2) yield curve risk, which arises from changes in the slope and shape of the yield curve; (3) basis risk, which arises from imperfect correlation in the adjustment of the rates earned and paid on different instruments with otherwise similar repricing characteristics; and (4) optionality, which arises from the express or implied options imbedded in many bank assets, liabilities and off-balance sheet portfolios. Although such risk is a normal part of banking, excessive interest rate risk can pose a significant threat to a bank's earnings and capital base. Managing this risk is of growing importance in sophisticated financial markets where customers actively manage their interest rate exposure. Special attention should be paid to this risk in countries where interest rates are being deregulated.

Liquidity Risk

Liquidity risk arises from the inability of a bank to accommodate decreases in liabilities or to fund increases in assets. When a bank has inadequate liquidity, it cannot obtain sufficient funds, either by increasing liabilities or by converting assets promptly, at a reasonable cost, thereby affecting profitability. In extreme cases, insufficient liquidity can lead to the insolvency of a bank.

Operational Risk

The most important types of operational risk involve breakdowns in internal controls and corporate governance. Such breakdowns can lead to financial losses through error, fraud, or failure to perform in a timely manner or cause the interests of the bank to be compromised in some other way, for example, by its dealers, lending officers or other staff exceeding their authority or conducting business in an unethical or risky manner. Other aspects of operational risk include major failure of information technology systems or events such as major fires or other disasters.

Legal Risk

Banks are subject to various forms of legal risk. This can include the risk that assets will turn out to be worth less or liabilities will turn out to be greater than expected because of inadequate or incorrect legal advice or documentation. In addition, existing laws may fail to resolve legal issues involving a bank; a court case involving a particular bank may have wider implications for banking business and involve costs to it and many or all other banks; and, laws affecting banks or other commercial enterprises may change. Banks are particularly susceptible to legal risks when entering new types of transactions and when the legal right of a counterparty to enter into a transaction is not established.

Reputational Risk

Reputational risk arises from operational failures, failure to comply with relevant laws and regulations, or other sources. Reputational risk is particularly damaging for banks since the nature of their business requires maintaining the confidence of depositors, creditors and the general marketplace.

Development and Implementation of Prudential Regulations and Requirements

The risks inherent in banking must be recognised, monitored and controlled. Supervisors play a critical role in ensuring that bank management does this. An important part of the supervisory process is the authority of supervisors to develop and utilise prudential regulations and requirements to control these risks, including those covering capital adequacy, loan loss reserves, asset concentrations, liquidity, risk management and internal controls. These may be qualitative and/or quantitative requirements. Their purpose is to limit imprudent risk-taking by banks. These requirements should not supplant management decisions but rather impose minimum prudential standards to ensure that banks conduct their activities in an appropriate manner. The dynamic nature of banking requires that supervisors periodically assess their prudential requirements and evaluate the continued relevance of existing requirements as well as the need for new requirements.

Capital Adequacy

Principle 6: Banking supervisors must set prudent and appropriate minimum capital adequacy requirements for all banks. Such requirements should reflect the risks that the banks undertake, and must define the components of capital, bearing in mind their ability to absorb losses. At least for internationally active banks, these requirements must not be less than those established in the Basle Capital Accord and its amendments.

Equity capital serves several purposes: it provides a permanent source of revenue for the shareholders and funding for the bank; it is available to bear risk and absorb losses; it provides a base for further growth; and it gives the shareholders reason to ensure that the bank is managed in a safe and sound manner. Minimum capital adequacy ratios are necessary to reduce the risk of loss to depositors, creditors and other stakeholders of the bank and to help supervisors pursue the overall stability of the banking industry. Supervisors must set prudent and appropriate minimum capital adequacy requirements and encourage banks to operate with capital in excess of the minimum. Supervisors should consider requiring higher than minimum capital ratios when it appears appropriate due to the particular risk profile of the bank or if there are uncertainties regarding the asset quality, risk concentrations or other adverse characteristics of a bank's financial condition.

If a bank's ratio falls below the minimum, banking supervisors should ensure that it has realistic plans to restore the minimum in a timely fashion. Supervisors should also consider whether additional restrictions are needed in such cases.

In 1988, the member countries of the Basle Committee on Banking Supervision agreed to a method of ensuring a bank's capital adequacy.

Many other countries have adopted the Capital Accord or something very close to it. The Accord addresses two important elements of a bank's activities: (1) different levels of credit risk inherent in its balance sheet and (2) off-balance sheet activities, which can represent a significant risk exposure.

The Accord defines what types of capital are acceptable for supervisory purposes and stresses the need for adequate levels of "core capital" (in the accord this capital is referred to as tier one capital) consisting of permanent shareholders' equity and disclosed reserves that are created or maintained by appropriations of retained earnings or other surplus (e.g. share premiums, retained profit, general reserves and reserves required by law).

Disclosed reserves also include general funds that meet the following criteria: (1) allocations to the funds must be made out of post-tax retained earnings or out of pre-tax earnings adjusted for all potential tax liabilities; (2) the funds and movements into or out of them must be disclosed separately in the bank's published accounts; (3) the funds must be available to a bank to meet losses; and (4) losses cannot be charged directly to the funds but must be taken through the profit and loss account. The Accord also acknowledges other forms of supplementary capital (referred to as tier two capital), such as other forms of reserves and hybrid capital instruments that should be included within a system of capital measurement.

The Accord assigns risk weights to on-and off-balance sheet exposures according to broad categories of relative riskiness. The framework of weights has been kept as simple as possible with only five weights being used: 0, 10, 20, 50 and 100%.

The Accord sets minimum capital ratio requirements for internationally active banks of 4% tier one capital and 8% total (tier one plus tier two) capital in relation to risk-weighted assets. These requirements are applied to banks on a consolidated basis.

It must be stressed that these ratios are considered a minimum standard and many supervisors require higher ratios or apply stricter definitions of capital or higher risk weights than set out in the Accord.

Credit Risk Management

Credit-granting Standards and Credit Monitoring Process

Principle 7: An essential part of any supervisory system is the evaluation of a bank's policies, practices and procedures related to the granting of loans and making of investments and the ongoing management of the loan and investment portfolios.

Supervisors need to ensure that the credit and investment function at individual banks is objective and grounded in sound principles. The maintenance of prudent written lending policies, loan approval and administration procedures, and appropriate loan documentation are essential to a bank's management of the lending function. Lending and investment activities should be based on prudent underwriting standards that are approved by the bank's board of directors and clearly communicated to the bank's lending officers and staff. It is also critical for supervisors to determine the extent to which the institution makes its credit decisions free of conflicting interests and inappropriate pressure from outside parties.

Banks must also have a well-developed process for ongoing monitoring of credit relationships, including the financial condition of borrowers. A key element of any management information system should be a data base that provides essential details on the condition of the loan portfolio, including internal loan grading and classifications.

Assessment of Asset Quality and Adequacy of Loan Loss Provisions and Reserves

Principle 8: Banking supervisors must be satisfied that banks establish and adhere to adequate policies, practices and procedures for evaluating the quality of assets and the adequacy of loan loss provisions and loan loss reserves.

Supervisors should assess a bank's policies regarding the periodic review of individual credits, asset classification and provisioning. They should be satisfied that these policies are being reviewed regularly and implemented consistently. Supervisors should also ensure that banks have a process in place for overseeing problem credits and collecting past due loans. When the level of problem credits at a bank is of concern to the supervisors, they should require the bank to strengthen its lending practices, credit-granting standards, and overall financial strength.

When guarantees or collateral are provided, the bank should have a mechanism in place for continually assessing the strength of these guarantees and appraising the worth of the collateral. Supervisors should also ensure that banks properly record and hold adequate capital against off-balance sheet exposures when they retain contingent risks.

Concentrations of Risk and Large Exposures

Principle 9: Banking supervisors must be satisfied that banks have management information systems that enable management to identify concentrations within the portfolio and supervisors must set prudential limits to restrict bank exposures to single borrowers or groups of related borrowers. Banking supervisors must set prudential limits to restrict bank exposures to single borrowers, groups of related borrowers and other significant risk concentrations. These limits are usually expressed in terms of a percentage of bank capital and, although they vary, 25% of capital is typically the most that a bank or banking group may extend to a private sector non-bank borrower or a group of closely related borrowers without specific supervisory approval. It is recognised that newly-established or very small banks may face practical limits on their ability to diversify, necessitating higher levels of capital to reflect the resultant risk. Supervisors should monitor the bank's handling of concentrations of risk and may require that banks report to them any such exposures exceeding a specified limit (e.g., 10% of capital) or exposures to large borrowers as determined by the supervisors. In some countries, the aggregate of such large exposures is also subject to limits.

Connected Lending

Principle 10: In order to prevent abuses arising from connected lending, banking supervisors must have in place requirements that banks lend to related companies and individuals on an arm's-length basis, that such extensions of credit are effectively monitored, and that other appropriate steps are taken to control or mitigate the risks.

Banking supervisors must be able to prevent abuses arising from connected and related party lending. This will require ensuring that such lending is conducted only on an arm's-length basis and that the amount of credit extended is monitored. These controls are most easily implemented by requiring that the terms and conditions of such credits not be more favourable than credit extended to non-related borrowers under similar circumstances and by imposing strict limits on such lending. Supervisors should have the authority, in appropriate circumstances, to go further and establish absolute limits on categories of such loans, to deduct such lending from capital when assessing capital adequacy, or to require collateralisation of such loans. Transactions with related parties that pose special risks to the bank should be subject to the approval of the bank's board of directors, reported to the supervisors, or prohibited altogether. Supervising banking organisations on a consolidated basis can in some circumstances identify and reduce problems arising from connected lending.

Supervisors should also have the authority to make discretionary judgements about the existence of connections between the bank and other parties. This is especially necessary in those instances where the bank and related parties have taken measures to conceal such connections.

Country and Transfer Risk

Principle 11: Banking supervisors must be satisfied that banks have adequate policies and procedures for identifying, monitoring and controlling country risk and transfer risk in their international lending and investment activities, and for maintaining appropriate reserves against such risks.

Market Risk Management

Principle 12: Banking supervisors must be satisfied that banks have in place systems that accurately measure, monitor and adequately control market risks; supervisors should have powers to impose specific limits and/or a specific capital charge on market risk exposures, if warranted.

Banking supervisors must determine that banks accurately measure and adequately control market risks. Where material, it is appropriate to provide an explicit capital cushion for the price risks to which banks are exposed, particularly those arising from their trading activities. Introducing the discipline that capital requirements impose can be an important further step in strengthening the soundness and stability of financial markets. There should also be well-structured quantitative and qualitative standards for the risk management process related to market risk.

Banking supervisors should also ensure that bank management has set appropriate limits and implemented adequate internal controls for their foreign exchange business.

Other Risk Management

Principle 13: Banking supervisors must be satisfied that banks have in place a comprehensive risk management process (including appropriate board and senior management oversight) to identify, measure, monitor and control all other material risks and, where appropriate, to hold capital against these risks.

Risk management standards are a necessary element of banking supervision, and increasingly important as financial instruments and risk measurement techniques become more complex. Moreover, the effect of new technologies on financial markets both permits and requires many banks to monitor their portfolios daily and adjust risk exposures rapidly in response to market and customer needs. In this environment, management, investors, and supervisors need information about a bank's exposures that is correct, informative, and provided on a timely basis. Supervisors can contribute to this process by promoting and enforcing sound policies in banks, and requiring procedures that ensure the necessary information is available.

Interest Rate Risk

Supervisors should monitor the way in which banks control interest rate risk including effective board and senior management oversight, adequate risk management policies and procedures, risk measurement and monitoring systems, and comprehensive controls. In addition, supervisors should receive sufficient and timely information from banks in order to evaluate the level of interest rate risk. This information should take appropriate account of the range of maturities and currencies in each bank's portfolio, as well as other relevant factors such as the distinction between trading and non-trading activities.

Liquidity Management

The purpose of liquidity management is to ensure that the bank is able to meet fully its contractual commitments. Crucial elements of strong liquidity management include good management information systems, central liquidity control, analysis of net funding requirements under alternative scenarios, diversification of funding sources, and contingency planning.

Supervisors should expect banks to manage their assets, liabilities and off-balance sheet contracts with a view to maintaining adequate liquidity. Banks should have a diversified funding base, both in terms of sources of funds and the maturity breakdown of the liabilities. They should also maintain an adequate level of liquid assets.

Operational Risk

Supervisors should ensure that senior management puts in place effective internal control and auditing procedures; also, that they have policies for managing or mitigating operational risk (e.g., through insurance or contingency planning). Supervisors should determine that banks have adequate and well-tested business resumption plans for all major systems, with remote site facilities, to protect against such events.

Internal Controls

Principle 14. Banking supervisors must determine that banks have in place internal controls that are adequate for the nature and scale of their business. These should include clear arrangements for delegating authority and responsibility; separation of the functions that involve committing the bank, paying away its funds, and accounting for its assets and liabilities; reconciliation of these processes; safeguarding its assets; and appropriate independent internal or external audit and compliance functions to test adherence to these controls as well as applicable laws and regulations.

Principle 15. Banking supervisors must determine that banks have adequate policies, practices and procedures in place, including strict "know-your-customer" rules, that promote high ethical and professional standards in the financial sector and prevent the bank being used, intentionally or unintentionally, by criminal elements.

The purpose of internal controls is to ensure that the business of a bank is conducted in a prudent manner in accordance with policies and strategies established by the bank's board of directors; that transactions are only entered into with appropriate authority; that assets are safeguarded and liabilities controlled; that accounting and other records provide complete, accurate and timely information; and that management is able to identify, assess, manage and control the risks of the business.

There are four primary areas of internal controls:

organisational structures (definitions of duties and responsibilities, discretionary limits for loan approval, and decision-making procedures);

accounting procedures (reconciliation of accounts, control lists, periodic trial balances, etc.);

the "four eyes" principle (segregation of various functions, cross-checking, dual control of assets, double signatures, etc.); and

physical control over assets and investments.

These controls must be supplemented by an effective audit function that independently evaluates the adequacy, operational effectiveness and efficiency of the control systems within an organisation. Consequently, the internal auditor must have an appropriate status within the bank and adequate reporting lines designed to safeguard his or her independence.

The external audit can provide a cross-check on the effectiveness of this process. Banking supervisors must be satisfied that effective policies and practices are followed and that management takes appropriate corrective action in response to internal control weaknesses identified by internal and external auditors.

Banks are subject to a wide array of banking and non-banking laws and regulations and must have in place adequate policies and procedures to ensure compliance. Otherwise, violations of established requirements can damage the reputation of the bank and expose it to penalties. In extreme cases, this damage could threaten the bank's solvency. Compliance failures also indicate that the bank is not being managed with the integrity and skill expected of a banking organisation. Larger banks in particular should have independent compliance functions and banking supervisors should determine that such functions are operating effectively.

Public confidence in banks can be undermined, and bank reputations damaged, as a result of association (even if inadvertent) with drug traders and other criminals. Consequently, while banking supervisors are not generally responsible for the criminal prosecution of money laundering offences or the ongoing anti-money laundering efforts in their countries, they have a role in ensuring that banks have procedures in place, including strict "know-your-customer" policies, to avoid association or involvement with drug traders and other criminals, as well as in the general promotion of high ethical and professional standards in the financial sector.

Specifically, supervisors should encourage the adoption of those recommendations of the Financial Action Task Force on Money Laundering (FATF) that apply to financial institutions. These relate to customer identification and record-keeping, increased diligence by financial institutions in detecting and reporting suspicious transactions, and measures to deal with countries with insufficient or no anti-money laundering measures. The occurrence of fraud in banks, or involving them, is also of concern to banking supervisors for three reasons. On a large scale it may threaten the solvency of banks and the integrity and soundness of the financial system. Second, it may be indicative of weak internal controls that will require supervisory attention. And thirdly, there are potential reputational and confidence implications which may also spread from a particular institution to the system. For these reasons, banks should have established lines of communication, both within the management chain and within an internal security or guardian function independent of management, for reporting problems. Employees should be required to report suspicious or troubling behaviour to a superior or to internal security.

Moreover, banks should be required to report suspicious activities and significant incidents of fraud to the supervisors. It is not necessarily the role of supervisors to investigate fraud in banks, and the skills required to do so are specialised, but supervisors do need to ensure that appropriate authorities have been alerted. They need to be able to consider and, if necessary, act to prevent effects on other banks and to maintain an awareness of the types of fraudulent activity that are being undertaken or attempted in order to ensure that banks have controls capable of countering them.

Methods of Ongoing Banking Supervision

Principle 16: An effective banking supervisory system should consist of some form of both on-site and off-site supervision.

Principle 17: Banking supervisors must have regular contact with bank management and a thorough understanding of the institution's operations.

Principle 18: Banking supervisors must have a means of collecting, reviewing and analysing prudential reports and statistical returns from banks on a solo and consolidated basis.

Principle 19: Banking supervisors must have a means of independent validation of supervisory information either through on-site examinations or use of external auditors.

Principle 20: An essential element of banking supervision is the ability of the supervisors to supervise the banking group on a consolidated basis.

Supervision requires the collection and analysis of information. This can be done on or off-site. An effective supervisory system will use both means. In some countries, on-site work is carried out by examiners and in others by qualified external auditors. In still other countries, a mixed system of on-site examinations and collaboration between the supervisors and the external auditors exists. The extent of on-site work and the method by which it is carried out depend on a variety of factors. Regardless of their mix of on-site and off-site activities or their use of work done by external accountants, banking supervisors must have regular contact with bank management and a thorough understanding of the institution's operations. Review of the reports of internal and external auditors can be an integral part of both on-site and off-site supervision. The various factors considered during the licensing process should be periodically assessed as part of on-going supervision. Banks should be required to submit information on a periodic basis for review by the supervisors, and supervisors should be able to discuss regularly with banks all significant issues and areas of their business. If problems develop, banks should also feel that they can confide in and consult with the supervisor, and expect that problems will be discussed constructively and treated in a confidential manner. They must also recognise their responsibility to inform supervisors of important matters in a timely manner.

Off-site Surveillance

Supervisors must have a means of collecting, reviewing and analysing prudential reports and statistical returns from banks on a solo and consolidated basis. These should include basic financial statements as well as supporting schedules that provide greater detail on exposure to different types of risk and various other financial aspects of the bank, including provisions and off-balance sheet activities. The supervisory agency should also have the ability to obtain information on affiliated non-bank entities. Banking supervisors should also make full use of publicly-available information and analysis.

These reports can be used to check adherence to prudential requirements, such as capital adequacy or single debtor limits. Off-site monitoring can often identify potential problems, particularly in the interval between on-site inspections, thereby providing early detection and prompting corrective action before problems become more serious. Such reports can also be used to identify trends not only for particular institutions, but also for the banking system as a whole. These reports can provide the basis for discussions with bank management, either at periodic intervals or when problems appear. They should also be a key component of examination planning so that maximum benefit is achieved from the limited time spent conducting an on-site review.

On-site Examination and/or use of External Auditors

Supervisors must have a means of validating supervisory information either through on-site examinations or use of external auditors. On-site work, whether done by examination staff of the banking supervisory agency or commissioned by supervisors but undertaken by external auditors, should be structured to provide independent verification that adequate corporate governance exists at individual banks and that information provided by banks is reliable.

On-site examinations provide the supervisor with a means of verifying or assessing a range of matters including:

the accuracy of reports received from the bank

the overall operations and condition of the bank

the adequacy of the bank's risk management systems and internal control procedures

the quality of the loan portfolio and adequacy of loan loss provisions and reserves

the competence of management

the adequacy of accounting and management information systems

issues identified in off-site or previous on-site supervisory processes

bank adherence to laws and regulations and the terms stipulated in the banking licence.

The supervisory agency should establish clear internal guidelines related to the frequency and scope of examinations. In addition, examination policies and procedures should be developed in order to ensure that examinations are conducted in a thorough and consistent manner with clear objectives.

Depending on its use of examination staff, a supervisory agency may use external auditors to fulfil the above functions in whole or in part. In some cases, such functions may be part of the normal audit process (e.g. assessing the quality of the loan portfolio and the level of provisions that need to be held against it). In other areas, the supervisor should have adequate powers to require work to be commissioned specifically for supervisory purposes (e.g. on the accuracy of reports filed with supervisors or the adequacy of control systems.)

However, the work of external auditors should be utilised for supervisory purposes only when there is a well-developed, professionally independent auditing profession with skills to undertake the work required. In these circumstances, the supervisory agency needs to reserve the right to veto the appointment of a particular firm of external auditors where supervisory reliance is to be placed on the firm's work. In addition, supervisors should urge banking groups to use common auditors and common accounting dates throughout the group, to the extent possible.

It is also important that the supervisors and external auditors have a clear understanding of their respective roles. Before problems are detected at a bank, the external auditors should clearly understand their responsibilities for communicating with the supervisory agency and should also be protected from personal liability for disclosures, in good faith, of such information. A mechanism should be in place to facilitate discussions between the supervisors and the external auditors.

In many instances, these discussions should also include the bank.

In all cases, the supervisory agency should have the legal authority and means to conduct independent checks of banks based on identified concerns.

Supervision on a Consolidated Basis

An essential element of banking supervision is the ability of the supervisors to supervise the consolidated banking organisation. This includes the ability to review both banking and non-banking activities conducted by the banking organisation, either directly or indirectly (through subsidiaries and affiliates), and activities conducted at both domestic and foreign offices. Supervisors need to take into account that non-financial activities of a bank or group may pose risks to the bank. Supervisors should decide which prudential requirements will be applied on a bank-only (solo) basis, which ones will be applied on a consolidated basis, and which ones will be applied on both bases. In all cases, the banking supervisors should be aware of the overall structure of the banking organisation or group when applying their supervisory methods.

Banking supervisors should also have the ability to coordinate with other authorities responsible for supervising specific entities within the organisation's structure.

Information Requirements of Banking Organisations

Principle 21: Banking supervisors must be satisfied that each bank maintains adequate records drawn up in accordance with consistent accounting policies and practices that enable the supervisor to obtain a true and fair view of the financial condition of the bank and the profitability of its business, and that the bank publishes on a regular basis financial statements that fairly reflect its condition.

For banking supervisors to conduct effective off-site supervision of banks and to evaluate the condition of the local banking market, they must receive financial information at regular intervals and this information must be verified periodically through on-site examinations or external audits. Banking supervisors must ensure that each bank maintains adequate accounting records drawn up in accordance with consistent accounting policies and practices that enable the supervisor to obtain a true and fair view of the financial condition of the bank and the profitability of its business. In order that the accounts portray a true and fair view, it is essential that assets are recorded at values that are realistic and consistent, taking account of current values, where relevant, and that profit reflects what, on a net basis, is likely to be received and takes into account likely transfers to loan loss reserves. It is important that banks submit information in a format that makes comparisons among banks possible although, for certain purposes, data derived from internal management information systems may also be helpful to supervisors. At a minimum, periodic reporting should include a bank's balance sheet, contingent liabilities and income statement, with supporting details and key risk exposures. Supervisors can be obstructed or misled when banks knowingly or recklessly provide false information of material importance to the supervisory process. If a bank provides information to the supervisor knowing that it is materially false or misleading, or it does so recklessly, supervisory and/or criminal action should be taken against both the individuals involved and the institution.

Accounting Standards

In order to ensure that the information submitted by banks is of a comparable nature and its meaning is clear, the supervisory agency will need to provide report instructions that clearly establish the accounting standards to be used in preparing the reports. These standards should be based on accounting principles and rules that command wide international acceptance and be aimed specifically at banking institutions.

Scope and Frequency of Reporting

The supervisory agency needs to have powers to determine the scope and frequency of reporting to reflect the volatility of the business and to enable the agency to track what is happening at individual banks on both a solo and consolidated basis, as well as with the banking system as a whole. The supervisors should develop a series of informational reports for banks to prepare and submit at regular intervals. While some reports may be filed as often as monthly, others may be filed quarterly or annually. In addition, some reports may be "event generated", meaning they are filed only if a particular event occurs (e.g. investment in a new affiliate). Supervisors should be sensitive to the burden that reporting imposes. Consequently, they may determine that it is not necessary for every bank to file every report. Filing status can be based on the organisational structure of the bank, its size, and the types of activities it conducts.

Confirmation of the Accuracy of Information Submitted

It is the responsibility of bank management to ensure the accuracy, completeness and timeliness of prudential, financial, and other reports submitted to the supervisors. Therefore, bank management must ensure that reports are verified and that external auditors determine that the reporting systems in place are adequate and provide reliable data. External auditors should express an opinion on the annual accounts and management report supplied to shareholders and the general public. Weaknesses in bank auditing standards in a particular country may require that banking supervisors become involved in establishing clear guidelines concerning the scope and content of the audit programme as well as the standards to be used. In extreme cases where supervisors cannot be satisfied with the quality of the annual accounts or regulatory reports, or with the work done by external auditors, they should have the ability to use supervisory measures to bring about timely corrective action, and they may need to reserve the right to approve the issue of accounts to the public.

In assessing the nature and adequacy of work done by auditors, and the degree of reliance that can be placed on this work, supervisors will need to consider the extent to which the audit programme has examined such areas as the loan portfolio, loan loss reserves, non-performing assets (including the treatment of interest on such assets), asset valuations, trading and other securities activities, derivatives, asset securitisations, and the adequacy of internal controls over financial reporting. Where it is competent and independent of management, internal audits can be relied upon as a source of information and may contribute usefully to the supervisors' understanding.

Confidentiality of Supervisory Information

Although market participants should have access to correct and timely information, there are certain types of sensitive information that should be held confidential by banking supervisors. In order for a relationship of mutual trust to develop, banks need to know that such sensitive information will be held confidential by the banking supervisory agency and its appropriate counterparts at other domestic and foreign supervisory agencies.

Disclosure

In order for market forces to work effectively, thereby fostering a stable and efficient financial system, market participants need access to correct and timely information. Disclosure, therefore, is a complement to supervision. For this reason, banks should be required to disclose to the public information regarding their activities and financial position that is comprehensive and not misleading. This information should be timely and sufficient for market participants to assess the risk inherent in any individual banking organisation.

FORMAL POWERS OF SUPERVISORS

Principle 22: Banking supervisors must have at their disposal adequate supervisory measures to bring about timely corrective action when banks fail to meet prudential requirements (such as minimum capital adequacy ratios), when there are regulatory violations, or where depositors are threatened in any other way. In extreme circumstances, this should include the ability to revoke the banking licence or recommend its revocation.

Corrective Measures

Despite the efforts of supervisors, situations can occur where banks fail to meet supervisory requirements or where their solvency comes into question. In order to protect depositors and creditors, and prevent more widespread contagion of such problems, supervisors must be able to conduct appropriate intervention. Banking supervisors must have at their disposal adequate supervisory measures to bring about timely corrective action and which enable a graduated response by supervisors depending on the nature of the problems detected. In those instances where the detected problem is relatively minor, informal action such as a simple oral or written communication to bank management may be all that is warranted. In other instances, more formal action may be necessary. These remedial measures have the greatest chance of success when they are part of a comprehensive programme of corrective action developed by the bank and with an implementation timetable; however, failure to achieve agreement with bank management should not inhibit the supervisory authority from requiring the necessary corrective action.

Supervisors should have the authority not only to restrict the current activities of the bank but also withhold approval for new activities or acquisitions. They should also have the authority to restrict or suspend dividend or other payments to shareholders, as well as to restrict asset transfers and a bank's purchase of its own shares. The supervisor should have effective means to address management problems, including the power to have controlling owners, directors, and managers replaced or their powers restricted, and, where appropriate, barring individuals from the business of banking. In extreme cases, the supervisors should have the ability to impose conservatorship over a bank that is failing to meet prudential or other requirements. It is important that all remedial actions be addressed directly to the bank's board of directors since they have overall responsibility for the institution. Once action has been taken or remedial measures have been imposed, supervisors must be vigilant in their oversight of the problems giving rise to it by periodically checking to determine that the bank is complying with the measures. There should be a progressive escalation of action or remedial measures if the problems become worse or if bank management ignores more informal requests from supervisors to take corrective action.

Liquidation Procedures

In the most extreme cases, and despite ongoing attempts by the supervisors to ensure that a problem situation is resolved, a banking organisation may no longer be financially viable. In such cases, the supervisor can be involved in resolutions that require a take-over by or merger with a healthier institution. When all other measures fail, the supervisor should have the ability to close or assist in the closing of an unhealthy bank in order to protect the overall stability of the banking system.

CROSS-BORDER BANKING

The Principles set out in this section are consistent with the so-called Basle Concordat and its successors.

The Concordat establishes understandings relating to contact and collaboration between home and host country authorities in the supervision of banks' cross-border establishments. The most recent of these documents, "The supervision of cross-border banking", was developed by the Basle Committee in collaboration with the Offshore Group of Banking Supervisors and subsequently endorsed by 130 countries attending the International Conference of Banking Supervisors in June 1996. This document contains twenty-nine recommendations aimed at removing obstacles to the implementation of effective consolidated supervision.

Obligations of Home Country Supervisors

Principle 23: Banking supervisors must practise global consolidated supervision over their internationally active banking organisations, adequately monitoring and applying appropriate prudential norms to all aspects of the business conducted by these banking organisations worldwide, primarily at their foreign branches, joint ventures and subsidiaries.

Principle 24: A key component of consolidated supervision is establishing contact and information exchange with the various other supervisors involved, primarily host country supervisory authorities.

As part of practising consolidated banking supervision, banking supervisors must adequately monitor and apply appropriate prudential norms to all aspects of the business conducted by their banking organisations worldwide including at their foreign branches, joint ventures and subsidiaries. A major responsibility of the parent bank supervisor is to determine that the parent bank is providing adequate oversight not only of its overseas branches but also its joint ventures and subsidiaries. This parent bank oversight should include monitoring compliance with internal controls, receiving an adequate and regular flow of information, and periodically verifying the information received. In many instances, a bank's foreign offices may be conducting business fundamentally different from the bank's domestic operations. Consequently, supervisors should determine that the bank has the expertise needed to conduct these activities in a safe and sound manner.

A key component of consolidated supervision is establishing contact and information exchange with the various other supervisors involved, including host country supervisory authorities. This contact should commence at the authorisation stage when the host supervisor should seek the approval from the home supervisor before issuing a licence. In many cases, bilateral arrangements exist between supervisors. These arrangements can prove helpful in defining the scope of information to be shared and the conditions under which such sharing would normally be expected. Unless satisfactory arrangements for obtaining information can be agreed, banking supervisors should prohibit their banks from establishing operations in countries with secrecy laws or other regulations prohibiting flows of information deemed necessary for adequate supervision.

The parent supervisor should also determine the nature and extent of supervision conducted by the host country of the local operations of the home country's banks. Where host country supervision is inadequate, the parent supervisor may need to take special additional measures to compensate, such as through on-site examinations, or by requiring additional information from the bank's head office or its external auditors. If these options can not be developed to give sufficient comfort, bearing in mind the risks involved, then the home supervisor may have no option but to request the closure of the relevant overseas establishment.

Obligations of Host Country Supervisors

Principle 25: Banking supervisors must require the local operations of foreign banks to be conducted to the same high standards as are required of domestic institutions and must have powers to share information needed by the home country supervisors of those banks for the purpose of carrying out consolidated supervision.

Foreign banks often provide depth and increase competition and are therefore important participants in local banking markets. Banking supervisors must require the local operations of foreign banks to be conducted to the same high standards as are required of domestic institutions and must have powers to share information needed by the home country supervisors of those banks for the purpose of carrying out consolidated supervision. Consequently, foreign bank operations should be subject to similar prudential, inspection and reporting requirements as domestic banks (recognising, of course, obvious differences such as branches not being separately capitalised).

As the host country supervisory agency supervises only a limited part of the overall operations of the foreign bank, the supervisory agency should determine that the home country supervisor practices consolidated supervision of both the domestic and overseas operations of the bank. In order for home country supervisors to practice effectively consolidated supervision, the host country supervisor must share information about the local operations of foreign banks with them provided there is reciprocity and protection of the confidentiality of the information.

In addition, home country supervisors should be given on-site access to local offices and subsidiaries for appropriate supervisory purposes. Where host country laws pose obstacles to sharing information or cooperating with home country supervisors, host authorities should work to have their laws changed in order to permit effective consolidated supervision by home countries.

SPECIAL ISSUES RELATED TO GOVERNMENT-OWNED BANKS

Many countries have some commercial banks that are owned, wholly or substantially, by the national government or by other public bodies.

In other countries, government-owned commercial banks comprise the majority of the banking system, usually for historic reasons. In principle, all banks should be subject to the same operational and supervisory standards regardless of their ownership; however, the unique nature of government-owned commercial banks should be recognised.

Government-owned commercial banks typically are backed by the full resources of the government. This provides additional support and strength for these banks. Although this government support can be advantageous, it should also be noted that the correction of problems at these banks is sometimes deferred and the government is not always in a position to recapitalise the bank when required. At the same time, this support may lead to the taking of excessive risks by bank management. In addition, market discipline may be less effective when market participants know that a particular bank has the full backing of the government and consequently has access to more extensive (and possibly cheaper) funding than would be the case for a comparable privately-owned bank.

Consequently, it is important that supervisors seek to ensure that government-owned commercial banks operate to the same high level of professional skill and disciplines as required of privately-owned commercial banks in order to preserve a strong credit and control culture in the banking system as a whole. In addition, supervisors should apply their supervisory methods in the same manner to government-owned commercial banks as they do to all other commercial banks.

Deposit Protection

Despite the efforts of supervisors, bank failures can occur. At such times, the possible loss of all or part of their funds increases the risk that depositors will lose confidence in other banks. Consequently, many countries have established deposit insurance plans to protect small depositors. These plans are normally organised by the government or central bank, or by the relevant bankers' association and are compulsory rather than voluntary.

Deposit insurance provides a safety net for many bank creditors thereby increasing public confidence in banks and making the financial system more stable. A safety net may also limit the effect that problems at one bank might have on other, healthier, banks in the same market, thereby reducing the possibility of contagion or a chain reaction within the banking system as a whole. A key benefit of deposit insurance is that, in conjunction with logical exit procedures, it gives the banking supervisors greater freedom to let problem banks fail. Deposit insurance can however increase the risk of imprudent behaviour by individual banks. Small depositors will be less inclined to withdraw funds even if the bank pursues high-risk strategies, thus weakening an important check on imprudent management. Government officials and supervisors need to recognise this effect of a safety net and take steps to prevent excessive risk-taking by banks. One method of limiting risk-taking is to utilise a deposit insurance system consisting of "co-insurance." Under such a system, the deposit insurance covers a percentage (e.g. 90%) of individual deposits and/or provides cover only up to a certain absolute amount so that depositors still have some funds at risk. Other methods include charging risk-based premiums or withholding deposit insurance from large, institutional depositors.

The actual form of such a programme should be tailored to the circumstances in, as well as historical and cultural features of, each country.

BANKING ON THE PRINCIPLES

This chapter studies whether compliance with the Basel Core Principles for Effective Banking Supervision (BCPs) improves bank soundness. BCP compliance assessments provide a unique source of information about the quality of bank supervision and regulation around the world. We find a significant and positive relationship between bank soundness (measured with Moody's financial strength ratings) and compliance with principles related to information provision. Specifically, countries which require banks to report regularly and accurately their financial data to regulators and market participants have sounder banks. This relationship is robust to controlling for broad indexes of institutional quality, macroeconomic variables, sovereign ratings, as well as reverse causality. Measuring soundness through z-scores yields similar results. These findings emphasize the importance of transparency in making supervisory processes effective and strengthening market discipline. Countries aiming to upgrade banking regulation and supervision should consider giving priority to information provision over other elements of the Core Principles.

INTRODUCTION

With increasing deregulation and globalization beginning in the 1980s, banking systems have become more fragile and banking crises have proliferated, causing or aggravating economic downturns and leading to significant fiscal costs (Caprio and Klingebiel, 1999). To improve crisis prevention and management, many countries are working to upgrade their bank regulation and supervision. This is a complex and difficult process, particularly in developing countries, where the required expertise may be scarce, the legal environment weak, and governance problems may lead to regulatory capture. But what exactly is good regulation and supervision? How can countries do it with limited resources? What should reforms focus on?

To answer the first question, in 1997 a group of representatives of bank supervisors from advanced countries ? the Basel Committee on Banking Supervision ? issued the Core Principles for Effective Bank Supervision (BCPs), a document summarizing best practices in the field (Table 1).1 Most countries in the world have endorsed the BCPs and have undertaken to comply with them, making them an almost universal standard for bank regulators. Beginning in 1999, the IMF and the World Bank have conducted joint evaluations of member countries' compliance with this standard, mainly within their joint Financial Sector Assessment Program (FSAP).2 These assessments provide a unique source of information about the quality of supervision and regulation around the world.

In this paper, we rely on assessments of compliance with the BCPs to study whether better banking supervision and regulation is associated with sounder banks. In addition, we look at which elements of the regulatory framework are most closely related to soundness. The goal is to shed light on how to prioritize efforts to improve supervision.

BCP compliance ratings have several advantages as measures of the quality of banking supervision and regulation. First, the BCPs are accepted as the blueprint of good supervision and regulation worldwide. Second, the assessment takes into account not only which laws and regulations are on the books, but also the extent to which they are implemented in practice. This is an important distinction. Third, separate compliance assessments are available for the 25 core principles, so that it is possible to separate out different aspects of supervision. The measure is only on a four-point scale, but to cut finer distinctions would likely be unrealistic. Because the evaluation reflects the judgment of the assessors, it inevitably contains an element of subjectivity. To limit subjectivity and ensure cross-country comparability, the Base Committee has developed a standardized methodology. In addition, the evaluations are conducted by expert supervisors from foreign countries and reviewed by internal teams at the Fund and the Bank. In any case, to the extent that measurement error is independent of bank soundness, it should not bias our results.

We measure bank soundness using Moody's financial strength ratings. This is a comprehensive measure of the ability of a bank to meet its obligations to depositors and other creditors as viewed by specialized analysts. To the extent that Moody's analysts have access to both quantitative and qualitative information about banks and their operating environment, ratings should be a more accurate measure of bank soundness than indicators built using only. The assessment methodology was published by the Basel Committee in 1999.

Another advantage of Moody's ratings is they aim at capturing bank solvency independent of the safety net, so that cross-country differences in the safety net, which are difficult to observe and measure, should not affect the results. A limitation of using Moody's ratings is that it restricts the sample to larger banks, as smaller banks are not rated. Thus, our investigation will not address the impact of the regulatory framework on smaller banks. As the latter are not likely to be of systemic importance, this limitation should be relatively minor. A more serious limitation is that a number of low-income countries have no rated banks, and thus are excluded from the sample.

Because so far data on BCP compliance are available only at one point in time, our study cannot rely on time series variation. This limitation forces us to be very careful in controlling for other potential sources of cross-sectional variation as well as joint endogeneity. One important problem is that the BCP compliance indicator may be associated with bank soundness because it proxies for the overall quality of the institutional and macroeconomic environment rather than capture specific features of supervision. While we recognize that this concern cannot be fully laid to rest, we perform extensive robustness tests controlling for broad indexes of institutional quality, macroeconomic variables, as well as sovereign credit ratings.

A second concern is the endogeneity of supervision. The level of compliance with the BCPs is chosen by the countries themselves, and countries with sounder banks may face less opposition in enacting more rigorous supervision than countries with distressed banks.6 On the other hand, it can also be argued that countries that have experienced episodes of distress, and whose banks are still weak, may have the strongest incentives to upgrade their supervisory capacity. So in principle the endogeneity of supervision may bias the relationship with soundness in either direction. To take endogeneity into account, we resort to instrumental variables estimation.

We find that an index of overall compliance with the BCPs is positively correlated with bank ratings after controlling for institutional quality, the macroeconomic environment, and bank characteristics. However, this relationship is not very robust. When we distinguish among groups of BCPs, on the other hand, we find a very robust positive relationship between compliance with information provision (BCP No. 21) and bank soundness. More specifically, countries in which banks have to report regularly and accurately their financial data to regulators and market participants have more highly rated banks. The relationship between bank soundness and transparency remains even after we instrument for transparency, suggesting it does not reflect reverse causality.

LITERATURE REVIEW

In their empirical studies of bank crisis determinants, Demirg-Kunt and Detragiache (1998, 2002) find that countries with better institutions are less likely to experience banking crises and are less affected by moral hazard due to deposit insurance. They interpret institutional variables such as rule of law and quality of bureaucracy as proxies for supervision and regulation, but do not include direct measures of this dimension, which were not available at the time.

Barth, Caprio, and Levine (2001) (BCL) assembled the first extensive cross-country database on the characteristics of the supervisory and regulatory framework. The data come from a survey of bank supervisors, and measure the presence or absence of a series of regulatory features. In the first comprehensive theoretical and empirical study of alternative approaches to bank supervision, BCL (2004) find that regulatory and supervisory practices that force accurate information disclosure, empower private sector monitoring of banks, and foster incentives for private agents to exert corporate control work best to promote bank performance and stability. Specifically, in a cross-country setting they show that regulatory and supervisory regimes with these features have suffered fewer crises in the past two decades, have lower non-performing loans, and have deeper credit markets.

One limitation of this study is that survey information reflects whether laws or regulations are on the books, but not to what extent they are implemented in practice.

Judging from FSAP reports, implementation is a serious concern in many countries. BCP compliance assessments allow us to better capture this important dimension, at least to the extent the assessors are able to evaluate it. Another difference between our approach and BCL is that we use bank ratings as measures of bank soundness in cross-sectional regressions, while BCL use the occurrence of systemic banking crises and non-performing loans. Because systemic crises are rare events, in BCL's analysis crises predate information on bank regulation and supervision which is available only for the end of the sample period. To the extent that bank regulation and supervision may have evolved over the sample, the relationships identified may not be accurate. Non-performing loans do not suffer from this problem, but are not usually comparable across countries, since countries have difference rules for marking loans as non-performing (Barth et al., 2006). On the other hand, an advantage of the BCL survey data is that it does not rely on the subjective views of compliance assessors.

Three papers have used information on BCP compliance to study bank performance: An early paper by Sundararajan, Marston, and Basu (2001) uses a sample of 25 countries to examine the relationship between an overall index of compliance and bank soundness measured by the size of non-performing loans (NPLs) and loan spreads. They found BCP compliance not be a significant determinant of soundness. Podpiera (2004) extends the set of countries and finds that better BCP compliance lowers NPLs. Das et al. (2004) broadens the measure of bank soundness to include also compliance with standards for monetary and financial policies, and shows that better regulatory governance is associated with sounder banks, particularly in countries with better institutions.

We claim that bank ratings are a more accurate measure of bank soundness across countries than NPLs, loan spreads, interest margins, or capital adequacy. Because different countries have different reporting rules, NPLs are notoriously difficult to compare across countries, as already mentioned above. On the other hand, loan spreads or interest margins, and capitalization are affected by a variety of forces other than fragility, such as market structure, differences in risk-free interest rates and operating costs, and varying capital regulation. Another departure from existing studies is that we conduct much more extensive robustness test to separate out the effects of banking regulation from those of other country characteristics, such as institutional quality and macroeconomic performance. Finally, and perhaps most importantly in light of the results, our work is the first to explore how compliance with different components of the BCPs affects soundness.

Our study is also related to the growing literature on transparency in financial markets. Patel, Balic, and Bwakira (2002) compare transparency and disclosure in emerging markets corporations. Mitton (2002) argues that transparency helps weather financial crises, as East Asian companies with auditors from major international accounting firms were found to have better stock performance after the crisis of 1997-98. Glennerster and Shin (2003) shows that countries that disclose more information to the IMF and the markets are rewarded through lower borrowing costs. More transparency also attracts more foreign portfolio investment (Gelos and Wei, 2005). Perotti and Von Thadden (2005) study how the presence of a dominant investor affects a firm decision of how much to disclose.

METHODOLOGY AND DATA

Basic Econometric Model

The empirical model is a basic cross-sectional regression using bank level data. The dependent variable is the bank's rating. Moody's rates banks' financial strength on a 15-point scale, ranging from E-(least sound) to A+ (most sound). Since this is a limited dependent variable, the appropriate econometric model is an ordered probit, which we use to estimate the baseline specification. We also show that the results do not change if we transform the ratings in a numerical index and estimate an OLS model. Standard errors are clustered by country to allow for correlated residuals within each country. Specifically, the regression equations we estimate are of the form:

Ratingij = + 1compliancej + 2bank characteristicsij +3institutions j + 4macroeconomiccontrolsj +ij, (1)

where the subscript j denotes the country and the subscript i denotes the bank.

The variable of interest is compliance with the BCPs. Assessors separately rate compliance with each principle using a four-point scale.7 We assign numerical values to these ratings, aggregate over all the principles, and standardize the sum to obtain an index that varies from zero to one. Since we are also interested in differentiating among the various dimensions of regulation and supervision, we compute compliance indexes for subgroups of principles following the grouping by chapters used by the Basel Committee. Compliance for each chapter is used as an alternative variable of interest.

The first set of control variables includes various bank characteristics that might affect financial strength: size, measured by the logarithm of bank assets; profitability, measured alternatively as return on assets or return on equity; and capitalization, measured by the ratio of equity to total assets. We also use the ratio of bank loans to total assets and the ratio of deposit to total liabilities to control for the type of intermediation and funding sources of each bank. Finally, we control for whether the bank is owned by the government or by foreigners and for whether the bank is not a commercial bank.

A second group of control variables captures the overall quality of the institutions. Combining information from a variety of available indexes, Kaufman, Kraay, and Mastruzzi (2003) create various broad measures of perception of institutional quality which have been widely used in empirical studies. In our baseline specification, we use an index capturing the extent to which the rule of law is respected. This index is strongly correlated with other institutional indexes from the same source, such as lack of corruption, contract enforcement, etc., and we obtain similar results using these alternative indexes or an average of all the indexes. As alternative control for the overall quality of institutions we use GDP per capita.

Bank soundness is also affected by the macroeconomic outlook, as slow output growth, high inflation, a depreciating currency, high real interest rates, and rapid credit expansion have been found to be associated with bank instability (see, for instance, Demirg-Kunt and Detragiache, 1998). Thus, as a third set of controls, we employ various combination of these macroeconomic variables in alternative specifications. We also use S&P's sovereign rating as a comprehensive indicator of the quality of macroeconomic policies and institutions which might affect bank stability in a country.

The sample includes a few mutual banks, investment houses, and similar institutions. Excluding non-commercial banks does not change the results.

Sample and Data Sources

BCP compliance data come from assessments carried out by the IMF and the World Bank beginning in 1999. Some of these assessments are public information and can be found on the institutions' websites. Others are kept confidential at the request of the country authorities. Moody's financial strength ratings have been compiled from Bankscope database. Bankscope reports the current rating, the last date in which the rating was revised, and the rating that prevailed before then, but no other historical rating information. Since we need to roughly match the timing of the BCP rating with that of Moody's ratings, we dropped from the sample banks that had a rating change after more than one year since the BCP compliance evaluation. Only a few banks fall in this category.

Bank-level variables have also been constructed from Bankscope, while macroeconomic variables are mainly from the IMF's International Financial Statistics. Information about bank ownership is obtained from Bankscope and other miscellaneous sources. Banks are considered state-owned if the government has a controlling share or is the sole owner, and similarly for foreign-owned banks.

We use BCP assessment data for 39 countries for which we have bank ratings from Moody's. Not surprisingly, this group includes mostly developed countries and emerging markets, while low-income countries are not represented. Some countries have only one or two banks in the sample, but since we are not relying on intra-country variation to identify the relationship of interest this should not be a major limitation. The total number of banks in the baseline sample is 203.

A First Look at the Data

Figure 1 shows the overall compliance index by region and level of development. As expected, advanced countries have the highest compliance. Among the other countries, East Asia and Sub-Saharan Africa are closer to meeting the Basel standards, while South Asia, the Middle East and North Africa and Latin America lag behind. If we examine subgroups of chapters, the highest compliance is with principles concerning the licensing of banks and the structure of the banking market. At the other extreme, principles regarding the formal powers of supervisors were implemented to the least degree. Differences in compliance are not very large across different categories of principles, but averages across countries may hide larger discrepancies within each country.

Compliance levels are all significantly and positively correlated. The strongest correlation (over 80 percent) is between compliance with principles concerning prudential regulation and those concerning methods of ongoing supervision. Other correlations are considerably weaker, even falling below 50 percent in the case of principles regarding the formal powers of supervisors. All in all, these correlations suggest that there is enough variation in compliance across chapters to investigate the effect of various aspects of supervision separately.

There is a strong positive correlation between bank size and bank soundness, as larger, better diversified banks are seen as more stable. This correlation may be partly driven by the fact that larger banks tend to be located in more advanced countries, which have more stable economies. More profitable and better capitalized banks with a lower ratio of loans to assets also receive higher ratings. State banks are seen as more vulnerable, while the presence of large liquid assets is associated with a less favorable rating. This may reflect the existence of high compulsory liquidity requirements or lack of opportunities to lend in some unstable emerging markets. Interestingly, foreign-owned banks do not receive significantly higher ratings.

Among country level variables, bank ratings have a strong positive correlation with the country sovereign rating, the index of rule of law, and GDP per capita. Rapid exchange rate depreciation is associated with lower ratings. The correlation with the variable of interest, compliance with the BCPs, is positive, large, and significant.

THE RESULTS

Results Using the Aggregate Index and their Robustness

The index enters the regressions positively and significantly both by itself and when bank characteristics are controlled for. Controlling for institutional development with GDP per capita does not alter the relationship, while when we control for the sovereign rating the coefficient of compliance becomes smaller and statistical significance drops from one percent to five percent. When the quality of institutions is controlled for through the rule of law index, the coefficient of compliance becomes even smaller and significance drops to ten percent, suggesting that rule of law is an important control variable. We take the specification including rule of law as the baseline in the rest of the paper.

Excluding advanced country banks from the sample does not change regression results much. However, when we exclude extreme observations, the coefficient of compliance becomes quite small and is no longer significant. Significance also disappears if we estimate the model using OLS instead of ordered probit.

As far as the control variables, larger banks are rated significantly higher and state-owned banks are considered more vulnerable. Foreign-owned banks are also rated more favorably and the coefficient is significant in the specification that includes the overall institutional quality of the country, but not if we restrict the sample to developing countries. These results suggest that once we control for bank size, ownership, and institutions, the additional explanatory power of bank balance sheet variables is small.

We conclude that while there is a positive correlation between bank soundness and the overall index of BCP compliance, this result is sensitive to controlling for the institutional quality of the country and to the exclusion of outliers. An interesting question is whether different principles that make up the overall BCP index affect bank soundness differently. We turn to this issue next.

Results by Group of Principles

Our results indicate that principles related to licensing and structure and information requirements are the most significantly associated with higher bank ratings at one percent significance. At the ten percent level, preconditions for effective bank supervision also enter significantly.

To check if these results are robust we control for compliance with the rest of the principles. When we include these aggregate indexes in the relevant regressions, we see that only compliance with information requirements remains significant. As an additional robustness test, we re-run these three specifications excluding individual countries one by one.

Assessing the magnitude of the effect of Chapter 5 compliance on ratings is somewhat complicated by the fact that the econometric model is non-linear and that the compliance indicator is discrete. Nonetheless, computing marginal effects at the sample mean of the regressors, and assuming a constant elasticity around the mean, a decline in compliance from largely compliant to materially non-compliant would lower by one notch the rating of a bank rated D (from D to D-).

ROBUSTNESS OF THE RELATIONSHIP BETWEEN BANK RATINGS AND COMPLIANCE WITH INFORMATION Provision

In this section we conduct additional robustness checks on the empirical relationship between information disclosure and bank soundness and investigate reverse causality.

Compliance with Chapter 5 of the BCPs is positively and significantly associated with bank ratings also when we exclude from the sample advanced countries or extreme observations. In further robustness tests, we add to the baseline regression additional macroeconomic controls, which have been found in the literature to be associated with bank fragility (Demirg-Kunt and Detragiache, 1998 and 2005): depreciation of the nominal exchange rate, the inflation rate and its standard deviation, real credit growth, real GDP per capita growth.13 Among the macro variables, exchange rate depreciation and inflation volatility are negatively and significantly associated with bank ratings, while the level of inflation, real GDP growth, and real credit growth are not significant (results not reported). Compliance with information requirements remains significant and positive throughout these different specifications, confirming that the impact of this principle is not sensitive to omitted macro controls.

In yet another specification, we include in the regressions two measures of the frequency and timeliness of macroeconomic data release obtained from IMF's Special Data Dissemination Standards (Allum and Aga, 2001). These measures might help us control for unobservable characteristics that make a country more transparent. The frequency index is positive and significant, while the timeliness is not (result not reported).

In the last set of regressions, we try to separate out compliance with Chapter 5 from other design features of supervision and regulation by introducing as regressors four indexes constructed using BCL's survey of bank regulators. Specifically, these indexes measure the presence in the laws and regulations of various provisions related to discipline, information disclosure, auditing requirements, and lack of banking restrictions (Barth, Caprio, Levine, 2001).

Endogeneity of BCP Compliance

In this paper, we use individual bank level information to test the impact of compliance with the BCPs. Since an individual bank's soundness rating is unlikely to have an impact on country-level measures of supervisory quality, reverse causality should not be a serious concern. However, soundness ratings are correlated within countries, so it is possible that assessors may assign better compliance ratings to countries whose large banks are generally considered to be financially sound. Furthermore, since the level of compliance is a policy choice made by the countries themselves, countries with sounder banks may face less political opposition in adopting more rigorous regulatory and supervisory processes compared to those countries with distressed banks. On the other hand, it can also be argued that countries with weak banks coming out of a financial crisis may have the strongest incentives and political support to reform their regulations and supervision. So in principle the endogeneity of supervision may bias the relationship with soundness in either direction. It should be emphasized that endogeneity concerns should not be overblown, particularly because we are examining only one of the chapters and using compliance with the other chapters as a control variable.

First, legal origin variables are jointly highly significant in the first stage regressions. In all specifications the F-test for the joint significance of the instruments is well above 10, suggesting that there is no concern about weak instruments (Stock and Yogo, 2005). In the second stage, compliance with information provision remains positive and significant in all specification. Following Moreira (2003), we have also computed CLR confidence intervals, which should be robust to weak instruments. Using religion as an alternative instrument gives similar results. On the other hand, other basic country characteristics, such as latitude or ethnic fractionalization, have poor predictive power for BCP compliance.

Measuring Bank Soundness with Z-Scores

As discussed in the introduction, Moody's ratings are a nice measure of bank financial strength, as they are prepared by specialists with access to variety of sources of information and whose business is to make accurate assessments. On the other hand, ratings are subjective, and it may be argued that analysts may be better disposed towards bank that provide more accurate and timely information even though these banks are not necessarily more sound. To address this concern, in this section we measure bank soundness using an alternative, objective, and commonly used indicator, namely the Z-score.16 We compute Z-scores for the banks in our sample and investigate if we continue to find evidence that compliance with information requirements is a significant correlate to bank soundness.

The specification is broadly similar to the previous baseline, although we dropped equity and return on assets from the set of regressors since these variables are now used to compute the left-hand-side variable. The z-scores have a positive and statistically significant correlation with Moody's ratings, but the correlation is not very high (about 20 percent). Nonetheless, the relationship between bank soundness and BCP compliance remains remarkably similar to the one uncovered using Moody's ratings: the overall compliance index is positive but not significant, and when we examine individual chapters the only one that is robust on information provision. Additional tests using more macroeconomic control variables (exchange rate depreciation, inflation, inflation volatility, credit growth) confirm this finding (results not reported).

To summarize, the positive relationship between compliance with information provision regulation is in evidence whether bank soundness is measured through Moody's ratings or through Z-scores.

CONCLUSIONS

Strong regulation and supervision plays an essential part in ensuring a safe and sound banking system. To curb bank fragility and improve crisis management, many countries are in the process of strengthening their regulatory and supervisory systems, a complicated and costly process for many developing countries where human resources are scarce and other supporting institutions are weak. What type of regulations and supervisory practices are most effective in ensuring bank soundness? This is the question that we have addressed in this study. Using bank-level investor ratings for 39 countries, we study whether compliance with Basel Core Principles (BCPs), the standard of best practices in bank supervision, is associated with bank soundness. BCP compliance assessments, carried out under the auspices of the World Bank and IMF Financial Sector Assessment Program, provide a unique source of information about the quality of bank supervision and regulation around the world.

An important aspect of our study is the attempt to differentiate among different elements of the regulatory framework, to help prioritize reform efforts. We find a significant and positive relationship between compliance with information provision and bank soundness, which is robust to controlling broad indexes of institutional quality, macroeconomic variables, sovereign ratings, as well as reverse causality. Specifically, countries which require their banks to report regularly and accurately their financial data to regulators and market participants have more highly rated banks, as timely disclosure of high quality information strengthens monitoring by regulators and markets alike.

Our results also suggest that countries aiming to upgrade banking regulation and supervision should consider giving priority to information provision over other elements of the Core Principles. Because information provision is a necessary condition for effective discipline, this policy recommendation is consistent with the approach to regulation and supervision recommended by Barth, Caprio, and Levine (2006), who stress the importance of mechanisms to empower market discipline and are skeptical of structures that assign too much power to regulators.

BASLE CORE PRINCIPLES–INFORMATION REQUIREMENTS OF BANKING ORGANIZATIONS

Principle 21: Banking supervisors must be satisfied that each bank maintains adequate records drawn up in accordance with consistent accounting policies and practices that enable the supervisor to obtain a true and fair view of the financial condition of the bank and the profitability of its business, and that the bank publishes on a regular basis financial statements that fairly reflect its condition.

For banking supervisors to conduct effective off-site supervision of banks and to evaluate the condition of the local banking market, they must receive financial information at regular intervals and this information must be verified periodically through on-site examinations or external audits. Banking supervisors must ensure that each bank maintains adequate accounting records drawn up in accordance with consistent accounting policies and practices that enable the supervisor to obtain a true and fair view of the financial condition of the bank and the profitability of its business. In order that the accounts portray a true and fair view, it is essential that assets are recorded at values that are realistic and consistent, taking account of current values, where relevant, and that profit reflects what, on a net basis, is likely to be received and takes into account likely transfers to loan loss reserves. It is important that banks submit information in a format that makes comparisons among banks possible although, for certain purposes, data derived from internal management information systems may also be helpful to supervisors. At a minimum, periodic reporting should include a bank's balance sheet, contingent liabilities and income statement, with supporting details and key risk exposures. Supervisors can be obstructed or misled when banks knowingly or recklessly provide false information of material importance to the supervisory process. If a bank provides information to the supervisor knowing that it is materially false or misleading, or it does so recklessly, supervisory and/or criminal action should be taken against both the individuals involved and the institution.

Accounting Standards

In order to ensure that the information submitted by banks is of a comparable nature and its meaning is clear, the supervisory agency will need to provide report instructions that clearly establish the accounting standards to be used in preparing the reports. These standards should be based on accounting principles and rules that command wide international acceptance and be aimed specifically at banking institutions.

Scope and Frequency of Reporting

The supervisory agency needs to have powers to determine the scope and frequency of reporting to reflect the volatility of the business and to enable the agency to track what is happening at individual banks on both a solo and consolidated basis, as well as with the banking system as a whole. The supervisors should develop a series of informational reports for banks to prepare and submit at regular intervals. While some reports may be filed as often as monthly, others may be filed quarterly or annually. In addition, some reports may be "event generated", meaning they are filed only if a particular event occurs (e.g. investment in a new affiliate). Supervisors should be sensitive to the burden that reporting imposes. Consequently, they may determine that it is not necessary for every bank to file every report. Filing status can be based on the organizational structure of the bank, its size, and the types of activities it conducts.

Confirmation of the Accuracy of Information Submitted

It is the responsibility of bank management to ensure the accuracy, completeness and timeliness of prudential, financial, and other reports submitted to the supervisors. Therefore, bank management must ensure that reports are verified and that external auditors determine that the reporting systems in place are adequate and provide reliable data. External auditors should express an opinion on the annual accounts and management report supplied to shareholders and the general public. Weaknesses in bank auditing standards in a particular country may require that banking supervisors become involved in establishing clear guidelines concerning the scope and content of the audit program as well as the standards to be used. In extreme cases where supervisors cannot be satisfied with the quality of the annual accounts or regulatory reports, or with the work done by external auditors, they should have the ability to use supervisory measures to bring about timely corrective action, and they may need to reserve the right to approve the issue of accounts to the public. In assessing the nature and adequacy of work done by auditors, and the degree of reliance that can be placed on this work, supervisors will need to consider the extent to which the audit program has examined such areas as the loan portfolio, loan loss reserves, nonperforming assets (including the treatment of interest on such assets), asset valuations, trading and other securities activities, derivatives, asset securitizations, and the adequacy of internal controls over financial reporting. Where it is competent and independent of management, internal audits can be relied upon as a source of information and may contribute usefully to the supervisors' understanding.

Confidentiality of Supervisory Information

Although market participants should have access to correct and timely information, there are certain types of sensitive information27 that should be held confidential by banking supervisors. In order for a relationship of mutual trust to develop, banks need to know that such sensitive information will be held confidential by the banking supervisory agency and its appropriate counterparts at other domestic and foreign supervisory agencies.

Disclosure

In order for market forces to work effectively, thereby fostering a stable and efficient financial system, market participants need access to correct and timely information. Disclosure, therefore, is a complement to supervision. For this reason, banks should be required to disclose to the public information regarding their activities and financial position that is comprehensive and not misleading. This information should be timely and sufficient for market participants to assess the risk inherent in any individual banking organization.

CORE PRINCIPLES OF EFFECTIVE BANKING SUPERVISION

The Basel Committee on Banking Supervision, which is a committee of banking supervisory authorities of G-10 countries, has been in the forefront of the international attempt in the development of standards and the establishment of a framework for bank supervision towards strengthening international financial stability. In 1997, in consultation with the supervisory authorities of a few non G-10 countries including India, it drew up the 25 "Core Principles for Effective Banking Supervision" which were in the nature of minimum requirements intended to guide supervisory authorities which were seeking to "strengthen their current supervisory regime".

Being one of the central banks which was involved in the exercise of drawing up the Core Principles, the Reserve Bank of India had assessed its own position with respect to these

Principles in 1998. The assessment had shown that most of the Core Principles were already enshrined in our existing legislation or current regulations. Gaps had been identified between existing practice and principle mainly in the areas of risk management in banks, inter-agency cooperation with other domestic/international regulators and consolidated supervision. Internal working groups were set up to suggest measures to bridge these gaps and their recommendations have been accepted by the Board for Financial Supervision and are now in the process of being implemented. Given the spread and reach of the Indian banking system, with over 60,000 branches of more than 100 banks, implementation is a challenge for the supervisors. However, the Reserve Bank of India is committed to the full implementation of the Core Principles.

The Bank also serves on the Core Principles Liaison Group of the BCBS, which has been formed "to promote the timely and complete implementation of these principles world-wide".

It gives me great pleasure to release this document which is intended to provide the reader with a framework within which one can view the developments in the Indian Banking System in a proper perspective. The document reflects the position as existing on date and will be updated to reflect future changes. As supervision is a dynamic process, readers may refer to the Reserve Bank of India for the latest position or for any clarifications.

CORE PRINCIPLES FOR BANKING SUPERVISION-STATUS IN INDIA

Preconditions for Effective Banking Supervision

Framework and Coordination

An effective system of banking supervision will have clear responsibilities and objectives for each agency involved in the supervision of banks. Each such agency should possess operational independence and adequate resources. A suitable legal framework for banking supervision is also necessary including provisions relating to authorisation of banking establishments and their ongoing supervision; powers to address compliance with laws as well as safety and soundness concerns; and legal protection for supervisors. Arrangements for sharing information between supervisors and protection for confidentiality of such information should be in place.

The Reserve Bank of India ("RBI"), an autonomous body created under an act of the Indian parliament i.e. The Reserve Bank of India Act, 1934, is entrusted, interalia, with the sole responsibility of regulation and supervision of banks under the Banking Regulation Act, 1949. Section 35 of the Banking Regulation Act vests powers in RBI for inspection of books of any banking company at any time.

Both the regulatory and supervisory functions of RBI were earlier carried out through its Department of Banking Operations and Development ("DBOD") till December 1993, when a separate department entitled 'Department of Supervision (DOS)' was formed to take over the supervisory function, leaving regulatory functions to DBOD. In November 1994, RBI constituted the Board for Financial Supervision (BFS) under RBI (BFS) Regulations 1994 to give undivided attention to the prudential supervision and regulation of banks, financial institutions and non-bank financial institutions in an integrated manner. DBOD continues to perform the regulatory function pertaining to banks.

However, DOS has since been bifurcated into Department of Banking Supervision (DBS) and Department of Non-Banking Supervision (DNBS). DBS is responsible for the supervision of commercial banks and their merchant banking subsidiaries. Both regulation and supervision of the development financial institutions (DFI's) are handled by the Financial Institutions Division (FID) of the DBS.

DNBS is responsible for supervision and regulation of Non-banking Financial Companies (NBFCs). No NBFC can commence or carry on the business of a non-banking financial institution without obtaining a certificate of registration from RBI. The NBFC with net owned funds of Rs.2.5 million and above (since enhanced to Rs.20 million effective from 20 April 1999) are mandatorily required to be registered with RBI. Maintenance of liquid assets at a specified percentage of public deposits is compulsory.

RBI is empowered to give directions to NBFCs and can even prohibit NBFCs which do not adhere to a set of prudential norms from accepting deposits and impose penalties under the provisions of the RBI Act. A system of on-site examination based on CAMELS rating model and off-site surveillance of various statutory returns of NBFCs is in place. Besides, special formats for off-site surveillance of NBFCs with asset size of Rs.1 billion and above have been devised.

The BFS has been constituted under the aegis of RBI. It is an autonomous body and directs the policies and operations relating to supervision of banks, DFIs and NBFCs. The Governor of the Reserve Bank is the Chairman of the BFS while the Deputy Governor in-charge of supervision is the Vice-chairman. The other two Deputy Governors of the Bank, together with four non-official directors from the Central Board of the Bank, are the members of the BFS. Since its formation in November 1994, the BFS, which meets every month, has positioned a new strategy for on-site supervision of banks and a system of off-site monitoring, based on quarterly reporting system.

RBI has been given broad powers under Section 35A of the Banking Regulation Act to issue directions to banking companies in general or to any banking company in particular, if it is satisfied that these are required-

(a) in the public interest; or

(b) in the interest of banking policy; or

(c) to prevent the affairs of any banking company being conducted in a manner detrimental to the interests of the depositors or in a manner prejudicial to the interests of the banking company; or

(d) to secure the proper management of any banking company generally.

The Central Government, after consultation with RBI, may acquire or amalgamate or reconstitute a banking company, which is being managed in a manner detrimental to the interest of its depositors or which has failed to comply with directions issued by RBI under the Banking Regulation Act. The RBI has powers to apply for winding up of a banking company that is unable to meet its commitments and / or its continuation is prejudicial to the interest of its depositors. The RBI can intervene in the bank's management if directors / management are not found to be 'fit and proper' in the course of operation. The RBI can cancel the licence of a banking company provided the conditions stated in Section 22(3) of the Banking Regulation Act are not fulfilled.

Section 7 of the RBI Act provides for operational independence to RBI while at the same time reserving the Central Government's right to issue directions to RBI from time to time in public interest. The management of RBI rests with the Central Board of Directors. The RBI is headed by the Governor who is appointed by the Central Government for a term not exceeding five years and is eligible for reappointment.

An annual report on the working of RBI with detailed analysis of its annual accounts and an assessment of the Indian economy is submitted to the Central Government under Section 53(2) of the RBI Act. The RBI compiles two financial statements viz. weekly statement of its affairs and annual balance sheet as at 30 June of each year in terms of Section 53 of the RBI Act, 1934 and transmits these to the Central Government. The Central Government publishes these statements in the Gazette of India. The RBI publishes fortnightly a consolidated statement containing aggregate liabilities and assets of all the scheduled commercial banks as per Section 43 of the RBI Act. The RBI brings out certain publications at regular intervals on the financial strength and performance of banking industry and state of economy. The publications include Banking Statistics, Report on Currency and Finance, Report on Trends and Progress of Banking in India (Section 36(2) of the Banking Regulation Act), Credit Information Review, and monthly RBI bulletin containing statistics on selective economic and banking indicators and weekly statistical supplements.

The RBI equips its officers with latest techniques of supervision through ongoing training programmes organised at its own staff colleges viz. Reserve Bank Staff College, Chennai; College of Agricultural Banking, Pune; Bankers Training College, Mumbai; and Institute for Development and Research of Banking Technology, Hyderabad. Besides, the RBI regularly deputes its officers to training programmes, seminars and conferences conducted by international bodies, Central Banks of other countries and international organisations like Bank for International Settlements and the International Financial Institutions.

On-going analysis of off-site returns is carried out in a computerised environment. The RBI has initiated steps to move from Local Area Networking (LAN) to Wide Area Networking (WAN) with a view to connect its Regional Offices and commercial banks through VSAT based connectivity by December 2000.

The banking laws are reviewed and updated from time to time considering the changing needs of the banking industry and economy. The Banking Regulation Act was last amended in 1994. An expert committee set up in February 1999 on the recommendations of the Committee on Banking Sector Reforms is engaged in the task of examining various banking laws and all relevant banking related legislations. The committee is expected to submit its recommendations by December, 1999.

The RBI has the necessary powers to issue licence to a company for carrying on the business of banking. The RBI is vested with powers to issue guidelines on any issue relating to functioning of banks. This helps the Bank in laying down prudential guidelines for sound management of banks. It has issued several mandatory guidelines on liquidity maintenance, capital adequacy, income recognition, asset classification and provisioning, connected lending and prudential norms on large exposures. The Banking Regulation Act vests powers in RBI to ensure compliance with its provisions. Non-compliance with mandatory guidelines can invite monetary and / or non-monetary penalties. The Banking Regulation Act provides for explicit protection to the supervisors under Section 54. No suit or other legal proceeding shall lie against RBI or any of its officers for anything or any damage caused or likely to be caused by anything done in good faith or intended to be done in pursuance of the Banking Regulation Act.

RBI shares relevant information with overseas supervisors on request. Information from overseas supervisors is received with the understanding that this would remain confidential. Information needs of domestic regulatory bodies like Securities and Exchange Board of India (SEBI), National Bank for Agricultural and Rural Development (NABARD), National Housing Bank (NHB), etc, are attended to on mutual understanding. A High level Committee on Capital Markets consisting of Governor of RBI, Chairman of SEBI and Economic

Affairs Secretary of the Central Government, serves as a forum for discussing common regulatory issues.

Licensing and Structure

Permissible Activities

The permissible activities of institutions that are licensed and subject to supervision as banks must be clearly defined and the use of word 'bank' in names should be controlled as far as possible.

The permissible activities of a banking company are listed in Section 6(1) of the Banking Regulation Act, 1949. Section 6(2) specifically prohibits a banking company from carrying on any form of business other than those referred to in Section 6(1). The term "banking" as defined in Section 5 means "the accepting, for the purpose of lending or investment, of deposits of money from the public, repayable on demand or otherwise and withdrawal by cheque, order or otherwise". A banking company means any company that transacts the business of banking in India. Any company other than a banking company accepting deposit of money from the public merely for the purpose of financing its business is not deemed to transact the business of banking. A banking company could be either a public sector bank, privately held bank, foreign bank or co-operative bank.

The first three types of banks are called 'commercial' banks. Commercial banks can be divided into certain distinct categories depending on their method of establishment and pattern of ownership, namely public sector banks, i.e.(State Bank of India, its 7 associate banks and 19 nationalised banks); 'old' private sector banks i.e. those which were in existence before the guidelines for floating new private banks were issued in 1993; 'new' private sector banks, foreign banks, and Regional Rural banks (RRBs). The scope of the supervision of the BFS in currently limited to all commercial banks other than RRBs. Recently, those urban co-operative banks which are included in the second schedule of the RBI Act, 1934, have also been brought under the ambit of the BFS.

The permissible activities of banks in India are defined in the Banking Regulation Act that allow banks to undertake both commercial banking and investment banking. However, banks are not allowed to undertake mutual fund business departmentally.

Similarly, banks cannot yet undertake insurance business. Banks are permitted to set up subsidiaries only for undertaking activities that are permissible under Section 19 of the Banking Regulation Act. Banks are not allowed to trade in commodities or become members of the stock exchange.

In India, besides banks that accept public deposits, there are other institutions like development financial institutions (DFIs) and non-banking financial companies that also accept deposits of money that are not repayable on demand. The DFIs have been brought under the supervisory ambit of the DBS since April 1995. The RBI has also recently framed detailed regulations for supervision of these entities that are part of the financial system. Besides these entities, corporate bodies other than banks can also accept retail deposits. The supervision of the RBI does not extend to such corporates, and the acceptance of deposits by corporates is regulated by the Government of India under Acceptance of Deposits Rules,1993 framed under the Companies Act, 1956.

Section 7 of the Banking Regulation Act limits the use of words such as "bank", "banker", or "banking" to a banking company only as part of its name or in connection with its business. Further, no company shall carry on the business of banking in India unless it uses as part of its name at least one of such words. The Central Government,on the recommendation of the RBI, may exempt any banking company or class of banking companies from any of the provisions of the Banking Regulation Act (Section 53 of the Banking Regulation Act).

Licensing of Banks

The licensing authority must have the right to set criteria and reject applications of establishments that do not meet the standards set. The licensing process at minimum should consist of an assessment of the bank's ownership structure, directors and senior management; its operating plan and internal controls and its projected financial conditions, including its capital base. Where the proposed owner or parent organisation is a foreign bank, the prior consent of its home country supervisor should be obtained.

Section 22 of the Banking Regulation Act provides that a company intending to carry on banking business must obtain a licence from RBI except such of the banks (public sector banks and RRBs), which are established under specific enactments. The RBI issues licence only after "tests of entry" are fulfilled. These tests include minimum capital, ownership structure, bank's operating plans and controls, ability of the bank to pay its present and future depositors in full, quality of management and whether the licensing of the bank would be in the public interest. Section 22(3) of the Banking Regulation Act provides that the RBI may require to be satisfied by an "inspection of books of the company and methods of operation of the company or otherwise" regarding the capital structure, proposed management etc. prior to grant of licence. By virtue of Section 10A(2) of the Banking Regulation Act, not less than 51% of the total number of members of the Board of Directors of a banking company should have special knowledge or practical experience in accountancy, agriculture, banking, co-operation, economics, finance, law, small scale industry, etc.

Foreign banks are allowed to operate through branches only. The 'tests of entry' criteria are also applied to branches of foreign banks. Besides these, the RBI examines dealings of the foreign bank with Indian parties, international and home country ranking where available, international presence, economic and trade relations with the home country and supervisory standards prevalent in the home country. The RBI also insists on prior consent of the home country regulator and ensures that the laws of the home country do not discriminate in any way against banks incorporated in India. A new foreign bank is required to bring in minimum assigned capital of USD 25 million, of which USD10 million shall be brought in at the time of opening each of the first two branches and balance USD 5 million at the time of opening of third branch. All the foreign banks are required to maintain minimum capital adequacy ratio of 8% on aggregate risk weighted assets of their Indian operations (being raised to 9% with effect from March 31, 2000). It is important to get home regulators' consent even in the case of opening a Representative Office, as once presence is allowed, it may be construed that the bank has fulfilled the tests of entry.

As far as opening of branches by Indian banks overseas is concerned, the bank in India has to take prior approval of RBI for setting up a branch or subsidiary or joint venture. The factors considered while granting such permission include importance of the country as a centre of international finance, pattern of India's trade with and investment in the country concerned, size of Indian population and expatriates in the country, prevailing local banking laws, exchange control regulations, etc.

For opening a new branch in India, RBI permission is needed after approval of the Board of the bank. However, banks that have achieved 8% capital adequacy ratio; have earned net profit for three consecutive years; have non-performing loans not exceeding 15% of the gross loans and have minimum owned funds of Rs.1 billion, may be permitted to set up new branches and update extension counters into full-fledged new branches.The policy in this regard is revised from time to time.

The norms for licensing of new banks have been tightened since 1993 when guidelines allowing entry of banks in private sector were formulated. The track record of the promoters is ascertained from other banks, supervisory/regulatory Departments as well as from SEBI, the Capital Market Regulator. Financial strength of the promoters (minimum paid-up capital required for new private banks is Rs.1 billion) and long-term viability are important factors.

The RBI is vested with powers under section 22(4) of the Banking Regulation Act to cancel a licence granted to a banking company provided the company ceases to carry on banking business; or is unable to pay its present or/and future depositors; or carrying on banking business by the company is detrimental to the public interest or to the interest of its depositors.

Ownership Pattern

Banking supervisors must have the authority to review and reject any proposals to transfer significant ownership or controlling interests in existing banks to other parties.

Section 12(2) of the Banking Regulation Act restricts shareholders in a banking company from exercising voting rights on poll in excess of ten per cent of the total voting rights of all the shareholders of the banking company. In terms of administrative circular issued by the RBI under Section 35(A) of the Banking Regulation Act, any transfer of shares in a banking company, which exceeds 5% of the paid-up capital of the bank requires acknowledgement by the RBI before the registration of the transfer in their books. While seeking acknowledgement from the RBI, the bank has to give a declaration that the proposed transferee is not likely to acquire, either singly or along with the companies and concerns in the group, a controlling interest in the bank.

Acquisition and Investments

Banking supervisors must have the authority to establish criteria for reviewing major acquisitions or investments by a bank and ensuring that corporate affiliations or structures do not expose the bank to undue risks or hinder effective supervision.

Banks are allowed to set up subsidiaries and make significant investment only in companies that are undertaking business authorized under section 19(1) of the Banking Regulation Act. This ensures that banks form subsidiaries only in financial services sector, and this requires prior approval of RBI. The RBI applies 'fit and proper' test and examines viability report of the proposed subsidiary before granting permission. Under Section 19(2) of the Banking Regulation Act, other investments by banks whether as pledgee, mortgagee or absolute owner in other companies cannot exceed 30% of the paid-up share capital or 30% of its own paid-up share capital, whichever is less. Investment by banks in a financial services company requires prior approval of RBI and is subject to a ceiling of 10% of the bank's paid-up capital and reserves. Aggregate investment in all the subsidiaries shall not exceed 20% of the bank's paid-up capital. In the case of investments in equity shares of companies not engaged in financial services, investment in a year should not exceed 5% of incremental deposits of the previous year. The RBI insists on arms length relationship between the bank and its subsidiary. As regards supervision, RBI has the authority to supervise companies undertaking non-banking financial services. The capital market related activities of such companies are also under the functional regulation of SEBI.

Prudential Regulations and Requirements

Capital Requirements

Banking supervisors must set minimum capital requirements for banks that reflect the risks that the banks undertake and must define the components of capital bearing in mind its ability to absorb losses. For internationally active banks these requirements should not be less than those established in the Basel Capital Accord.

The RBI has prescribed a minimum Capital Adequacy Ratio (CAR) of 8% to be maintained by banks on a solo basis as per Basel norms, covering both on and off-balance sheet items. The components of CAR have been defined as per Basel norms and detailed guidelines were issued in 1992. Compliance with CAR for banks was phased in a gradual manner to give them time to raise the capital level. These transitional arrangements were different for banks with international presence, foreign banks and local banks. Presently all the banks except those dealing in gold / silver / platinum are required to maintain 8% CAR. For banks dealing in gold / silver /platinum, minimum CAR is 9%. Banks' foreign exchange open position limit as well as open position limit in gold should carry 100% risk weight with effect from March 31, 1999.

Absolute amount of capital for new private sector banks and those dealing in gold / silver / platinum should not fall below Rs.1 billion and Rs.3 billion respectively. All the banks are required to attain 9% CAR by March 31, 2000. Certain structural adjustments have also been made in risk weights like assigning risk weight on investments in Government and other approved securities, and loans and advances guaranteed by the State Governments depending on the status of payment of interest and principal, effective from March 31, 2000.

Compliance with CAR is monitored through quarterly prudential reporting and on-site inspection of banks. Non-compliance and possible ways to achieve compliance are discussed with the top management of the banks. The banks not complying with the CAR norms may trigger supervisory / regulatory intervention.

The question of computation of capital adequacy on a consolidated basis is under examination of the Bank.

Loan & Investment Policy

An essential part of any supervisory system is the evaluation of a bank's policies and procedures related to the granting of loans and making of investments and the ongoing management of the loan and investment portfolios.

Under Section 21 of the Banking Regulation Act, the RBI is charged with the responsibility of determining the policy relating to advances by banks and of giving directions to them in this regard. Accordingly, RBI has asked banks to lay down transparent policies and guidelines for credit dispensation in respect of each of the broad category of economic activity. Similarly, RBI has issued guidelines on drawing up policies and procedure for managing investment portfolio. The banks are required to delegate powers to various functionaries for credit dispensation and investment decision making.

In the course of On-site Examination, these policies and adherence thereto are looked into. The examination of the investment portfolio is done against the background of instructions issued by the RBI from time to time on investment policy, internal control systems, separation of client deals from the bank's own portfolio, prescription of accounting standards and overseeing systems of audit, review and reporting.

The examination of the loan portfolio centres around adequacy of policies, practices and procedures, operation of the scheme of delegation, classification of assets, loan loss provisioning for loans and investments, concentration risk, adherence to prudential exposure norms, scope and adequacy of audit and loan review functions and compliance with laws and regulations. Banks are also expected to put in place detailed operational guidelines based on the policy framework for day-to-day management of the portfolios. The adequacy of provisions for loan losses and for marking of investments to market, and concentration of credit are also assessed on quarterly basis through off-site monitoring returns. Concurrent audit of treasury operations by external auditors to confirm adherence to RBI guidelines is mandatory. Such reports are required to be put up to the top management of the bank on monthly basis.

The RBI has recently issued comprehensive guidelines on Risk Management Systems in banks after discussions with the banks. These guidelines propose vesting of risk management function with Credit Policy and Asset-Liability Management committees. The banks have been advised to articulate risk-return philosophy, adopt credit risk mitigating tools like setting up of multi-tier credit approving system, prudential portfolio limits, loan grading, risk pricing, portfolio management and loan review mechanism.

The RBI has issued a manual of instructions to guide its inspection teams in analysing various portfolios of a bank.

Asset Quality

Banking supervisors must be satisfied that banks establish and adhere to adequate policies, practices and procedures for evaluating the quality of assets and the adequacy of loan loss provisions and loan loss reserves.

The RBI has laid down detailed guidelines on income recognition, asset classification and provisioning covering both on and off-balance sheet exposures in line with international standards. The non-performing assets (NPAs) are required to be classified into substandard, doubtful and loss assets depending on the age of irregularity and provisions are required to be made taking into account the potential threat to realisability of the asset, as per RBI norms for each of the category and for each of the borrower. A credit facility is classified as non-performing if interest and / or instalment of principal have remained unpaid for two quarters after it has become past due. Any off-balance sheet exposure that is likely to devolve on bank has to be provided for. While computing NPA figures, value of collateral is not deducted from the balance outstanding. The banks have now been advised to provide for standard assets at a minimum of 0.25% with effect from March 31, 2000. Provisioning norms and age for classification of an asset as doubtful have also been made more stringent, and these are to be implemented in phases effective from March 31, 2001. An asset will be required to be classified as doubtful if it has remained in the sub-standard category for 18 months, instead of 24 months as at present. Further, banks will have to provide for not less than 50% on the assets which have become doubtful on account of these norms by March 31, 2000. The balance of the provisions required on this account will have to be made by March 31, 2002. The banks are required to lay down loan recovery policy, compromise / settlement policy and norms for valuation of collateral.

The system of on-site Inspection comprises of appraisal of asset quality and the impairment in the value of assets. The appraisal is an assessment of adherence to the prudential norms on income recognition, asset classification and adequacy of provisions for erosion in value of assets and adequacy of recovery policy. Significant divergence, if any, noticed in asset classification is not only taken up with the bank management, but also with the statutory auditors of the bank. The quality of assets is also monitored on quarterly basis through off-site monitoring returns. These returns not only help in monitoring the NPAs category-wise, but also movement in some of the top non-performing loans (NPLs) and provisioning therefor.

It is the sole responsibility of the bank management to ensure that adequate provisions as per the prudential norms are made. The statutory auditors of the bank have to certify adequacy of provisions as per RBI norms.

Portfolio Concentration and Large Exposures

Banking supervisors must be satisfied that banks have Management Information Systems that enable management to identify concentrations within the portfolio and supervisors must set prudential limits to restrict bank exposures to single borrowers or groups of related borrowers.

Prudential exposure norms have been prescribed both in respect of operations of foreign branches as well as for domestic lending to individual/group borrowers at 25/50 per cent of the bank's capital funds. To encourage flow of funds to the infrastructure sector, group borrower norm is fixed at higher level of 60% for companies engaged in this area. The banks may fix internally lower exposure norms with the approval of their Boards. The banks have also been advised to fix internal aggregate limits for exposure to different sectors as part of the Loan Policy. In case loans and advances are granted to Indian subsidiaries or joint ventures abroad, aggregate of such loans and advances shall not exceed 5% of unimpaired Tier I capital of the bank. The adequacy of such limits and the reporting system in this regard is studied during the on-site inspection of loan portfolio. A quarterly reporting to RBI on the exposure ceilings for off-site monitoring is in place. The banks are required to report top 20 borrowers with balances outstanding exceeding 15% of their capital funds. Besides, overseas offices of Indian banks report exposures to all large borrowers together with a separate statement for new borrowers.

Connected Lending

In order to prevent abuses arising from connected lending, banking supervisors must have in place requirements that banks lend to related companies and individuals on arms-length basis, that such extensions of credit are effectively monitored, and that other appropriate steps are taken to control or mitigate the risks.

Section 20 of the Banking Regulation Act prohibits loans and advances (other than for personal use) to directors or to any firm or company in which directors are interested or individuals in respect of whom any of its directors is a partner or guarantor. In respect of non-fund based facilities, which are not regarded as loans and advances within the meaning of Section 20 of the Banking Regulation Act, any devolvement on the bank resulting in creditor-debtor relationship between the bank and the director, etc. shall attract Section 20 of the Banking Regulation Act. Therefore, RBI has issued guidelines to ensure that no liability under non-fund based facility devolves on the bank. Further, in order to check unethical practices of granting loans and advances to relatives of directors of the bank, directors of other banks and / or their relatives, RBI has issued guidelines that such loans aggregating Rs.2.5 million and above should be invariably approved by the Board of the bank and the related Director shall not participate at the time of sanction of such loan. Loans for less than Rs.2.5 million which can be sanctioned by competent authorities as per delegation of powers, should be reported to the Board. These restrictions do not apply to loans and advances to the directors of foreign banks. However, aggregate of such loans and advances should not exceed 5% of the foreign bank's advances in India.

As regards loans to related companies i.e. the bank's own subsidiaries or joint ventures, the banks are required to maintain arms-length relationship and sanction of such loans and advances is subject to procedures applicable to sanction of loans and advances to directors of other banks and their relatives. The subsidiary company is treated as any other company and all loans to such companies have to be made at commercial rates and are subject to limits that apply to similar companies.

The investments in subsidiaries are deducted from Tier I Capital of the banks. The banks are also required to maintain arm's length relationship with promoter companies and cannot extend finance for acquisition of shares except for acquiring shares in overseas wholly owned subsidiaries or joint ventures provided such facility is backed by an approved refinance facility from EXIM bank.

Sanction of loans and advances to senior officers of a bank and their relatives should ordinarily be sanctioned by next higher sanctioning authority and the same should be reported to the Board. The above norms equally apply to award of contracts. The RBI examines connected lendings as part of on-site inspection and through an off-site return on half-yearly basis.

In order to strengthen these provisions and making their application more stringent, the Bank is seeking legislative amendment to empower it to take appropriate steps to safeguard against siphoning of banks' funds through connected lending and to initiate criminal prosecution in such cases.

Country and Transfer Risk

Banking supervisors must be satisfied that banks have adequate policies and procedures for identifying monitoring and controlling country risk and transfer risk in their international lending and investment activities and for maintaining reserves against such risks.

Indian banks having overseas operations are required to lay down internal guidelines on country risk management and fix limits based on risk rating of the country. Limits should also be fixed for a group of countries in a particular risk category subject to a maximum ceiling fixed by RBI. In the normal course, prudential exposure norms apply to all loans and investments overseas including loans to sovereign entities. The overseas branches are governed by the host country regulations also. Adequacy of the bank's policy on identification, measurement and control of country risk is assessed during on-site inspection. It is also monitored through a quarterly return on country-wise counterparty exposure.

The RBI has formed a working group on risk management systems (including country risk). The group is also examining the issue of bringing about uniformity in the method of assessing country risk as also the reporting systems on key parameters.

Market Risk

Banking supervisors must be satisfied that banks have in place systems that accurately control market risks. Supervisors should have powers to impose specific limits and/ or a specific capital charge on market risk exposures if warranted.

RBI has powers under Section 35A of the Banking Regulation Act to impose specific limits and /or specific capital charge on market risk exposures as part of the general powers to issue directions to banks on any aspect of their functioning. RBI has prescribed detailed operational guidelines on Asset-Liability Management System in banks, effective from April 1, 1999.

The capital charge for some of the market risks already exist. Market risks in the Investment Portfolio are controlled through quantitative restrictions on the extent of exposure that banks can have in equity. Investment portfolio is classified into 'Permanent' and 'Current' categories with effect from 1992. At present, the banks are required to mark to market at least 70% of all approved securities and 100% of non-approved securities. The ratio of marking to market has been fixed at 75% of approved securities with effect from 31 March 2000. In addition, effective from March 31, 2000 Government and other approved securities are to be assigned 2.5% risk weight instead of 'nil' risk weight as earlier and requisite capital will have to be maintained thereon. The banks in general are not allowed to trade in commodities. Recently however, select banks have been permitted to deal in gold / silver / platinum. These banks must maintain 9% capital adequacy on all risk weighted assets including on the open position in gold / silver / platinum that carries 100% risk weight with effect from 31 March 1999.

Capital charge on market risk arising from open foreign exchange position is captured by assigning 100% risk weight.

The banks have been advised to lay down maximum limits for Value at Risk (VaR) with the approval of their Boards. However, no additional capital charge is required based on VaR. The Basle Committee is looking into various risks and in the new Capital Accord, various methods are suggested to address these risks. Once these issues are finalized, RBI will come out with detailed guidelines on these issues.

The banks revalue their foreign exchange portfolios on monthly basis. The investments in securities / equities are valued quarterly.

Risk Management Process

Banking supervisors must be satisfied that banks have in place a comprehensive risk management process (including appropriate Board and Senior Management oversight) to identify measures monitor and control all other material risks and where appropriate to hold capital against these risks.

The RBI has issued detailed guidelines to banks for putting in place effective Asset-Liability Management (ALM) system with effect from April 1, 1999. Every bank has an Asset-Liability Committee (ALCO), headed by the Chief Executive Officer / Chairman and Managing Director or the Executive Director of the bank. The banks are expected to lay down policy on identification, measurement, monitoring and control of various kinds of risks such as liquidity risk, interest rate risk and currency risk and to review the policy from time to time to incorporate changes in business environment and the perception of the top management about the risks. To put in place a uniform ALM system, it is imperative for banks to have good management information system. To start with, the banks are required to ensure coverage of at least 60% of their assets and liabilities on actual basis. Liquidity risk, currency risk and interest rate risk should be measured through simple gap statements. The banks are required to achieve coverage of their entire business by April 1, 2000.

Liquidity Risk Management

All banks are required to maintain Cash Reserve Ratio (CRR) and Statutory Liquidity Ratio (SLR) as per section 42(1) of RBI Act, 1934 and Section 24(2A) of the Banking Regulation Act, 1949 respectively. The method of computing these ratios has been defined in the respective sections of the Acts. The RBI has powers to modify CRR between 3% to 20% and SLR between 25% to 40% by notification in the Official Gazette. The RBI has advised the banks to monitor liquidity through maturity or cash flow mismatches. Future cash flows are to be bracketed in different time buckets. The banks are required to fix tolerance levels for various maturity mismatches depending upon the bank's asset-liability profile, extent of stable deposit base, nature of cash flows, etc. Further, prudential limit on mismatches (negative gap) in cash flows during 1-14 days and 15-28 days should not exceed 20% of each of the cash out-flows during these time buckets as per RBI guidelines. These tolerance levels are to be strictly enforced by April 1, 2000 when all the banks are supposed to be covering their entire business for ALM purposes. The RBI will be monitoring the liquidity position of banks through a periodic return on structural liquidity. The objective of RBI is to move to fortnightly reporting by April 1, 2000.

Interest rate Risk Management

The banks are expected to measure interest rate risk through traditional gap analysis supplemented by sophisticated techniques wherever possible. Each bank is required to set prudential limits on gaps for each time bucket considering total assets, earning assets and equity. The bank may fix prudent level for earnings at risk (EaR) or Net Interest Margin (NIM). The RBI intends to move over to modern techniques of interest rate risk measurement like Duration Gap Analysis, Simulation and Value at Risk when banks acquire sufficient expertise and sophistication in collating requisite information. The banks are required to submit a quarterly return on interest rate sensitivity for exposures in Rupee as well as in foreign currencies to RBI with effect from June 1999. The reporting periodicity is proposed to be made monthly by April 1, 2000.

Currency Risk Management

The banks are required to assign 100% risk weight to their open position limit in foreign exchange with effect from March 31, 1999. Besides, they are required to fix aggregate and individual gap limits for each currency with the approval of RBI. They are required to adopt Value at Risk approach to measure the risk associated with forward exposures. The RBI monitors currency risk through a monthly return on maturity and positions for both on and off balance sheet items in foreign exchange.

The RBI has recently issued guidelines on overall risk management covering the major risks faced by the banks. Introduction of appropriate Risk Management Systems in the banks is on top of the regulatory agenda of the RBI and RBI is fully committed to introducing these systems on par with international practices. Efforts made by banks in introducing and enforcing risk management system are being monitored at regular intervals and during on-site inspections.

Internal Controls

Banking supervisors must determine that banks have in place internal controls that are adequate for the nature and scale of their business. These should include clear arrangements for delegating authority and responsibility, separation of the functions that involve committing the bank, paying away its funds, and proper accounts for its assets and liabilities reconciliation of these processes; safeguarding its assets; and appropriate independent internal or external audit and compliance functions to test adherence to these controls as well as applicable laws and regulations.

RBI has issued a number of instructions/guidelines to banks to streamline their inspection and audit machinery, introduce concurrent audit, monitor treasury operations, introduce internal control system for prevention of frauds, monitor cash flows in accounts, promptly reconcile inter-branch accounts, and balance books periodically. The RBI has also issued guidelines from time to time on segregation of duties and responsibilities in front office, mid office and back office for treasury operations. Each bank is required to have a written policy on delegation of powers for managing credit, investments, money market operations, foreign exchange operations, etc.

All exceptionally large branches (whose total of deposits and advances are Rs1 billion and above) and large branches (whose total of deposits and advances are Rs 0.15 billion and above but below Rs 1 billion) are subjected to concurrent audit so as to cover at least 50% of bank's business operations (total of deposits and advances). The treasury related transactions and specialized activities like portfolio management services and credit card business are also subjected to concurrent audit. Each bank has an internal audit department that undertakes audit of bank's operations periodically. With a view to strengthening the corporate governance function, the banks have set up an Audit Committee of the Board (ACB) for supervising the internal audit function. The non-official Chartered Accountant Director is necessarily to be member of the ACB. The Chairman / Managing Director / Chief Executive Officer does not participate in Audit Committee meetings.

Examination and evaluation of the adequacy and effectiveness of the Internal Control System in the banks form one of the important aspects during on-site inspection by the RBI.

All domestic banks have been advised to name the General Manager in-charge of Audit and Inspection function as Compliance Officer, who should ensure ongoing compliance with instructions issued by the RBI and Government of India.

The RBI is vested with powers to remove managerial and other persons from the office of a banking company and appoint additional directors on the Board of a bank to secure proper management of the banking company in public interest as per Section 36-AA and 36-AB of the Banking Regulation Act.

Know Your Customer

Banking supervisors must determine that banks have adequate policies, practices and procedures in place including strict 'Know Your Customer' rules that promote high ethical and professional standards in the financial sector and prevent the bank being used intentionally and unintentionally by criminal elements.

In India 'Know Your Customer' Rules are in place right from the beginning. There are specific directions for obtaining proper introduction while opening Deposit Accounts. Requirement of obtaining photographs of account holders before opening accounts has been prescribed. Numbered accounts are not permitted in India. The banks have also been advised to be careful while dealing with clients who deposit and withdraw large sums of money in cash. Such transactions of Rs1 million and above are to be closely monitored. Number of instructions have been issued by the RBI and the Government of India to discourage money laundering. A draft bill on money laundering has also been prepared based on the recommendations of a committee set up for the purpose for enactment.

A system of reporting frauds on banks involving an aggregate of Rs.0.1 million and above to RBI on a case by case basis is in place. All frauds below Rs.0.1 million are also to be reported to the RBI in consolidated form, category wise. Frauds are required to be classified in seven categories viz. misappropriation and criminal breach of trust, fraudulent encashment through forged instruments, manipulation of books of accounts, operation of fictitious accounts and conversion of property, unauthorized credit facilities extended for reward or for illegal gratification, negligence and cash shortages, cheating and forgery, irregularities in foreign exchange transactions and any other type of fraud. Banks are also required to report all cases of frauds to the concerned investigative agencies immediately. The RBI maintains a database of frauds and their modus operandi and this information is shared with banks to enable them to prevent occurrences of such frauds.

Methods of Ongoing Banking Supervision

Instruments of Supervision

An effective banking supervisory system should consist of some form of both on-site and off-site supervision. The main instrument of supervision in India is the periodical on-site inspection of banks that is supplemented by off-site monitoring and surveillance. Since 1995, on-site inspections are based on CAMELS (Capital adequacy, asset quality, management, earning, liquidity and systems and controls) model and aim at achieving the following objectives:

i) Evaluation of bank's safety and soundness,

ii) Appraisal of the quality of Board and top management,

iii) Ensuring compliance with prudential regulations,

iv) Identifying the areas where corrective action is required to strengthen the bank

v) Appraisal of soundness of bank's assets,

vi) Analysis of key financial factors such as capital, earnings, and liquidity and determine bank's solvency,

vii) Assessment of the quality of its management team and evaluation of the bank's policies, systems of management, internal operations and control, and

viii) Review of compliance with banking laws and regulations as well as supervisory guidance conveyed on specific policies.

The domestic banks are rated on CAMELS model while foreign banks are rated on CACS model (capital adequacy, assets quality, compliance and systems). The frequency of inspections is generally annual, which can be increased / reduced depending on the financial position, methods of operation and compliance record of the bank. The inspection teams base their reports on the primary records at selective representative cross section of branches, controlling offices and the head office of the bank. Besides, the inspection team uses pre-inspection feedback from other departments of the RBI about specific aspects to be looked into. Other inputs used for on-site inspection are off-site surveillance reports, market reports, internal audit and concurrent audit reports of the bank, Long Form Audit Reports (LFAR) and report forming part of annual accounts given by the statutory auditors and RBI nominee directors' reports/communications. On-site findings and areas of concern are discussed with top management of the bank and corrective steps taken by the bank are followed up by RBI.

To ensure continuity in supervision, RBI also undertakes targeted appraisals of specific portfolios at control site, commissioned audits of specific areas by external auditors and monitoring visits for follow-up or review of selected areas of concern.

RBI is gradually moving towards a risk-based supervisory framework that is based on both off-site and on-site inputs. Pursuant to the new supervision strategy approved by the BFS, the RBI has introduced a formal Supervisory Reporting System. The reporting is essentially prudential in content and tri-monthly in periodicity. The total package of Supervisory Returns for commercial banks (designated DSB Returns) comprises 12 Reports (9 to be filed at Quarterly intervals, 2 at half-yearly intervals and 1 at yearly interval). Analysis of the returns is done for individual bank, peer group and industry as a whole. These analysis help in detecting early warning signals.

In the first tranche, 7 returns (5 for foreign banks) on assets and liabilities, capital adequacy, profitability, asset quality, large exposures, connected lendings and ownership and control were introduced in November 1995 and came into effect as from end-December 1995. The annual return on bank profile came into effect from 1997. The second tranche of four ALM returns covering interest rate sensitivity for on balance sheet and off-balance sheet exposures in rupee and foreign exchange, structural liquidity for rupee exposures and maturity and positions for exposure in foreign exchange have been introduced from end-June 1999.

Supervisory Contact

Banking supervisors must have regular contact with bank management and thorough understanding of the institution's operations.

The contact between supervisors and banks is almost continuous. Senior executives at Regional office of RBI meet the bank management if serious supervisory issues crop up. Senior Executives at Central Office of RBI meet annually top management of banks to discuss matters of supervisory concerns identified during on-site inspection. The overall CAMELS rating is communicated to the bank management. Supervisory concerns emanating out of off-site supervision are also communicated to banks on an ongoing basis.

Meetings are also held with banks for various purposes like discussions on Resource Management. Banks are often consulted before introduction of major reporting changes and senior bank officers are often associated with the working groups and committees set up by the RBI to examine / deliberate on regulatory / supervisory issues. RBI Nominee Directors on the Boards of banks are also required to report bimonthly on the important policy decisions taken by the bank in particular highlighting supervisory issues, if any.

Prudential Reports and Statistical Returns

Banking supervisors must have means of collecting reviewing and analysing prudential reports and statistical returns from banks on a solo and consolidated basis.

Under Section 27 of the Banking Regulation Act, RBI has powers to call for any information at any time from a banking company relating to its affairs. Presently, RBI receives prudential reports and statistical returns from banks on a solo basis only. Although financial and operating results are not currently drawn on a consolidated basis, the introduction of this is being examined by the RBI. During the course of on-site examinations, the operations of the subsidiaries and joint ventures and the control of the parent banks over them are studied. RBI undertakes inspection of merchant banking subsidiaries of banks. The off-site supervisory returns received by RBI are used to prepare bank-wise, peer group-wise and sector-wide analysis reports, which are seen by the top management of RBI and matters of supervisory concerns emanating from such analysis are taken up with the banks.

Any inconsistency or inaccuracy in reporting is taken up with top management of the bank. Submission of any wrong information to RBI can invite imposition of penalties specified in Section 46(1) of the Banking Regulation Act.

Independent Validation & External Audit

Banking supervisors must have a means of independent validation of supervisory information either through on-site examination or use of external auditors.

The supervisory information is mainly received in the form of off-site (DSB) Returns. The prima facie validation of the information is taken care of in the EDP software itself. Besides this, during the inspection of banks, the DSB Returns and other information furnished by the bank are verified with regard to their accuracy.

The balance sheet and profit and loss account of the bank are to be audited by statutory auditors appointed by RBI in case of public sector banks. Private sector banks and foreign banks in India appoint their auditors with prior approval of RBI. Any divergence, noticed during on-site inspection in compliance with laid down prudential norms, is required to be discussed with statutory auditors of the bank by the bank management.

The RBI has powers to order for special audit for specific area or a specific period (Section 30 (1A) of the Banking Regulation Act). The statutory auditors may be directed to certify correctness of any information furnished by the banks to RBI. The statutory auditors, among other things, are at present required to verify the calculation of the net demand and time liabilities made by banks for maintenance of Cash Reserve Ratio (CRR) and Statutory Liquidity Ratio (SLR) by them. The auditors also certify the accuracy of Income Recognition and Asset Classification, Capital Adequacy calculations, etc. In the recent past, the external audit mechanism has been used for verification of inter-branch/inter-bank reconciliation, FCNR (A) accounts, import bills, etc.

Consolidated Supervision

An essential element of bank supervision is the capability of the supervisors to supervise the banking group on a consolidated basis.

The on-site inspection reports of the banks include comments on earning performance of the bank's subsidiaries and joint ventures. In addition, the RBI conducts inspection of merchant banking subsidiaries of banks. The banks are required to conduct internal audit / inspection of their subsidiaries as a measure of control over them. Periodical review notes on these subsidiaries put up to the banks' Board are sent to RBI.

Private sector banks are required to annex the balance sheet and profit and loss accounts of their subsidiaries to the annual report of the bank. Public sector banks generally give a brief description of the performance of their subsidiaries in the Directors' report that forms part of the annual accounts of the bank. The question of publishing balance sheet and profit and loss account of subsidiaries as an annexure to the annual report of the public sector banks is also being examined in connection with the introduction of a system of consolidated supervision.

Information Requirements

Adequate Records & Financial Statements

Bank supervisors must be satisfied that each bank maintains adequate records drawn up in accordance with consistent accounting policies and practices that enable the supervisor to obtain a true and fair view of the financial condition of the bank and the profitability of its business and that the bank publishes on a regular basis financial statements that fairly reflect its condition. RBI is committed to enhance and improve increasing the levels of transparency and disclosure in the annual accounts of banks. The formats for preparation of financial statements are prescribed under Section 29 of the Banking Regulation Act. The financial statements are prepared based on accounting standards prescribed by Institute of Chartered Accountants of India (ICAI) except those that have been specifically modified by RBI in consultation with ICAI keeping in view the nature of banking industry. The banks are mandated to disclose additional information as part of annual financial statements:

Capital Adequacy Ratio;

Tier I ratio;

Tier II ratio;

Percentage of shareholding of the Government of India in nationalised banks;

Net NPL ratio;

Amount of provision made towards NPLs and provisions for income-tax for the year;

Amount of subordinated debt raised as Tier II capital;

Gross value of investments, provision for depreciation on investments and net value of investments separately for within India and outside India;

Interest income as percentage to working funds;

Non-interest income as a percentage to working funds;

Operating profit as a percentage to working funds;

Return on assets; business (deposits and advances) per employee Profit per employee;

Maturity pattern of certain assets and liabilities;

Movement in NPLs;

Foreign currency assets and liabilities;

Lending to sensitive sectors as defined from time to time.

It is mandatory for all the banks to get their annual accounts audited every year by statutory auditors appointed by the RBI or appointed with approval of RBI. The auditors are required to report whether the financial statements exhibit a true and fair view of affairs of the bank. Adequacy and accuracy of records maintained are verified during on-site inspection. Guidelines on minimum record maintenance in computerised environment have been issued by RBI.

As per Section 31 of the Banking Regulation Act, banks incorporated in India are required to publish their balance sheet and profit and loss account together with the auditor's report in a newspaper in circulation at the place where the bank has its principal office. Further, banks have been advised to publish its annual accounts in abridged form in additional newspapers, journals, etc. to give wider coverage to bank's operations. They should also furnish copies to the concerned Regional Office and Central Office of RBI, where these are examined and taken up with the bank, if considered necessary.

Formal Powers of Supervisors

Supervisory Intervention

Banking supervisors must have at their disposal adequate supervisory measures to bring about timely corrective action when banks fail to meet prudential requirements such as minimum capital adequacy ratios when there are regulatory violations or where depositors are threatened in any other way. In extreme circumstances this should include the ability to revoke the banking licence or recommend its revocation.

The RBI is vested with powers to issue directions under the Banking Regulation Act where necessary in the interest of banking policy, in public interest or where the affairs of the banking company are being conducted in a manner detrimental to the interest of the depositors. The Banking Regulation Act also gives RBI wide powers to obtain any information from the supervised institutions (Section 27), issue directions on any aspect of their business (Section 35A), appoint nominees on their boards, cause change of management (Section 36AA and 36AB), cancel their licence (Section 22(4)), take monetary and non-monetary penal measures (Section 46 to 48), cause merger / amalgamations, impose restrictions or even close the bank.

Regulatory violations in complying with prudential requirements could lead to imposition of monetary penalties and issue of letters of displeasure to the bank's management.

In extreme cases, the Top Management of the bank or the Directors on the Board may be replaced. In the case of banks which do not meet capital adequacy regulations, restrictions on branch expansion, assets expansion and setting up of subsidiaries are imposed. RBI also has the authority to restrict declaration of dividend by private banks to bring about corrective action.

Cross-border Banking

Global Consolidated Supervision

Banking supervisors must practice global consolidated supervision over their internationally active banks, adequately monitoring and applying appropriate prudential norms to all aspects of the business conducted by these banking organisations worldwide, primarily at their foreign branches, joint ventures and subsidiaries.

Since 1983, detailed instructions on operations of overseas branches and merchant banking subsidiaries of Indian banks-ranging from asset-liability mismatches to country exposure limits etc. have been issued. Special Off-site Monitoring Returns have to be submitted by the banks to RBI at quarterly intervals on the working of foreign branches. The overseas segment of a bank is targeted for annual appraisal by the RBI based on records maintained at Head Office, to ensure that they comply with regulations and prudential norms framed by the home and host countries. Besides, the foreign branches of Indian banks are subjected to inspection by RBI when deemed necessary and by the bank regularly. As indicated earlier, the RBI is examining the question of putting in place a prudential reporting system on global consolidated basis.

International Coordination

A key component of consolidated supervision is establishing contact and information exchange with the various other supervisors involved (primarily host-country supervisory authorities).

RBI maintains regular contact with overseas supervisors and also serves on important international forums connected with bank supervision. It was one of the non-G 10 member countries consulted in the Core Principles formulation exercise and is now represented on the Core Principles Liaison Group set up by the BCBS (Basel Committee on Banking Supervision). It has also been represented on key international forums of Central Bankers / Bank Supervisors such as the Working Group on Strengthening Financial Systems. Supervisory officials, during visits to foreign countries, generally call on the overseas supervisory authorities for exchange of views. While issuing licence to a foreign bank to open a branch in India, the RBI considers adequacy of supervisory and regulatory systems in existence in the home country. A system of exchange of information is being put in place.

Host Country Obligations

Banking supervisors must require the local operations of foreign banks to be conducted to the same high standards as are required of domestic institutions and must have powers to share information needed by the home country supervisors of those banks for the purpose of carrying out consolidated supervision.

Country of origin does not confer any special status on foreign banks operating in India. They are generally subject to the same legislation and regulatory requirements as applicable to domestic banks. RBI has the necessary powers to share information with overseas supervisors.

2

Compliance with Basel Core Principles and Bank Soundness

The views expressed in this Working Paper are those of the authors and do not necessarily represent those of the IMF, the World Bank, or IMF policy. Working Papers describe research in progress by the authors and are published to elicit comments and to further debate.

This paper studies whether compliance with the Basel Core Principles for Effective Banking Supervision (BCPs) improves bank soundness. The authors find a significant and positive relationship between bank soundness (measured with Moody's financial strength ratings) and compliance with principles related to information provision. Specifically, countries that require banks to regularly and accurately report their financial data to regulators and market participants have sounder banks. This relationship is robust to controlling for broad indexes of institutional quality, macroeconomic variables, sovereign ratings, and reverse causality. Measuring soundness through Z-scores yields similar results. These findings emphasize the importance of transparency in making supervisory processes effective and strengthening market discipline. Countries aiming to upgrade banking regulation and supervision should consider giving priority to information provision over other elements of the core principles.

INTRODUCTION

With increasing deregulation and globalization beginning in the 1980s, banking systems have become more fragile and banking crises have proliferated, causing or aggravating economic downturns and leading to significant fiscal costs

(Caprio and Klingebiel, 1999). To improve crisis prevention and management, many countries are working to upgrade their bank regulation and supervision. This is a complex and difficult process, particularly in developing countries, where the required expertise may be scarce, the legal environment weak, and governance problems may lead to regulatory capture. But what exactly is good regulation and supervision? How can countries do it with limited resources? What should reforms focus on?

To answer the first question, in 1997 a group of representatives of bank supervisors from advanced countries-the Basel Committee on Banking Supervision-issued the Core Principles for Effective Bank Supervision (BCPs), a document summarizing best practices in the field.

Most countries in the world have endorsed the BCPs and have undertaken to comply with them, making them an almost universal standard for bank regulators. Since 1999, the IMF and the World Bank have conducted evaluations of member countries' compliance with this standard, mainly within their joint Financial Sector Assessment Program (FSAP).

These assessments provide a unique source of information about the quality of supervision and regulation around the world.

This paper relies on assessments of compliance with the BCPs to study whether better banking supervision and regulation is associated with sounder banks. In addition, we look at which elements of the regulatory framework are most closely related to soundness. The goal is to shed light on how to prioritize efforts to improve supervision.

BCP compliance ratings have several advantages as measures of the quality of banking supervision and regulation. First, the BCPs are accepted as the blueprint of good supervision and regulation worldwide. Second, the assessment takes into account not only which laws and regulations are on the books, but also the extent to which they are implemented in practice. This is an important distinction. Third, separate compliance assessments are available for the 25 core principles, so that it is possible to separate out different aspects of supervision. The measure is only on a four-point scale, but to cut finer distinctions would likely be unrealistic. Because the evaluation reflects the judgment of the assessors, it inevitably contains an element of subjectivity. To limit subjectivity and ensure cross-country comparability, the Basel Committee has developed a standardized methodology.

In addition, evaluations are conducted by expert supervisors from foreign countries and reviewed by internal teams at the IMF and the World Bank. In any case, to the extent that measurement error is independent of bank soundness, it should not bias our results. We measure bank soundness using Moody's financial strength ratings. This is a comprehensive measure of the ability of a bank to meet its obligations to depositors and other creditors as viewed by specialized analysts. To the extent that Moody's analysts have access to both quantitative and qualitative information about banks and their operating environment, ratings should be a more accurate measure of bank soundness than indicators built using only balance sheet variables (such as reported nonperforming loans, profitability, or Z-scores).

Another advantage of Moody's ratings is that they evaluate bank solvency independent of the safety net, so that cross-country differences in the safety net, which are difficult to observe and measure, should not affect the results. A limitation of using Moody's ratings is that it restricts the sample to larger banks, as smaller banks are not rated. Thus, our investigation will not address the impact of the regulatory framework on smaller banks. As the latter are not likely to be of systemic importance, this limitation should be relatively minor. A more serious limitation is that a number of low-income countries have no rated banks, and thus are excluded from the sample.

Because data to date on BCP compliance are available only at one point in time, our study cannot rely on time series variation. This limitation forces us to be very careful in controlling for other potential sources of cross-sectional variation as well as joint endogeneity. One important problem is that the BCP compliance indicator may be associated with bank soundness because it proxies for the overall quality of the institutional and macroeconomic environment rather than the quality of supervision. While we recognize that this concern cannot be fully laid to rest, we perform extensive robustness tests controlling for broad indexes of institutional quality, macroeconomic variables, and sovereign credit ratings. A second concern is the endogeneity of supervision. The level of compliance with the BCPs is chosen by the countries themselves, and countries with sounder banks may face less opposition in enacting more rigorous supervision than countries with distressed banks.

On the other hand, it can also be argued that countries that have experienced episodes of distress, and whose banks are still weak, may have the strongest incentives to upgrade their supervisory capacity. So in principle the endogeneity of supervision may bias the relationship with soundness in either direction. To take endogeneity into account, we resort to instrumental variables estimation.

We find that an index of overall compliance with the BCPs is positively correlated with bank ratings after controlling for institutional quality, the macroeconomic environment, and bank characteristics. However, this relationship is not very robust. When we distinguish among groups of BCPs, on the other hand, we find a very robust positive relationship between compliance with information provision (BCP No. 21) and bank soundness. More specifically, countries where banks have to regularly and accurately report their financial data to regulators and market participants have more highly rated banks. This result holds even after we control for joint endogeneity of soundness and compliance through instrumental variables and when we measure bank soundness using Z-scores rather than Moody's rating.

LITERATURE REVIEW

In their empirical studies of bank crisis determinants, Demirgüç-Kunt and Detragiache (1998, 2002) find that countries with better institutions are less likely to experience banking crises and are less affected by moral hazard due to deposit insurance. They interpret institutional variables such as rule of law and quality of bureaucracy as proxies for supervision and regulation, but do not include direct measures of this dimension, which were not available at the time.

Barth, Caprio, and Levine (2001) assembled the first extensive cross-country database on the characteristics of the supervisory and regulatory framework. The data come from a survey of bank supervisors, and measure the presence or absence of a series of regulatory features. In the first comprehensive theoretical and empirical study of alternative approaches to bank supervision, Barth, Caprio, and Levine (2004) find that regulatory and supervisory practices that force accurate information disclosure, empower private sector monitoring of banks, and foster incentives for private agents to exert corporate control work best to promote bank performance and stability. Specifically, in a cross-country setting they show that regulatory and supervisory regimes with these features have suffered fewer crises in the past two decades, have lower non-performing loans, and have deeper credit markets.

One limitation of this study is that survey information reflects whether laws or regulations are on the books, but not to what extent they are implemented in practice. Judging from FSAP reports, implementation is a serious concern in many countries. BCP compliance assessments allow us to better capture this important dimension, at least to the extent the assessors are able to evaluate it. Another difference between our approach and that of Barth, Caprio, and Levine, is that we use bank ratings as measures of bank soundness in cross-sectional regressions, while they use the occurrence of systemic banking crises and non-performing loans. Because systemic crises are rare events, in the analysis by Barth, Caprio, and Levine (2001) crises predate information on bank regulation and supervision which is available only for the end of the sample period. To the extent that bank regulation and supervision may have evolved over the sample, the relationships identified may not be accurate. Nonperforming loans do not suffer from this problem, but are difficult to compare across countries, since rules for classifying loans as nonperforming are not uniform (Barth, Carpio, and Levine, 2006). On the other hand, an advantage of the latter's survey data is that it does not rely on the subjective views of compliance assessors.

Three papers to date have used information on BCP compliance to study bank performance:

Sundararajan, Marston, and Basu (2001) uses a sample of 25 countries to examine the relationship between an overall index of BCP compliance and non-performing loans (NPLs) and loan spreads. They found BCP compliance not to be a significant determinant of soundness. Podpiera (2004) extends the set of countries and finds that better BCP compliance lowers NPLs. Das and others, (2005) relates bank soundness to a broader concept of regulatory governance, which encompasses both compliance with the BCPs and with standards and codes for monetary and financial policies. Better regulatory governance is found to be associated with sounder banks, particularly in countries with better institutions.

We claim that bank ratings are a more accurate measure of bank soundness across countries than those utilized in previous studies, namely NPLs, loan spreads, interest margins, and capital adequacy. Because different countries have different reporting rules, NPLs are notoriously difficult to compare across countries, as already discussed. On the other hand, loan spreads or interest margins, and capitalization are affected by a variety of forces other than fragility, such as market structure, differences in risk-free interest rates and operating costs, and varying capital regulation. Thus, we believe our work improves upon existing studies by using a more accurate measure of bank soundness.

Another departure from existing studies is that we conduct much more extensive robustness tests to separate out the effects of banking regulation from those of other country characteristics, such as institutional quality and macroeconomic performance. Finally, and perhaps most importantly in light of the results, our work is the first to explore how compliance with different components of the BCPs affects soundness.

Our study is also related to the growing literature on transparency in financial markets. Patel, Balic, and Bwakira (2002) compare transparency and disclosure in emerging markets corporations. Mitton (2002) argues that transparency helps weather financial crises, as East Asian companies with auditors from major international accounting firms were found to have better stock performance after the crisis of 1997-98. Glennerster and Shin (2004) shows that countries that disclose more information to the IMF and the markets are rewarded through lower borrowing costs. More transparency also attracts more foreign portfolio investment (Gelos and Wei, 2005). Perotti and Von Thadden (2005) study how the presence of a dominant investor affects a firm decision of how much to disclose. Another recent theoretical study is Feltenstein and Lagunoff (2005), which takes up the question of whether bank information disclosure should be voluntary, verified by a national auditor (such as a central bank), or by an international auditor (such as an international institution). The finding is that an international auditor is the best institutional set-up.

METHODOLOGY AND DATA

Basic Econometric Model

The empirical model is a basic cross-sectional regression using bank level data. The dependent variable is the bank's rating. Moody's rates banks' financial strength on a 15-point scale, ranging from E-(least sound) to A+ (most sound). Since this is a limited dependent variable, the appropriate econometric model is an ordered probit, which we use to estimate the baseline specification. In a robustness test, we transform the ratings in a numerical index and estimate an OLS model. Standard errors are clustered by country to allow for correlated residuals within each country.

We assign numerical values to these ratings, aggregate over all the principles, and standardize the sum to obtain an index that varies between zero and one. Since we are also interested in differentiating among the various dimensions of regulation and supervision, we compute compliance indexes for subgroups of principles following the grouping by chapters used by the Basel Committee. Compliance for each chapter is used as an alternative variable of interest.

The first set of control variables includes various bank characteristics that might affect financial strength: size, measured by the logarithm of bank assets; profitability, measured alternatively as return on assets or return on equity; and capitalization, measured as the ratio of equity to total assets. We also use the ratio of bank loans to total assets to control how much the bank does. Finally, we control for whether the bank is owned by the government or by foreigners and for whether the bank is not a commercial bank.

A second group of control variables captures the overall quality of the institutions in the country. Combining information from a variety of available indexes, Kaufman, Kraay, and Mastruzzi (2003) create various broad measures of perception of institutional quality which have been widely used in empirical studies. In our baseline specification, we use an index capturing the extent to which the rule of law is respected. This index is strongly correlated with other institutional indexes from the same source, such as lack of corruption, contract enforcement, etc., and we obtain similar results using these alternative indexes, an average of the indexes, or GDP per capita.

Bank soundness is also affected by the macroeconomic outlook, as slow output growth, high inflation, a depreciating currency, high real interest rates, and rapid credit expansion have been found to be associated with bank instability (see, for instance, Demirgüç-Kunt and Detragiache, 1998). Thus, in robustness tests we employ various combination of these macroeconomic variables in alternative specifications. We also use S&P's sovereign rating as a comprehensive indicator of the quality of macroeconomic policies and institutions which might affect bank stability in a country.

Sample and Data Sources

BCP compliance data comes from assessments carried out by the IMF and the World Bank beginning in 1999. Some of these assessments are public information and can be found on the institutions' websites. Others are kept confidential at the request of the country authorities. Moody's financial strength ratings have been compiled from the Bankscope database. Bankscope reports the current rating, the last date in which the rating was revised, and the rating that prevailed before then, but no other historical rating information. Since we need to roughly match the timing of the BCP rating with that of Moody's ratings, we dropped from the sample banks that had a rating change after more than one year since the BCP compliance evaluation. Only a few banks fall in this category.

Bank-level variables have also been constructed from Bankscope, while macroeconomic variables are mainly from the IMF's International Financial Statistics. Information about bank ownership is obtained from Bankscope and other miscellaneous sources. Banks are considered state-owned if the government has a controlling share or is the sole owner, and similarly for foreign-owned banks. We use BCP assessment data for 39 countries for which we have bank ratings from

Moody's. Not surprisingly, this group includes mostly developed countries and emerging markets, while low income countries are not represented. Some countries have only one or two banks in the sample, but since we are not relying on intra-country variation to identify the relationship of interest this should not be a major limitation. The total number of banks in the baseline sample is 203.

A First Look at the Data

As expected, advanced countries have the highest compliance. Among the other countries, East Asia and Sub-Saharan Africa are closer to meeting the Basel standards, while South Asia, the Middle East and North Africa and Latin America lag behind. If we examine subgroups of chapters, the highest compliance is with principles concerning the licensing of banks and the structure of the banking market (Figure 2). At the other extreme, principles regarding the formal powers of supervisors were implemented to the least degree. Differences in compliance are not very large across different categories of principles, but averages across countries may hide larger discrepancies within each country.

Table 3 presents correlations about compliance levels in different subgroups of chapters. Compliance levels are all significantly and positively correlated. The strongest correlation (over 80 percent) is between compliance with principles concerning prudential regulation and those concerning methods of ongoing supervision. Other correlations are considerably weaker, even falling below 50 percent in the case of principles regarding the formal powers of supervisors. All in all, these correlations suggest that there is enough variation in compliance across chapters to investigate the effect of various aspects of supervision separately.

There is a strong positive correlation between bank size and bank soundness, as larger, better diversified banks are seen as more stable. This correlation may be partly driven by the fact that larger banks tend to be located in more advanced countries, which have more stable economies. More profitable and better capitalized banks with a lower ratio of loans to assets also receive higher ratings. State banks are seen as more vulnerable, while the presence of large liquid assets is associated with a less favorable rating. This may reflect the existence of high compulsory liquidity requirements or lack of opportunities to lend in some unstable emerging markets. Interestingly, foreign-owned banks do not receive significantly higher ratings.

Among country level variables, bank ratings have a strong positive correlation with the country sovereign rating, the index of rule of law, and GDP per capita. Rapid exchange rate depreciation is associated with lower ratings. The correlation with the variable of interest, compliance with the BCPs, is positive, large, and significant.

THE RESULTS

Results Using the Aggregate Index and their Robustness

Regressions of bank financial strength ratings on the overall index of BCP compliance are in Table 6. The index enters the regressions positively and significantly both by itself and when bank characteristics are controlled for. Controlling for institutional development with GDP per capita does not alter the relationship, while when we control for the sovereign rating the coefficient of compliance becomes smaller and statistical significance drops from one percent to five percent. When the quality of institutions is controlled for through the rule of law index, the coefficient of compliance becomes even smaller and significance drops to ten percent, suggesting that rule of law is an important control variable. We take the specification including rule of law as the baseline in the rest of the paper.

Excluding advanced country banks from the sample does not change regression results much. However, when we exclude extreme observations, the coefficient of compliance becomes quite small and is no longer significant. Significance also disappears if we estimate the model using OLS instead of ordered probit. As far as the control variables, larger banks are rated significantly higher and state-owned banks are considered more vulnerable. Foreign-owned banks are also rated more favorably and the coefficient is significant in the specification that includes the overall institutional quality of the country, but not if we restrict the sample to developing countries.

These results suggest that once we control for bank size, ownership, and institutions, the additional explanatory power of bank balance sheet variables is small.

We conclude that while there is a positive correlation between bank soundness and the overall index of BCP compliance, this result is sensitive to controlling for the institutional quality of the country and to the exclusion of outliers. An interesting question is whether different principles that make up the overall BCP index affect bank soundness differently. We turn to this issue next.

Results by Group of Principles

Our results indicate that principles related to licensing and structure and information requirements are the most significantly associated with higher bank ratings at one percent significance. At the ten percent level, preconditions for effective bank supervision also enter significantly.

To check if these results are robust we control for compliance with the rest of the principles. When we include these aggregate indexes in the relevant regressions, we see that only compliance with information requirements remains significant. As an additional robustness test, we re-run these three specifications excluding individual countries one by one. The results show that, the principle measuring compliance with transparency, is the only principle that remains significantly associated with bank soundness.

Robustness of the Relationship Between Bank Ratings and Compliance with Information Provision

In this section we conduct additional robustness checks on the empirical relationship between information disclosure and bank soundness and investigate reverse causality. Compliance with Chapter 5 of the BCPs is positively and significantly associated with bank ratings also when we exclude from the sample advanced countries or extreme observations. In further robustness tests, we add to the baseline regression additional macroeconomic controls, which have been found in the literature to be associated with bank fragility (Demirgüç-Kunt and Detragiache, 1998, 2005): depreciation of the nominal exchange rate, the inflation rate and its standard deviation, real credit growth, real GDP per capita growth.

Among the macro variables, exchange rate depreciation and inflation volatility are negatively and significantly associated with bank ratings, while the level of inflation, real GDP growth, and real credit growth are not significant (results not reported). Compliance with information requirements remains significant and positive throughout these different specifications, confirming that the impact of this principle is not sensitive to omitted macro controls. In yet another specification, we include in the regressions two measures of the frequency and timeliness of macroeconomic data release obtained from IMF's Special Data Dissemination Standards (Allum and Agça, 2001). These measures might help us control for unobservable characteristics that make a country more transparent. The frequency index is positive and significant, while the timeliness is not (result not reported). More importantly, compliance with chapter 5 remains significant and positive also in these regressions.

In the last set of regressions, we try to separate out compliance with Chapter 5 from other design features of supervision and regulation by introducing as regressors four indexes constructed using the survey of bank regulators by Barth, Caprio, and Levine (2001). Specifically, these indexes measure the presence in the laws and regulations of various provisions related to discipline, information disclosure, auditing requirements, and lack of banking restrictions (Barth, Caprio, Levine, 2001).

Endogeneity of BCP Compliance

In this paper, we use individual bank level information to test the impact of compliance with the BCPs. Since an individual bank's soundness rating is unlikely to have an impact on country-level measures of supervisory quality, reverse causality should not be a serious concern. However, soundness ratings are correlated within countries, so it is possible that assessors may assign better compliance ratings to countries whose large banks are generally considered to be financially sound. Furthermore, since the level of compliance is a policy choice made by the countries themselves, countries with sounder banks may face less political opposition in adopting more rigorous regulatory and supervisory processes compared to those countries with distressed banks. On the other hand, it can also be argued that countries with weak banks coming out of a financial crisis may have the strongest incentives and political support to reform their regulations and supervision. So in principle the endogeneity of supervision may bias the relationship with soundness in either direction. Endogeneity concerns should not be overblown, particularly because we focus on the relationship between soundness and transparency, using compliance with the other BCP chapters as a control variable. The latter variable should work as a comprehensive control for unobserved country characteristics or shocks that make the country more likely to comply with Barth, Caprio, and Levine (2001). It is only omitted factors specific to compliance with information disclosure that remain to be controlled for.

We follow the established practice in the literature on institutions and use legal origin dummy variables as instruments. The idea is that fundamental historical country characteristics, such as legal origin, affect a country's institutions, and thus have a bearing on the particular institutions of bank regulation and supervision. On the other hand, bank soundness is unlikely to be affected by these historical characteristics, particularly after controlling for broad institutional quality and supervision itself.

First, legal origin variables are jointly highly significant in the first stage regressions. In all specifications the F-test for the joint significance of the instruments is well above 10, suggesting that there is no concern about weak instruments (Stock and Yogo, 2005). In the second stage, compliance with information provision remains positive and significant in all specification. Following Moreira (2003), we have also computed CLR confidence intervals, which should be robust to weak instruments. Using religion as an alternative instrument gives similar results. On the other hand, other basic country characteristics, such as latitude or ethnic fractionalization, have poor predictive power for BCP compliance.

Measuring Bank Soundness with Z-Scores

As discussed in the introduction, Moody's ratings are an appealing measure of bank financial strength, as they are prepared by specialists with access to variety of sources of information and whose business is to make accurate assessments. On the other hand, ratings are subjective, and it may be argued that analysts may be better disposed towards bank that provide more accurate and timely information even though these banks are not necessarily more sound. To address this concern, in this section we measure bank soundness using an alternative, objective, and commonly used indicator, namely the Z-score. Specifically, we compute Z-scores for the banks in our sample and investigate if we continue to find evidence that compliance with information requirements is a significant correlate to bank soundness.

The Z-score is defined as (average return on assets +equity/ assets)/(standard deviation of the return on assets). It can be interpreted as the number of standard deviations below the mean by which returns would have to fall to wipe out bank equity (see Boyd and Runkle, 1993). The average and standard deviation of bank returns are computed 1995-2003 whenever data are available. Since coverage varies across banks, the average number of years used is slightly above 6 years. In the regressions, we use as the dependent variable ln(1+ Z-score) to smooth out higher values of the z score and to avoid truncating the dependent variable at zero.

The specification is broadly similar to the previous baseline, although we dropped equity and return on assets from the set of regressors since these variables are now used to compute the left-hand-side variable. The Z-scores have a positive and statistically significant correlation with Moody's ratings, but the correlation is not very high (about 20 percent). Nonetheless, the relationship between bank soundness and BCP compliance remains remarkably similar to the one uncovered using Moody's ratings: the overall compliance index is positive but not significant. Additional tests using more macroeconomic control variables (exchange rate depreciation, inflation, inflation volatility, credit growth) confirm this finding (results not reported). To summarize, the positive relationship between compliance with information provision regulation is in evidence whether bank soundness is measured through Moody's ratings or through Z-scores.

CONCLUSIONS

Strong regulation and supervision plays an essential part in ensuring a safe and sound banking system. To curb bank fragility and improve crisis management, many countries are in the process of strengthening their regulatory and supervisory systems, a complex and costly process for many developing countries where human resources are scarce and other supporting institutions are weak. What type of regulation and supervisory practices are most effective in ensuring bank soundness? This is the question that we have addressed in this study.

Using bank-level investor ratings for 39 countries, we have explored whether countries that comply more closely with the Basel Core Principles (BCPs)-the universally accepted standard of best practices in bank supervision-have sounder banks. BCP compliance assessments, carried out under the auspices of the World Bank and IMF Financial Sector Assessment Program, provide a unique source of information about the quality of bank supervision and regulation around the world.

An important aspect of our study is the attempt to differentiate among different elements of the regulatory framework to help prioritize reform efforts. We find a significant and positive relationship between compliance with information provision and bank soundness.

This relationship is robust to controlling for broad indexes of institutional quality, macroeconomic variables, sovereign ratings, and reverse causality. Specifically, countries that require their banks to regularly and accurately report their financial data to regulators and market participants have more highly rated banks, as timely disclosure of high quality information strengthens monitoring by regulators and markets alike.

Our results suggest that countries aiming to upgrade banking regulation and supervision should consider giving priority to information provision over other elements of the core principles.

Because information provision is a necessary condition for effective discipline, this policy recommendation is consistent with the approach to regulation and supervision recommended by Barth, Caprio, and Levine (2006), who stress the importance of mechanisms to empower market discipline and are skeptical of structures that assign too much power to regulators.

THE PATH TO MODERN ISLAMIC BANKING

First National Bank recently announced a sharia compliant banking facility through its IslamicFinance bank accounts. This is the first time one of the big four banks has offered devout Muslim customers an opportunity to have a fully fledged bank account. The account is also available to non-Muslim customers who are tired of feathering the nests of the banks and want to do banking a little differently.

According to sharia, charging interest is not permitted and wealth must be generated through legitimate trade and investment in assets. The sharia financial model works on the basis of risk sharing so that the customer and the bank share the risk of any investment on agreed terms and divide any profit between them. In the case of ordinary banks, the interest they charge is often seen as excessive, especially as the banks make sure they take very little risk when lending, yet charge interest as if they were taking risk. However, for a depositor, sharia compliant banking can be a riskier investment than a conventional bank account although there is more upside potential-though this pertains more to a savings account as transactional accounts, in general, do not offer high returns.

'Customers will benefit in profits in the business but will also share the losses,' says Ebi Patel, CEO of Wesbank Islamic Finance at FNB. However, Patel says, there are ways of reducing the risk by carrying over losses into the next year in the hope that the business is more profitable.

In FNB's case, customers invest directly in Wesbank Islamic Finance and receive dividends based on the profits of the company. The percentage of the dividend pool a customer is entitled to is based on his or her average monthly balance. Although this is a riskier way of investing your cash, your dividends are tax free. In a strong economic environment such as we are experiencing in South Africa, car sales do particularly well, which has all vehicle financing houses smiling. Wesbank Islamic Finance, the vehicle financing arm of FNB's IslamicFinance, works on sharia principles. When you wish to purchase a vehicle the bank buys it first and sells it to you for a higher price which builds in the cost of financing. You, in turn, pay off the vehicle in equal monthly instalments.

Although FNB does not currently offer home loans that are sharia compliant, they will be doing so in the near future. Albaraka Bank, based in Durban, has been operating since June 1989 and was pioneered in response to the need for a system of banking in line with Islamic economic principles. Like FNB, Albaraka does not exclude any individual or business from banking with them.

Albaraka offers its customers two options to purchase a home in accordance with sharia.

Under Ijara (which means 'rental' in Arabic), the bank will buy and own your chosen property. It will then sell it to you for the same price over a period of up to 25 years. While you are paying off the property, the bank will also charge you rent for living in property which it owns. The bank therefore makes its profit from the rent it receives from you. Once you have paid the full purchase price, the property becomes yours.

Murabaha (essentially 'cost plus sales'), an alternative form of Islamic financing, works in the same way as vehicle financing. The bank buys the property from the seller for the original price and then sells it to you for a higher price. The higher price can be paid monthly to the bank over a period of up to 15 years. The bank therefore makes its profit from the higher sale price of the property. According to Patel, purchasing a vehicle or home in this manner can be advantageous to non-Muslim investors as well. Although the original costing is market related and will be determined by current interest rates, it does allow the opportunity to fix your repayments for the length of the bond or vehicle finance so you are not caught unawares by rising interest rates. 'Our products are open to anyone of any religious denomination. Currently five per cent of our customers are non-Muslim,' says Patel.

Apart from banks there are also investment houses which follow the sharia investment principles allowing Muslims to invest in the share market while avoiding investing in companies which conflict with sharia principles. Sharia compliant products are also available to non-Muslim investors. The screening out of certain types of companies makes sharia compliant funds an option for people with certain ethical or social sensibilities and as a result many non-Muslim investors are showing interest.

For example, Futuregrowth Specialist Asset Management manages the Albaraka Equity Fund on behalf of the Albaraka Bank and the fund abides by the principles that govern Islamic investment funds. They receive approximately 45 per cent of their investments through Linked Investment Services Providers (LISPs) which allows investment in a broad range of underlying unit trusts. 'We assume that Muslim investors would come to us directly so a large percentage of LISP investors would be non-Muslim,' says portfolio manager Ashraf Mohamed.

The fund is permitted to deal in the shares of a company whose main business is one permitted in sharia. This means that the fund cannot invest in companies such as banks that are involved in interest-based money lending transactions nor in insurance companies. Companies that trade in alcohol, gambling, nightclubs, pornography or pork products are all excluded from the fund.

Apart from these restrictions the fund is managed in accordance with prudential investment guidelines as with any normal unit trust fund and aims to out-perform the market over the long term. Despite its restrictions, or perhaps because of them, the fund has performed relatively well over the last five years providing investors a 30 per cent return per annum compared to the all share index's return of 19 per cent.

SHARI'AH

The term 'shari'ah' derives from the verb 'shara'a', which according to Omar's Dictionary of the Holy Qur'an connects to the idea of 'spiritual law' and 'system of divine law; way of belief and practice' in the Qur'an. The authority of sharia (conventional spelling) is drawn from two primary sources: first, the specific guidance in the Qur'an; and second, the Sunnah (literally 'the way' i.e. the way the Prophet Muhammad lived his life). The compilation of all that Muhammad said, did or approved of is called the Hadith. Sharia has largely been codified by the schools (madhabs) of Islamic Jurisprudence (which is called fiqh).

3

IMF and its Operations

A bank is an institution that provides financial service, particularly taking deposits and extending credit.

Currently the term bank is generally understood as an institution that holds a banking license. Banking licenses are granted by bank regulatory authorities and provide rights to conduct the most fundamental banking services such as accepting deposits and making loans. There are also financial institutions that provide certain banking services without meeting the legal definition of a bank, a so called non-banking financial company.

Banks have a long history, and have influenced economies and politics for centuries. The word bank is derived from the Italian banca, which is derived from German language and means bench. The terms bankrupt and broke are similarly derived from banca rotta, which refers to an out-of-business bank, having its bench physically broken. Money lenders in Northern Italy originally did business in open areas, or big open rooms, with each lender working from his own bench or table. Traditionally, a bank generates profits from transaction fees on financial services and from the interest it charges for lending. In recent history, with historically low interest rates limiting banks' ability to earn money by lending deposited funds, much of a bank's income is provided by overdraft fees and riskier investments.

INTERNATIONAL MONETARY FUND

The International Monetary Fund (IMF) is an international organization that oversees the global financial system by monitoring exchange rates and balance of payments, as well as offering technical and financial assistance when asked. Its headquarters are in Washington, D.C.

ORGANIZATION AND PURPOSE

The IMF describes itself as "an organization of 184 countries, working to foster global monetary cooperation, secure financial stability, facilitate international trade, promote high employment and sustainable economic growth, and reduce poverty". With the exception of North Korea, Cuba, Liechtenstein, Andorra, Monaco, Tuvalu and Nauru, all UN member states either participate directly in the IMF or are represented by other member states.

In the 1930s, as economic activity in the major industrial countries dwindled, countries started adopting mercantilist practices, attempting to defend their economies by increasing restrictions on imports. To conserve dwindling reserves of gold and foreign exchange, some countries curtailed foreign imports, some devalued their currencies, and some introduced complicated restrictions on foreign exchange accounts held by their citizens. These measures were arguably detrimental to the countries themselves as the Ricardian comparative advantage states that everyone gains from trade without restrictions. It is noteworthy to mention that, although the "size of the pie" is enhanced according to this theory of free trade, when distributional concerns are taken into account, there are always industries that lose out even as others benefit. World trade declined sharply, as did employment and living standards in many countries.

As World War II came to a close, the leading allied countries considered various plans to restore order to international monetary relations, and at the Bretton Woods conference the IMF emerged. The founding members drafted a charter (or Articles of Agreement) of an international institution to oversee the international monetary system and to promote both the elimination of exchange restrictions relating to trade in goods and services, and the stability of exchange rates.

The IMF came into existence in December 1945, when the first 29 countries signed its Articles of Agreement. The statutory purposes of the IMF today are the same as when they were formulated in 1944. From the end of World War II until the late-1970s, the capitalist world experienced unprecedented growth in real incomes. (Since then, China's integration into the capitalist system has added substantially to the growth of the system.) Within the capitalist system, the benefits of growth have not flowed equally to all (either within or among nations) but most capitalist countries have seen recent increases in prosperity that contrast starkly with the conditions within capitalist countries during the interwar period. The lack of a recurring global depression is likely due to improvements in the conduct of international economic policies that have encouraged the growth of international trade and helped smooth the economic cycle of boom and bust.

In the decades since World War II, apart from rising prosperity, the world economy and monetary system have undergone other major changes that have increased the importance and relevance of the purposes served by the IMF, but that has also required the IMF to adapt and reform. Rapid advances in technology and communications have contributed to the increasing international integration of markets and to closer linkages among national economies. As a result, financial crises, when they erupt, now tend to spread more rapidly among countries. The IMF's influence in the global economy steadily increased as it accumulated more members. The number of IMF member countries has more than quadrupled from the 44 states involved in its establishment, reflecting in particular the attainment of political independence by many developing countries and more recently the collapse of the Soviet bloc. The expansion of the IMF's membership, together with the changes in the world economy, have required the IMF to adapt in a variety of ways to continue serving its purposes effectively.

HISTORY

Agreement for the creation of the International Monetary Fund came at the United Nations Monetary and Financial Conference. The United Nations was at the time only a wartime alliance, not yet an international organization in Bretton Woods, New Hampshire, United States, on July 22, 1944. The principal architects of the IMF at the conference were British economist John Maynard Keynes and the chief international economist at the US Treasury Department, Harry Dexter White.

The Articles of Agreement: Articles of Agreement of the International Monetary Fund came into force on December 27, 1945, the organization came into existence on May 1, 1946, as part of a post-WWII reconstruction plan, and it began financial operations on March 1, 1947. It is sometimes referred to as a Bretton Woods institution, along with the International Bank for Reconstruction and Development (now part of the larger World Bank Group). The IMF is the referee and, when the need arises, rescuer of the world's financial system. It was set up to supervise the newly established fixed exchange rate system. After this fell apart in 1971-73, the IMF became more involved with its member countries' economic policies, doling out advice on fiscal policy and monetary policy as well as microeconomic changes such as privatisation, of which it became a forceful advocate. In the 1980s, it played a leading part in sorting out the problems of developing countries' mounting debt. More recently, it has several times co-ordinated and helped to finance assistance to countries with a currency crisis.

The Fund has been criticised for the conditionality of its support, which is usually given only if the recipient country promises to implement IMF-approved economic reforms. Unfortunately, the IMF has often approved "one size fits all" policies that, not much later, turned out to be inappropriate. It has also been accused of creating moral hazard, in effect encouraging governments (and firms, banks and other investors) to behave recklessly by giving them reason to expect that if things go badly the IMF will organise a bail-out. Indeed, some financiers have described an investment in a financially shaky country as a "moral-hazard play" because they were so confident that the IMF would ensure the safety of their money, one way or another. Following the economic crisis in Asia during the late 1990s, and again after the crisis in Argentina early in this decade, some policymakers argued (to no avail) for the IMF to be abolished, as the absence of its safety net would encourage more prudent behaviour all round. More sympathetic folk argued that the IMF should evolve into a global lender of last resort.

MEMBERSHIP QUALIFICATIONS

Any country may apply for membership of the IMF. The application will be considered, first, by the IMF's Executive

Board. After its consideration, the Executive Board will submit a report to the Board of Governors of the IMF with recommendations in the form of a "Membership Resolution." These recommendations cover the amount of quota in the IMF, the form of payment of the subscription, and other customary terms and conditions of membership. After the Board of Governors has adopted the "Membership Resolution," the applicant state needs to take the legal steps required under its own law to enable it to sign the IMF's Articles of Agreement and to fulfill the obligations of IMF membership.

A member's quota in the IMF determines the amount of its subscription, its voting weight, its access to IMF financing, and its allocation of SDRs.

As of 2006, participating nations were discussing changes to the voting formula, to increase equity.

ASSISTANCE AND REFORMS

The primary mission of the IMF is to provide financial assistance to countries that experience serious financial difficulties. Member states with balance of payments problems may request loans and/or organizational management of their national economies. In return, the countries are usually required to launch certain reforms, an example of which is the "Washington Consensus". These reforms are generally required because countries with fixed exchange rate policies can engage in fiscal, monetary, and political practices which may lead to the crisis itself. For example, nations with severe budget deficits, rampant inflation, strict price controls, or significantly over-valued or under-valued currencies run the risk of facing balance of payment crises in their future. Thus, the structural adjustment programs are at least ostensibly intended to ensure that the IMF is actually helping to prevent financial crises rather than merely funding financial recklessness.

However, this approach is not without its critics, as described below. Many proponents of the IMF contend that some criticisms are the result of the fact that many people are not familiar with the operations and objectives of the IMF, and blame a lack of transparency within the IMF for this, as well as the dense nature of international finance in general. Suggestions for improving these understandings have included greater community outreach efforts, tighter accounting standards, possible regulatory oversight, and changes in the organizational structure of the IMF to include fewer economists, whom many fear are attempting to use developing countries as nothing more than lab raccoons. Some fear, however, that some of these reforms to the IMF itself introduce political considerations rather than economic considerations, many of which may have resulted in the financial crises in the first place.

CRITICISM

The role of the two Bretton Woods institutions has been controversial to many since the late Cold War period. Critics claim that IMF policy makers deliberately supported capitalistic military dictatorships friendly to American and European corporations. Critics also claim that the IMF is generally apathetic or hostile to their views of democracy, human rights, and labor rights. These criticisms generated a controversy that helped spark the anti-globalization movement. Others claim the IMF has little power to democratize sovereign states, nor is that its stated objective: to advise and promote financial stability. Arguments in favor of the IMF say that economic stability is a precursor to democracy.

Two criticisms from economists have been that financial aid is always bound to so-called "Conditionalities", including Structural Adjustment Programs. Conditionalities, it is claimed, retard social stability and hence inhibit the stated goals of the IMF. Typically the IMF and its supporters advocate a Keynesian approach. As such, adherents of supply-side economics generally find themselves in open disagreement with the IMF. The IMF frequently advocates currency devaluation, criticized by proponents of supply-side economics as inflationary. Secondly they link higher taxes under "austerity programmes" with economic contraction.

Currency devaluation is recommended by the IMF to the governments of poor nations with struggling economies. Supply-side economists claim these Keynesian IMF policies are destructive to economic prosperity, although many other economists disagree.

Complaints are also directed toward International Monetary Fund gold reserve being undervalued. At its inception in 1945, the IMF pegged gold at 35 dollars per Troy ounce of gold. In 1973 the Nixon administration lifted the fixed asset value of gold in favour of a world market price. Hence the fixed exchange rates of currencies tied to gold were switched to a floating rate, also based on market price and exchange. This largely came about because Petrodollars outside the United States were more than could be backed by the gold at Fort Knox under the fixed exchange rate system. The fixed rate system only served to limit the amount of assistance the organization could use to help debt-ridden countries.

That said, the IMF sometimes advocates "austerity programmes," increasing even when the economy is weak, in order to generate government revenue and balance budget deficits, which is the opposite of Keynesian policy. These policies were criticised by Joseph E. Stiglitz, former chief economist at the World Bank, in his book Globalization and Its Discontents. He argued that by converting to a more Monetarist approach, the fund no longer had a valid purpose, as it was designed to provide funds for countries to carry out Keynesian reflations.

Most altermondialists, like ATTAC, believe that IMF interventions aggravate the poverty and debt of Third World and developing countries. According to the analysis by Yves Engler, the IMF is considered to be responsible for worsening or actually creating famine in Malawi (2002), Ethiopia (2003) and Niger (2005).

Opposition to the IMF is often fragmented. For instance, advocates of supply-side economics would generally regard the policies advocated by ATTAC to be little different in form to the ideas peddled by the IMF. In other words, they would see ATTAC tax-and-spend policies and the IMF's austerity policies as being fundamentally similar.

Argentina, which had been considered by the IMF to be a model country in its compliance to policy proposals by the Bretton Woods institutions, experienced a catastrophic economic crisis in 2001, generally believed to have been caused by IMF-induced budget restrictions-which undercut the government's ability to sustain national infrastructure even in crucial areas such as health, education, and security-and privatization of strategically vital national resources. The crisis added to widespread hatred of this institution in Argentina and other South American countries, with many blaming the IMF for the region's economic problems. The current-as of early 2006-trend towards moderate left-wing governments in the region and a growing concern with the development of a regional economic policy largely independent of big business pressures has been ascribed to this crisis.

Another example of where IMF Structural Adjustment Programmes aggravated the problem was in Kenya. Before IMF got involved in the country, the Kenya central bank oversaw all currency movement in and out of the country. IMF mandated that Kenya central bank had to allow easier currency movement. However, the adjustment resulted in very little foreign investment, but allowed Kamlesh Manusuklal Damji Pattni, with the help of corrupt government officials, to siphon out billions of Kenya shillings in what came to be known as the Goldenberg scandal, leaving the country in a state worse than that which it was in before the IMF reforms were implemented.

That the IMF intervenes only in countries that experience years of dire economic conditions has certainly hurt its reputation. The financial collapses it intervenes in are products of uneven capitalist development sometimes exacerbated by government mismanagement, but mismanagement is often cited by rich nations as the source of the financial crises. These collapses tend to lead to years of economic difficulty that can be addressed in various ways, but IMF Structural Adjustment Policies consistently serve to open up or "liberalize" economies to foreign capital rather than provide for economic recovery through statist policies such as government financed projects to achieve full employment. Thus, IMF policies further the notion that economic development in underdeveloped countries is dependent on attracting foreign investment rather than through a state-managed approach centered on full employment and progressive taxation. It is also true that politicians have used the IMF as an easy target for blame when they themselves have erred, using nationalism to gain easy political points.

Overall the IMF success record is limited. While it was created to help stabilize the global economy, since 1980 over 100 countries have experienced a banking collapse that reduced GDP by four percent or more, far more than at any previous time in history. The considerable delay in IMF response to a crisis, and the fact that it tends to only respond to rather than prevent them, has led many economists to argue for reform.

Whatever the feelings people in the Western world have for the IMF, research by the Pew Research Center shows that more than 60 percent of Asians and 70 percent of Africans feel that the IMF and the World Bank have a positive effect on their country. Such research has made proponents of IMF claim the IMF-critique misleading, as it would be difficult to speak of suffering if the sufferers don't feel hurt.

The documentary Life and Debt deals with the IMF's policies' influence on Jamaica and its economy, from a critical point of view.

PAST MANAGING DIRECTORS

An unwritten rule establishes that the IMF's managing director must be European and that the president of the World Bank must be from the United States. Executive Directors, who confirm the managing director are voted in by Finance Ministers from countries they represent.

Dates	Name	Country
May 6, 1946-May 5, 1951	Camille Gutt	Belgium
August 3, 1951-October 3, 1956	Ivar Rooth	Sweden
November 21, 1956-May 5, 1963	Per Jacobson	Sweden
September 1, 1963-August 31, 1973	Pierre-Paul Schweitzer	France
September 1, 1973-June 16, 1978	Johannes Witteveen	Netherlands
June 17, 1978-January 15, 1987	Jacques de Larosiare	France
January 16, 1987-February 14, 2000	Michel Camdessus	France
May 1, 2000-March 4, 2004	Horst Kahler	Germany
June 7, 2004-present	Rodrigo de Rato	Spain

The IMF is for the most part controlled by the major Western Powers, with voting rights on the Executive board based on a quota derived from a monetary stake in the institution. Rarely does the board vote and pass issues contradicting the will of the US or Europeans. There have been some exceptions in the past. Dr. Mohamed Finaish from Libya, the Executive Director representing the majority of the Arab World and Pakistan, was a tireless defender of the developing nations' rights at the IMF. He stood steadfast in his beliefs and principles for fourteen years until his defeat in the 1992 elections to an Egyptian IMF Staff Member.

COMPARATIVE ADVANTAGE

In economics, the theory of comparative advantage explains why it can be beneficial for two parties (usually countries) to trade, even though one of them may be able to produce every kind of item more cheaply than the other. What matters is not the absolute cost of production, but rather the ratio between how easily the two countries can produce different kinds of things. The concept is highly important in modern international trade theory.

Comparative advantage may be compared to absolute advantage. When one entity (be it a company or a country) is able to produce more efficiently than another entity it has an absolute advantage: that is, assuming equal inputs, the entity with an absolute advantage will have a greater output.

ORIGIN OF THE THEORY

Comparative advantage was first described by Robert Torrens in 1815 in an essay on the corn trade. He concluded that it was to England's advantage to trade various goods with Poland in return for corn, even though it might be possible to produce that corn more cheaply in England than Poland.

However, the theory is usually attributed to David Ricardo who created a systematic explanation in his 1817 book The Principles of Political Economy and Taxation using an example involving England and Portugal. In Portugal it is possible to produce both wine and cloth with less work than it takes in England. However, the relative costs of producing those two goods are different in the two countries. In England it is very hard to produce wine, and only moderately difficult to produce cloth. In Portugal both are easy to produce. Therefore, while it is cheaper to produce cloth in Portugal than England, it is cheaper still for Portugal to produce excess wine, and trade that for English cloth. Conversely, England benefits from this trade because its cost for producing cloth has not changed but it can now get wine at closer to the cost of cloth.

Stanislaw Ulam once challenged Nobel laureate Paul Samuelson to name one theory in all of the social sciences which is both true and nontrivial. Several years later, Samuelson responded with David Ricardo's theory of comparative advantage:

> *"That it is logically true need not be argued before a mathematician; that it is not trivial is attested by the thousands of important and intelligent men who have never been able to grasp the doctrine for themselves or to believe it after it was explained to them." —Paul Samuelson.*

CRITICAL ANALYSIS OF RICARDO'S THEORY

Ricardo's principle relies on a variety of implicit assumptions that are debatable, such as that there is no (or a low) cost for transportation, and that the advantages of increased production outweigh externalities such as environmental contamination or social inequities. It is also necessary that there be restrictions on the flow of capital-otherwise, there would be no incentive to invest in the manufacture of either wine or cloth in England, since both are more costly to produce there.

Opponents of free trade often point out that globalized communications and transportation unavailable in Ricardo's time invalidate the assumption of capital immobility and cause capital to gravitate toward absolute advantage. Another concern is that comparative advantage only works when competition is absolutely perfect. It has also been argued that comparative advantage may reduce economic diversity to risky levels.

Free trade advocates would dissent, however, and say that modernization has decreased transportation and logistics costs through inventions such as the airplane and internet unavailable in Ricardo's time making his theory ever more sound with time, furthermore, despite the increased movement of capital, differences in capacities of production are still wide, in fact, free trade creates a wider gap of production in many areas despite the larger increases it makes in absolute wealth. In theory, along a country has one more worker, one more machine, or one extra source of natural resources comparative advantage will still apply. As to perfect competition, supporters of free trade claim that perfect competition is the result of universal free trade, not its precondition. For free trade advocates, comparative advantage is what a capitalist country must embrace to gain an advantage in an existing mercantalist world.

On a final note, Gottfried Haberler showed in the 1930s that Ricardo's thinking on comparative advantage could also be expressed in neoclassical terms of opportunity cost.

Examples

The following worked examples explain the reasoning behind the theory. In Example 3 all assumptions are italicized for easy reference, and some are explained at the end of the example.

Example 1

Two men land alone in an isolated island. To survive they must undertake a few basic economic activities like water carrying, fishing, cooking and shelter construction and maintenance. The first man is young, strong, and educated and is faster, better, more productive at everything. He has an absolute advantage in all activities. The second man is old, weak, and uneducated. He has an absolute disadvantage in all economic activities. In some activities the difference between the two is great; in others it is small. Is it in the interest of either of them to work in isolation? No, specialization and exchange (trade) can benefit both of them.

How should they divide the work? According to comparative, not absolute advantage: the young man must spend more time on the tasks in which he is much better and the old man must concentrate on the tasks in which he is only a little worse. Such an arrangement will increase total production and/or reduce total labour. It will make both of them richer. Specialisation and exchange will not be possible if there is an absolute resource constraint. If, for example, the amount of fresh water available on the island is enough for one man only there will be war.

Example 2

A Needs 100 P1 and 100 P2

B Needs 100 P1 and 100 P2

A: No trade

Product	Cost	Produced	Cost
P1	10	100	1000
P2	20	100	2000
Net	-	200	3000

B: No trade

Product	Cost	Produced	Cost
P1	15	100	1500
P2	25	100	2500
Net	-	200	4000

A with trade: 100P1 for 56 P2

Product	Cost	Produced	Cost
P1	10	200	2000
P2	20	44	880
Net	-	244	2880

B With trade: 56 P2 for 100 P1

Product	Cost	Produced	Cost
P1	15	0	0
P2	25	156	3900
Net	-	156	3900

So A saved 120 cost units or 4% and B saved 100 cost units or 2.5%. Clearly A gained more from the trade, but both parties experienced growth. Now if B adds some taxes to protect the producers of P1 he can try to get a larger percentage of the trade but his savings goes down as do the overall savings.

Example 3

Suppose for example we have two countries of equal size, Northland and Southland, that both produce and consume two goods, Food and Clothes. The productive capacities and efficiencies of the countries are such that if both countries devoted all their resources to Food production, output would be as follows:

* Northland: 100 tonnes
* Southland: 200 tonnes

Conversely if all of the resources of the countries were allocated to the production of Clothes, output would be:

* Northland: 100 tonnes
* Southland: 100 tonnes

We need to assume that each of the countries has constant opportunity costs of production between the two products, and that both economies have full employment at all times. Also all factors of production are perfectly mobile within the countries between clothing and food industries, but are immobile between the countries. Finally the price mechanism must be working to provide perfect competition.

So Southland has an absolute advantage over Northland in the production of Food, and both countries are equally efficient in the production of Clothes. Intuitively it would seem that there is no mutual benefit in trade between the economies. But an examination of the opportunity costs shows something different. For Northland the opportunity cost of producing one tonne of Food is one tonne of Clothes and vice versa. But for Southland the opportunity cost of one tonne of Food is 0.5 tonne of Clothes; and the opportunity cost of one tonne of Clothes is 2 tonnes of Food. Looked at this way, Southland has a comparative advantage in Food production because of its lower opportunity cost of production with respect to Northland. And Northland also has a comparative advantage over Southland in the production of Clothes, the opportunity cost of which is lower in Southland with respect to Food than in Northland.

To show that these different opportunity costs can lead to mutual benefit if the countries specialise production and trade, consider the following starting position. Both countries produce and consume only domestically. The volumes are:

Production and Consumption before Trade

	Food	Clothes
Northland	50	50
Southland	100	50
World total	150	100

We now examine the consequences of trade between the two countries. This example includes no formulation of the preferences of consumers in the two economies which would allow the determination of the international exchange rate of Clothes and Food. But given the production capabilities of each country, in order for trade to be worthwhile Northland requires a price of at least one tonne of Food in exchange for one tonne of Clothes; and Southland requires at least one tonne of Clothes for two tonnes of Food. It follows that the actual exchange price will be somewhere between the two. The remainder of the example works with an international trading price of one tonne of Food for 2/3 tonne of Clothes. If both countries specialise completely in the goods in which they have comparative advantage, their outputs will be:

Production After Trade

	Food	Clothes
Northland	0	100
Southland	200	0
World total	200	100

Note that world production of Food had increased and Clothing production has remained the same. Using the exchange rate of one tonne of Food for 2/3 tonne of Clothes, Northland and Southland are able to trade to yield the following level of consumption:

Consumption After Trade

	Food	Clothes
Northland	75	50
Southland	125	50
World total	200	100

Northland has traded 50 tonnes of Clothing for 75 tonnes of Food. Both countries have benefited. In fact, both countries are now consuming at points outside their production possibility frontiers.

Assumptions in Example 3

* Two countries, two goods-the theory is no different for larger numbers of countries and goods, but the principles

are clearer and the argument easier to follow in this simpler case.

* Equal size economies-again, this is a simplification to produce a clearer example.
* Full employment-if one or other of the economies has less than full employment of factors of production, then this excess capacity must usually be used up before the comparative advantage reasoning can be applied.
* Constant opportunity costs-a more realistic treatment of opportunity costs the reasoning is broadly the same, but specialization of production can only be taken to the point at which the opportunity costs in the two countries become equal. This does not invalidate the principles of comparative advantage, but it does limit the magnitude of the benefit.
* Perfect mobility of factors of production within countries-this is necessary to allow production to be switched without cost. In real economies this cost will be incurred: capital will be tied up in plant (sewing machines are not sowing machines) and labour will need to be retrained and relocated. This is why it is sometimes argued that 'nascent industries' should be protected from fully liberalised international trade during the period in which a high cost of entry into the market (capital equipment, training) is being paid for.
* Immobility of factors of production between countries-why are there different rates of productivity? Capital includes production technology and know-how. If it can be moved between countries then the production capabilities of the countries will change. Similarly the movement of labour will change that factor cost and productivity. Perfect transnational mobility of factors of production would invalidate comparative advantage. Imperfect transnational mobility reduces the mutual benefit of trade.
* Perfect competition-this is a standard assumption that allows perfectly efficient allocation of productive resources in an idealized free market.

More Complexities

While the Ricardian model has only one input, we could extend the model both increasing the number of goods from two goods to n goods and by allowing the productivity coefficient to vary.

FREE TRADE

In international trade, free trade is an idealized market model, often stated as a political objective, wherein trade of goods and services between countries flows unhindered by government-imposed artificial costs. Intellectually, this arrangement is supported by followers of the neoclassical and microeconomic schools of thought. It is opposed by anti-globalization and labor due to shown tendencies for abuse by wealthier states.

The term is given to economic policies, as well as political parties that support increases in such trade.

Free trade is a concept in economics and government, encompassing:

* International trade of goods without tariffs (taxes on imports) or other trade barriers (e.g., quotas on imports)
* International trade in services without tariffs or other trade barriers
* The free movement of labour between countries
* The free movement of capital between countries
* The absence of trade-distorting policies (such as taxes, subsidies, regulations or laws) that give domestic firms, households or factors of production an advantage over foreign ones
* Trade-distorting policies to enforce property rights so as to ensure the above conditions

The relative costs, benefits and beneficiaries of free trade are debated by academics, economists, governments and interest groups. Aspects of the ongoing debate are addressed below.

WIDER MEANING

Depending on the specific context, use of the term free trade can signify one or more of the above conditions. However, it is fundamental that only governments can restrict trade:

they have the legal monopoly over the use of physical force in a geographical area. The term free trade has become very politically based, and it is not uncommon for so-called "free trade agreements" to impose additional trade restrictions. Such restrictions on trade are often due to domestic political pressure by powerful corporate, environmental or labor interest groups seeking special protections of their perceived interests.

Free trade agreements are a key element of customs unions and free trade areas. The details and differences of these agreements are covered in their respective articles.

HISTORY OF FREE TRADE

The history of free trade is a history of international trade focusing on the developments of open markets.

It is known that various prosperous world cultures throughout history have engaged in trade. Based on this, theoretical rationalizations as to why a policy of free trade would be beneficial to nations developed over time. These theories were developed in its academic modern sense from the commercial culture of England, and more broadly Europe, in the past five centuries. In opposition to free trade, a policy of mercantilism was developed in Europe in the 1500s and persists in various forms to this day. Early free trade theorists who were opposed to mercantilism were David Ricardo and Adam Smith. Free trade theorists offered trade as the reason why certain cultures prospered economically. Adam Smith, for example, pointed to increased trading as being the reason for the flourishing of not just Mediterranean cultures such as Egypt, Greece, and Rome, but also of Bengal (East Indies) and China.

Free trade policies have battled with mercantilist, protectionist, isolationist, communist, and other policies over the centuries. Wars, such as the Opium Wars, have been fought primarily over trade.

All developed countries have used protectionism, but usually reduced it as they gained more wealth. Some critics say that having more wealth guarantees that the country would benefit from free trade, although the majority of scientists think that also poor countries would benefit from free trade.

FREE TRADE AND INTELLECTUAL PROPERTY

Historically, the free trade movement was skeptical and even hostile to the notion of intellectual property, regarding it as monopolistic and harmful to a free, competitive economy. Indeed, during the late 19th century, free trade advocates succeeded in reducing the length of the patents available in many European countries. The Netherlands, remarked for its laissez-faire policies in the 19th century, even abolished its patent system (mostly used by foreign companies) in 1867. Under the stipulations of the Convention of Paris however did the Netherlands have to re-introduce the patent system (made law in 1910), and was the last European country to do so (after Switzerland). The 19th century anti-patent cause failed largely because the recession of 1874 weakened the free trade movement of the time Fritz Machlup & Edith Penrose, "The Patent Controversy in the 19th Century", Journal of Economic History, 10 (1) pp. 1-29, 1950]]. (and also because patent advocates used a public relations campaign which was remarkably sophisticated for its time). It is thus remarkable (maybe even ironic) that corporations lobbying for expanded intellectual property rights have succeeded in including Agreement on Trade-Related Aspects of Intellectual Property Rights (TRIPS), a very strong treaty on intellectual property rights, as a membership requirement for the World Trade Organization, the international organization dedicated to furthering the cause of free trade (although some modern free traders would argue that markets are impossible without property protections, and that incentives to produce highly capitalized intellectual property would be diminished if inventors could not profit from inventions).

CRITICISM OF FREE TRADE

Free trade is one of the most debated topics of the 20th and 21st century. Different arguments are used by those who favour and by those who oppose free trade, or feel that more constraints are needed. These arguments can be divided in economic, moral and socio-political arguments.

ALTERNATIVES TO FREE TRADE

Tobin Tax: A Tobin tax is the suggested tax on all trade of currency across borders. This is supposed to put a penalty on short-term speculation in currencies.

Fair Trade: The fair trade movement, also known as the trade justice movement, promotes international labor, environment and social standards for the production of traded goods and services. The movement focuses in particular on exports from the Third and Second Worlds to the First World.

Balanced Trade: Balanced trade is an alternative economic model to free trade. Under balanced trade, nations are required to provide a fairly even reciprocal trade pattern; they cannot run large trade deficits. If deficits appear, the surplus nation must find a way to balance out trade or risk sanctions, fees, or quotas. Critics say this may discourage innovation as one country may reduce its efforts to produce products needed by the other.

International Barter

Some nations have prohibited trade under monetary terms of trade. For example, Hjalmar Schacht arranged barter for Nazi Germany to bypass the free market which he thought was rigged by Anglo-American capitalists. Officially, the 1933 bilateral-barter policy was designed to ensure that foreign countries bought as much from industrial Germany as she bought from them. However, Milton Friedman has argued that Hjalmar Schacht's exchange controls were primarily designed to restrict capital flight. The former Soviet Union occasionally arranged bilateral barter within its sphere of influence. See Comprehensive Program for Socialist Economic Integration or Comecon. Arab League nations have also occasionally replaced monetary trade with barter.

Increase the Credit Risk to International Loans

George Soros and others argue that some of the most destructive free trade, such as developing world agricultural monoculture, is driven by export-oriented production targets set by the International Monetary Fund (IMF) and the governments it supports. He suggests that the volume of this trade would be lower if the lending banks were liable for credit default instead of receiving IMF bail-outs. If banks were responsible for default, the levels of lending would be lower and lead to more sustainable export programs due to the discipline of the free market, he believes.

International Price Floors

Some argue that free trade is responsible for the decline in international commodity prices. One reason for these low prices is the over-production of subsidized commodities in the developed world. Rather than removing the production subsidy for farmers in the rich world some suggest extending them to farmers in the developing world. For instance, producers in Poland lobbied to be included in the Common Agriculture Policy. The reason that rich-country farmers need subsidies to thrive is the comparative advantage of cheap land and labour enjoyed by their poor-country competitors.

Separating World Prices from Domestic Prices

Foreign trade of Communist Czechoslovakia was conducted at "free trade" import prices, with the Ministry of Foreign Trade selling the goods on, into the internal market, at pre-determined prices for each good. In this way, Czechoslovakian consumers were insulated from shifts in world prices whilst having some access to foreign products.

It is difficult for governments to sustain different internal prices over the long term. If the internal price is set below world prices, smugglers try to profit from the differential by illegally exporting the product to nations where they can sell it at a higher price. To the extent smugglers succeed, the domestic government is indirectly subsidizing foreign consumers. This problem has been vividly illustrated in nations where fuel prices are subsidized below world prices; domestic shortages frequently occur as a significant portion of the good is illegally smuggled out of the country. Rationing and black markets are stimulated by artificially low prices; in Iraq the famously long petrol pump queues for petrol at 50 dinars/litre can be bypassed by buying on the black market at 250 dinars/litre. Unofficial markets are a common problem wherever the "official" price is below the free trade price.

Despite the difficulties of maintaining fixed commodity prices, many Governments that attempt it claim that doing so "immunizes" their economies against destabilizing price shocks. It is sometimes argued that the social and economic benefits alone, outweigh the disadvantages (of import-price stability). On the other hand, international prices tell the costs of producing certain products and the benefits of consuming them. By separating the prices this flow of information is halted and therefore the local decisions are decoupled from the global needs and possibilities, thus hindering the producers in the country to produce the products where they have a comparative advantage and the consumers to consume the products that can elsewhere be produced so cheaply that they would like to consume them at those prices instead of consuming some other kind of products or less products (or services).

FREE TRADE AREA

A free trade area is a designated group of countries that have agreed to eliminate tariffs, quotas and preferences on most (if not all) goods between them.

It is the second stage of economic integration.

Countries choose this kind of economic integration form, if their economical structures are complementary. If they are competitive, they will choose customs union.

Unlike a customs union, members of a free trade area do not have the same policies with respect to non-members, meaning different quotas and customs. To avoid evasion (through re-exportation) the countries use the system of certification of origin most commonly called Rules of Origin, where there is a requirement for the minimum extent of local material inputs and local transformations adding value to the goods. Goods that don't cover these minimum requirements are not entitled for the special treatment envisioned in the free trade area provisions.

Cumulation is the relationship between different FTAs regarding the Rules of Origin sometimes different FTAs supplement each other, in other cases there is no cross-cumulation between the FTAs.

The Free Trade Area is a result of a Free Trade Agreement (a form of trade pact) between two or more countries. Free Trade Areas/Agreements (FTA) are cascadable to some degree if some countries sign agreement to form free trade area and choose to negotiate together (either as a trade bloc or as a forum of individual members of their FTA) another free trade agreement with some external country (or countries) then the new FTA will consist of the old FTA plus the new country (or countries). A Free Trade Area is a region in which obstacles to unrestricted trade have been reduced to a minimum.

Within an industrialized country there are usually few if any significant barriers to the easy exchange of goods and services between parts of that country. For example, there are usually no trade tariffs or import quotas; there are usually no delays as goods pass from one part of the country to another (other than those that distance imposes); there are usually no differences of taxation and regulation.

Between countries on the other hand, many of these barriers to the easy exchange of goods can and often do occur. It is commonplace for there to be import duties of one kind or another (as goods enter a country) and the levels of sales tax and regulation often vary by country.

The aim of a free trade area is to so reduce barriers to easy exchange that trade can grow as a result of specialisation, division of labour, and most importantly via (the theory and practice of) comparative advantage. The theory of comparative advantage argues that in an unrestricted marketplace (in equilibrium) each source of production will tend to specialize in that activity where it has comparative (rather than absolute) advantage. The theory argues that the net result will be an increase in income and ultimately wealth and well-being for everyone in the free trade area. However the theory refers only to aggregate wealth and says nothing about the distribution of wealth. In fact there may be significant losers, in particular among the recently protected industries with a comparative disadvantage. The proponent of free trade can, however, retort that the gains of the gainers exceed the losses of the losers.

FREE TRADE ZONE

A free trade zone (FTZ) or export processing zone is one or more areas of a country where tariffs and quotas are eliminated and bureaucratic requirements are lowered in order to attract companies by raising the incentives for doing business there.

Most FTZs are located in developing countries. They are special zones where (some) normal trade barriers such as import or export tariffs do not apply, bureaucracy is typically minimized by outsourcing it to the FTZ operator and corporations setting up in the zone may be given tax breaks as an additional incentive. Usually, these zones are set up in underdeveloped parts of the host country, the rationale being that the zones will attract employers and thus reduce poverty and unemployment and stimulate the area's economy. These zones are often used by multinational corporations to set up factories to produce goods (such as clothing or shoes).

Criticism

The creation of special free-trade zones is criticized as giving business which set up operations under influence of already corrupt governments, and as giving foreign corporations more economic liberty than is given ordinary citizens, who face large and sometimes insurmountable "regulatory" hurdles in most third-world nations. Because the multinational corporation is able to choose between many underdeveloped or depressed countries in setting up an overseas factory, and most of these countries do not have limited governments, bidding wars of sorts erupt between their governments. Often the government pays part of the initial cost of factory setup, loosens environmental protections and rules regarding negligence and the treatment of workers, and promises not to ask payment of taxes for the next few years. When the taxation-free years are over the corporation which set up the factory without fully assuming its costs is often able to set up operations elsewhere for less expense than the taxes to be paid, giving it leverage to take the host government to the bargaining table with more demands in order for it to continue operations in the country. The widespread use of free trade zones by companies such as Nike has received criticism from numerous writers such as Naomi Klein in her No logo book.

Free Trade Zones

* South American Community of Nations (planned for 2007)
* Mercosur
* Andean Community
* Jamaican Free Zones
* Jebel Ali Free Zone
* Shannon Free Zone

INTERNATIONAL TRADE

For other uses of that term, International trade is the exchange of goods and services across international boundaries or territories. In most countries, it represents a significant share of GDP. While international trade has been present throughout much of history, its economic, social, and political importance has been on the rise in recent centuries. Industrialization, advanced transportation, globalization, multinational corporations, and outsourcing are all having a major impact. Increasing international trade is the usually primary meaning of "globalization". International trade is also a branch of economics, which, together with international finance, forms the larger branch of international economics.

INTERNATIONAL TRADE THEORY

Several different models have been proposed to predict patterns of trade and to analyze the effects of trade policies such as tariffs.

Ricardian Model

The Ricardian model focuses on comparative advantage and is perhaps the most important concept in international trade theory. In a Ricardian model, countries specialize in producing what they produce best. Unlike other models, the Ricardian framework predicts that countries will fully specialize instead of producing a broad array of goods. Also, the Ricardian model does not directly consider factor endowments, such as the relative amounts of labor and capital within a country.

Heckscher-Ohlin Model

The Heckscher-Ohlin model was produced as an alternative to the Ricardian model of basic comparative advantage. Despite its greater complexity it did not prove much more accurate in its predictions. However from a theoretical point of view it did provide an elegant solution by incorporating the neoclassical price mechanism into international trade theory.

The theory argues that the pattern of international trade is determined by differences in factor endowments. It predicts that countries will export those goods that make intensive use of locally abundant factors and will import goods that make intensive use of factors that are locally scarce. Empirical problems with the H-O model, known as the Leontief paradox, were exposed in empirical tests by Wassily Leontief who found that the United States tended to export labor intensive goods despite having a capital abundance.

Specific Factors

While labor can move freely between sectors, there are other factors specific to sectors, there are other factors specific to particular industries. This model is ideal for particular industries. This model is ideal forunderstanding income distribution but awkward for discussion the pattern of trade.

Gravity Model

The Gravity model of trade presents a more empirical analysis of trading patterns rather than the more theoretical models. The gravity model, in its basic form, predicts trade based on the distance between countries and the interaction of the countries' economic sizes. The model mimics the Newtonian law of gravity which also considers distance and physical size between two objects. The model has been proven to be empirically strong through econometric analysis. Other factors such as income level, diplomatic relationships between countries, and trade policies are also included in expanded versions of the model.

REGULATION OF INTERNATIONAL TRADE

Traditionally trade was regulated through bilateral treaties between two nations. For centuries under the belief in Mercantilism most nations had high tariffs and many restrictions on international trade. In the 19th century, especially in Britain, a belief in free trade became paramount and this view has dominated thinking among western nations for most of the time since then. In the years since the Second World War multilateral treaties like the GATT and World Trade Organization have attempted to create a globally regulated trade structure.

Free trade is usually most strongly supported by the most economically powerful nations in the world, though they often engage in selective protectionism for those industries which are politically important domestically, such as the protective tariffs applied to agriculture and textiles by the United States and

Europe. The Netherlands and the United Kingdom were both strong advocates of free trade when they were economically dominant, today the United States, the United Kingdom and Japan are its greatest proponents. However, many other countries (such as India, China and Russia) are increasingly becoming advocates of free trade as they become more economically powerful themselves. As tariff levels fall there is also an increasing willingness to negotiate non tariff measures, including foreign direct investment, procurement and trade facilitation. The latter looks at the transaction cost associated with meeting trade and customs procedures.

Traditionally agricultural interests are usually in favour of free trade while manufacturing sectors often support protectionism. This has changed somewhat in recent years, however. In fact, agricultural lobbies, particularly in the United States, Europe and Japan, are chiefly responsible for particular rules in the major international trade treaties which allow for more protectionist measures in agriculture than for most other goods and services. During recessions there is often strong domestic pressure to increase tariffs to protect domestic industries. This occurred around the world during the Great Depression leading to a collapse in world trade that many believe seriously deepened the depression. The regulation of international trade is done through the World Trade Organization at the global level, and through several other regional arrangements such as MERCOSUR in South America, NAFTA between the United States, Canada and Mexico, and the European Union between 25 independent states.

The 2005 Buenos Aires talks on the planned establishment of the Free Trade Area of the Americas (FTAA) failed largely due to opposition from the populations of Latin American nations. Similar agreements such as the MAI (Multilateral Agreement on Investment) have also failed in recent years.

RISKS INVOLVED

The risks that exist in international trade can be divided into two major groups:

Economic Risks

* Risk of insolvency of the buyer,

* Risk of protracted default-the failure of the buyer to pay the amount due within six months after the due date, and
* Risk of non-acceptance
* Surrendering economic sovereignty

Political Risks

* Risk of cancellation or non-renewal of export or import licences
* War risks
* Risk of expropriation or confiscation of the importer's company
* Risk of the imposition of an import ban after the shipment of the goods
* Transfer risk-imposition of exchange controls by the importer's country or foreign currency shortages
* Surrendering political sovereignty.

Customs Union

A customs union is a free trade area with a Common External Tariff. The participant countries set up common external trade policy, but in some cases they use different import quotas. Common competition policy is also helpful to avoid competition deficiency.

Purposes for establishing a customs union normally include increasing economic efficiency and establishing closer political and cultural ties between the member countries.

It is the third stage of economic integration.

Customs union is established through trade pact.

BRETTON WOODS SYSTEM

The Bretton Woods system of international monetary management established the rules for commercial and financial relations among the world's major industrial states. The Bretton Woods system was the first example of a fully negotiated monetary order intended to govern monetary relations among independent nation-states.

Preparing to rebuild the international economic system as World War II was still raging, 730 delegates from all 44 Allied nations gathered at the Mount Washington Hotel in Bretton Woods, New Hampshire for the United Nations Monetary and Financial Conference. The delegates deliberated upon and signed the Bretton Woods Agreements during the first three weeks of July 1944.

Setting up a system of rules, institutions, and procedures to regulate the international monetary system, the planners at Bretton Woods established the International Bank for Reconstruction and Development (IBRD) (now one of five institutions in the World Bank Group) and the International Monetary Fund (IMF). These organizations became operational in 1946 after a sufficient number of countries had ratified the agreement.

The chief features of the Bretton Woods system were an obligation for each country to adopt a monetary policy that maintained the exchange rate of its currency within a fixed value-plus or minus one percent-in terms of gold; and the ability of the IMF to bridge temporary imbalances of payments. In the face of increasing strain, the system collapsed in 1971, following the United States' suspension of convertibility from dollars to gold.

Until the early 1970s, the Bretton Woods system was effective in controlling conflict and in achieving the common goals of the leading states that had created it, especially the United States.

ORIGINS

The political bases for the Bretton Woods system are in the confluence of several key conditions: the shared experiences of the Great Depression, the concentration of power in a small number of states, and the presence of a dominant power willing and able to assume a leadership role in global monetary affairs.

THE GREAT DEPRESSION

A high level of agreement among the powerful on the goals and means of international economic management facilitated the decisions reached by the Bretton Woods Conference. The foundation of that agreement was a shared belief in capitalism. Although the developed countries differed somewhat in the type of capitalism they preferred for their national economies

(France, for example, preferred greater planning and state intervention, whereas the United States favored relatively limited state intervention), all relied primarily on market mechanisms and on private ownership.

Thus, it is their similarities rather than their differences that appear most striking. All the participating governments at Bretton Woods agreed that the monetary chaos of the interwar period had yielded several valuable lessons.

The experience of the Great Depression, when proliferation of foreign exchange controls and trade barriers led to economic disaster, was fresh on the minds of public officials. The planners at Bretton Woods hoped to avoid a repeat of the debacle of the 1930s, when foreign exchange controls undermined the international payments system that was the basis for world trade. The "beggar thy neighbor" policies of 1930s governments-using currency devaluations to increase the competitiveness of a country's export products in order to reduce balance of payments deficits-worsened national deflationary spirals, which resulted in plummeting national incomes, shrinking demand, mass unemployment, and an overall decline in world trade. Trade in the 1930s became largely restricted to currency blocs (groups of nations that use an equivalent currency, such as the "Sterling Area" of the British Empire). These blocs retarded the international flow of capital and foreign investment opportunities. Although this strategy tended to increase government revenues in the short run, it dramatically worsened the situation in the medium and longer run.

Thus, for the international economy, planners at Bretton Woods all favored a liberal system, one that relied primarily on the market with the minimum of barriers to the flow of private trade and capital. Although they disagreed on the specific implementation of this liberal system, all agreed on an open system.

ECONOMIC SECURITY

Also based on experience of interwar years, U.S. planners developed a concept of economic security-that a liberal international economic system would enhance the possibilities of postwar peace. One of those who saw such a security link was Cordell Hull, the U.S. secretary of state from 1933 to

1944.1 Hull believed that the fundamental causes of the two world wars lay in economic discrimination and trade warfare. Specifically, he had in mind the trade and exchange controls (bilateral arrangements) of Nazi Germany and the imperial preference system practiced by Britain (by which members or former members of the British Empire were accorded special trade status). Hull argued

Unhampered trade dovetailed with peace; high tariffs, trade barriers, and unfair economic competition, with warif we could get a freer flow of tradefreer in the sense of fewer discriminations and obstructions so that one country would not be deadly jealous of another and the living standards of all countries might rise, thereby eliminating the economic dissatisfaction that breeds war, we might have a reasonable chance of lasting peace.

THE RISE OF GOVERNMENTAL INTERVENTION

The developed countries also agreed that the liberal international economic system required governmental intervention. In the aftermath of the Great Depression, public management of the economy had emerged as a primary activity of governments in the developed states. Employment, stability, and growth were now important subjects of public policy. In turn, the role of government in the national economy had become associated with the assumption by the state of the responsibility for assuring of its citizens a degree of economic well-being. The welfare state grew out of the Great Depression, which created a popular demand for governmental intervention in the economy, and out of the theoretical contributions of the Keynesian school of economics, which asserted the need for governmental intervention to maintain an adequate level of employment.

At the international level, these ideas evolved from the experience of the 1930s. The priority of national goals, independent national action in the interwar period, and the failure to perceive that those national goals could not be realized without some form of international collaboration resulted in "beggar-thy-neighbor" policies such as high tariffs and competitive devaluations which contributed to economic breakdown, domestic political instability, and international war.

The lesson learned was that, as New Dealer Harry Dexter White, the principal architect of the Bretton Woods system, put it: the absence of a high degree of economic collaboration among the leading nations will inevitably result in economic warfare that will be but the prelude and instigator of military warfare on an even vaster scale.

To ensure economic stability and political peace, states agreed to cooperate to regulate the international economic system. The pillar of the U.S. vision of the postwar world was free trade. Free trade involved lowering tariffs and among other things a balance of trade favorable to the capitalist system.

Thus, the more developed market economies agreed with the U.S. vision of postwar international economic management, which was to be designed to create and maintain an effective international monetary system and foster the reduction of barriers to trade and capital flows.

THE RISE OF U.S. HEGEMONY

International economic management relied on the dominant power to lead the system. The concentration of power facilitated management by confining the number of actors whose agreement was necessary to establish rules, institutions, and procedures and to carry out management within the agreed system. That leader was the United States. As the world's foremost economic and political power, the United States was clearly in a position to assume the responsibility of leadership.

The United States had emerged from the Second World War as the strongest economy, experiencing rapid industrial growth and capital accumulation. The U.S. had remained untouched by the ravages of World War II and had built a thriving manufacturing industry and grown wealthy selling weapons and lending money to the other combatants; in fact, U.S. industrial production in 1945 was more than double that of annual production between the prewar years of 1935 and 1939. In contrast, Europe and East Asia were militarily and economically shattered.

As the Bretton Woods Conference convened, the relative advantages of the U.S. economy were undeniable and overwhelming. The U.S. held a majority of investment capital, manufacturing production and exports. In 1945, the U.S.

produced half the world's coal, two-thirds of the oil, and more than half of the electricity. The U.S. was able to produce great quantities of ships, airplanes, vehicles, armaments, machine tools, chemicals, and so on. Reinforcing the initial advantage-and assuring the U.S. unmistakable leadership in the capitalist world-the U.S. held 80% of gold reserves and had not only a powerful army but also the atomic bomb.

As the world's greatest industrial power and one of the few nations unravaged by the war, the U.S. stood to gain more than any other country from the opening of the entire world to unfettered trade. The U.S. would have a global market for its exports, and it would have unrestricted access to vital raw materials.

The U.S. was not only able, it was also willing to assume this leadership role. Although the U.S. had more gold, more manufacturing capacity and more military power than the rest of the world put together, U.S. capitalism could not survive without markets and allies. William Clayton, the assistant secretary of state for economic affairs, was among myriad U.S. policymakers who summed up this point: "We need markets-big markets-around the world in which to buy and sell."

There had been many predictions that peace would bring a return of depression and unemployment, as war production ceased and returning soldiers flooded the labor market. Compounding the economic difficulties was a sharp rise in labor unrest. Determined to avoid another economic catastrophe like that of the 1930s, U.S. President Franklin D. Roosevelt saw the creation of the postwar order as a way to ensure continuing U.S. prosperity.

THE ATLANTIC CHARTER

Throughout the war, the United States envisaged a postwar economic order in which the U.S. could penetrate markets that had been previously closed to other currency trading blocs, as well as to expand opportunities for foreign investments for U.S. corporations by removing restrictions on the international flow of capital.

The Atlantic Charter, drafted during U.S. President Roosevelt's August 1941 meeting with British Prime Minister Winston Churchill on a ship in the North Atlantic, was the most notable precursor to the Bretton Woods Conference. Like Woodrow Wilson before him, whose "Fourteen Points" had outlined U.S. aims in the aftermath of the First World War, Roosevelt set forth a range of ambitious goals for the postwar world even before the U.S. had entered the Second World War.

The Atlantic Charter affirmed the right of all nations to equal access to trade and raw materials. Moreover, the charter called for freedom of the seas (a principal U.S. foreign policy aim since France and Britain had first threatened U.S. shipping in the 1790s), the disarmament of aggressors, and the "establishment of a wider and permanent system of general security."

As the war drew to a close, the Bretton Woods conference was the culmination of some two and a half years of planning for postwar reconstruction by the Treasuries of the U.S. and the UK. U.S. representatives studied with their British counterparts the reconstitution of what had been lacking between the two world wars: a system of international payments that would allow trade to be conducted without fear of sudden currency depreciation or wild fluctuations in exchange rates-ailments that had nearly paralyzed world capitalism during the Great Depression.

Without a strong European market for U.S. goods and services, most policymakers believed, the U.S. economy would be unable to sustain the prosperity it had achieved during the war. In addition, U.S. unions had only grudgingly accepted government-imposed restraints on their demand during the war, but they were willing to wait no longer, particularly as inflation cut into the existing wage scales with painful force. (By the end of 1945, there had already been major strikes in the automobile, electrical, and steel industries.)

Financier and self-appointed adviser to presidents and congressmen, Bernard Baruch, summed up the spirit of Bretton Woods in early 1945: if we can "stop subsidization of labor and sweated competition in the export markets," as well as prevent rebuilding of war machines, "oh boy, oh boy, what long term prosperity we will have." Thus, the United States would use its predominant position to restore an open world economy, unified under U.S. control, which gave all nations unhindered access to markets and raw materials.

WARTIME DEVASTATION OF EUROPE AND EAST ASIA

Furthermore, U.S. allies-economically exhausted by the war-accepted this leadership. They needed U.S. assistance to rebuild their domestic production and to finance their international trade; indeed, they needed it to survive.

Before the war, the French and the British were realizing that they could no longer compete with U.S. industry in an open marketplace. During the 1930s, the British had created their own economic bloc to shut out U.S. goods. Churchill did not believe that he could surrender that protection after the war, so he watered down the Atlantic Charter's "free access" clause before agreeing to it. Yet, U.S. officials were determined to break open the empire. Combined, British and U.S. trade accounted for well over half the world's exchange of goods. If the British bloc could be split apart, the U.S. would be well on its way to opening the entire global marketplace. But as the 19th century had been economically dominated by Britain, the second half of the 20th was to be one of U.S. hegemony.

A devastated Britain had little choice. Two world wars had destroyed the country's principal industries that paid for the importation of half the nation's food and nearly all its raw materials except coal. The British had no choice but to ask for aid. In 1945, the U.S. agreed to a loan of $3.8 billion. In return, weary British officials promised to negotiate the agreement.

For nearly two centuries, French and U.S. interests had clashed in both the Old World and the New World. During the war, French mistrust of the United States was embodied by General Charles de Gaulle, president of the French provisional government. De Gaulle bitterly fought U.S. officials as he tried to maintain his country's colonies and diplomatic freedom of action. In turn, U.S. officials saw de Gaulle as a political extremist. But in 1945 de Gaulle-the leading voice of French nationalism-was forced to grudgingly ask the U.S. for a billion-dollar loan. Most of the request was granted; in return France promised to curtail government subsidies and currency manipulation that had given its exporters advantages in the world market.

On a far more profound level, as the Bretton Woods conference was convening, the greater part of the Third World remained politically and economically subordinate. Linked to the developed countries of the West economically and politically-formally and informally-these states had little choice but to acquiesce to the international economic system established for them. In the East, Soviet hegemony in Eastern Europe provided the foundation for a separate international economic system.

In short, the confluence of these three favorable political conditions-the concentration of power, the cluster of shared interests and ideas, and the hegemony of the United States-provided the political capability to equal the task of managing the international economy.

Design

Free trade relied on the free convertibility of currencies. Negotiators at the Bretton Woods conference, fresh from what they perceived as a disastrous experience with floating rates in the 1930s, concluded that major monetary fluctuations could stall the free flow of trade.

The liberal economic system required an accepted vehicle for investment, trade, and payments. Unlike national economies, however, the international economy lacks a central government that can issue currency and manage its use. In the past this problem had been solved through the gold standard, but the architects of Bretton Woods did not consider this option feasible for the postwar political economy. Instead, they set up a system of fixed exchange rates managed by a series of newly created international institutions using the U.S. dollar (which was a gold standard currency for central banks) as a reserve currency.

INFORMAL REGIMES

Previous Regimes

In the 19th and early 20th centuries gold played a key role in international monetary transactions. The gold standard was used to back currencies; the international value of currency was determined by its fixed relationship to gold; gold was used to settle international accounts. The gold standard maintained fixed exchange rates that were seen as desirable because they reduced the risk of trading with other countries.

Imbalances in international trade were theoretically rectified automatically by the gold standard. A country with a deficit would have depleted gold reserves and would thus have to reduce its money supply. The resulting fall in demand would reduce imports and the lowering of prices would boost exports; thus the deficit would be rectified. Any country experiencing inflation would lose gold and therefore would have a decrease in the amount of money available to spend. This decrease in the amount of money would act to reduce the inflationary pressure. Supplementing the use of gold in this period was the British pound. Based on the dominant British economy, the pound became a reserve, transaction, and intervention currency. But the pound was not up to the challenge of serving as the primary world currency, given the weakness of the British economy after the Second World War.

The architects of Bretton Woods had conceived of a system wherein exchange rate stability was a prime goal. Yet, in an era of more activist economic policy, governments did not seriously consider permanently fixed rates on the model of the classical gold standard of the nineteenth century. Gold production was not even sufficient to meet the demands of growing international trade and investment. And a sizable share of the world's known gold reserves were located in the Soviet Union, which would later emerge as a Cold War rival to the United States and Western Europe.

The only currency strong enough to meet the rising demands for international liquidity was the US dollar. The strength of the US economy, the fixed relationship of the dollar to gold ($35 an ounce), and the commitment of the U.S. government to convert dollars into gold at that price made the dollar as good as gold. In fact, the dollar was even better than gold: it earned interest and it was more flexible than gold.

THE BRETTON WOODS SYSTEM OF FIXED EXCHANGE RATES

The Bretton Woods system sought to secure the advantages of the gold standard without its disadvantages. Thus, a compromise was sought between the polar alternatives of either freely floating or irrevocably fixed rates-an arrangement that might gain the advantages of both without suffering the disadvantages of either while retaining the right to revise currency values on occasion as circumstances warranted.

The rules of Bretton Woods, set forth in the articles of agreement of the International Monetary Fund (IMF) and the International Bank for Reconstruction and Development (IBRD), provided for a system of fixed exchange rates. The rules further sought to encourage an open system by committing members to the convertibility of their respective currencies into other currencies and to free trade.

The "pegged rate" or "par value" currency regime

What emerged was the "pegged rate" currency regime. Members were required to establish a parity of their national currencies in terms of gold (a "peg") and to maintain exchange rates within plus or minus 1% of parity (a "band") by intervening in their foreign exchange markets (that is, buying or selling foreign money).

The "reserve currency"

In practice, however, since the principal "reserve currency" would be the U.S. dollar, this meant that other countries would peg their currencies to the U.S. dollar, and-once convertibility was restored-would buy and sell U.S. dollars to keep market exchange rates within plus or minus 1% of parity. Thus, the U.S. dollar took over the role that gold had played under the gold standard in the international financial system.

Meanwhile, in order to bolster faith in the dollar, the U.S. agreed separately to link the dollar to gold at the rate of $35 per ounce of gold. At this rate, foreign governments and central banks were able to exchange dollars for gold. Bretton Woods established a system of payments based on the dollar, in which all currencies were defined in relation to the dollar, itself convertible into gold, and above all, "as good as gold." The U.S. currency was now effectively the world currency, the standard to which every other currency was pegged. As the world's key currency, most international transactions were denominated in dollars.

The U.S. dollar was the currency with the most purchasing power and it was the only currency that was backed by gold. Additionally, all European nations that had been involved in World War II were highly in debt and transferred large amounts of gold into the United States, a fact that contributed to the supremacy of the United States. Thus, the U.S. dollar was strongly appreciated in the rest of the world and therefore became the key currency of the Bretton Woods system. Member countries could only change their par value with IMF approval, which was contingent on IMF determination that its balance of payments was in a "fundamental disequilibrium."

Formal Regimes

The Bretton Woods Conference led to the establishment of the IMF and the IBRD (now the World Bank), which still remain powerful forces in the world economy.

As mentioned, a major point of common ground at the Conference was the goal to avoid a recurrence of the closed markets and economic warfare that had characterized the 1930s. Thus, negotiators at Bretton Woods also agreed that there was a need for an institutional forum for international cooperation on monetary matters. Already in 1944 the British economist John Maynard Keynes emphasized "the importance of rule-based regimes to stabilize business expectations"-something he accepted in the Bretton Woods system of fixed exchange rates. Currency troubles in the interwar years, it was felt, had been greatly exacerbated by the absence of any established procedure or machinery for intergovernmental consultation.

As a result of the establishment of agreed upon structures and rules of international economic interaction, conflict over economic issues was minimized, and the significance of the economic aspect of international relations seemed to recede.

THE INTERNATIONAL MONETARY FUND

Officially established on December 27, 1945, when the 29 participating countries at the conference of Bretton Woods signed its Articles of Agreement, the IMF was to be the keeper of the rules and the main instrument of public international management. The Fund commenced its financial operations on March 1, 1947. IMF approval was necessary for any change in exchange rates. It advised countries on policies affecting the monetary system.

Designing the IMF

The big question at the Bretton Woods conference with respect to the institution that would emerge as the IMF was the issue of future access to international liquidity and whether that source should be akin to a world central bank able to create new reserves at will or a more limited borrowing mechanism.

Although attended by 44 nations, discussions at the conference were dominated by two rival plans developed by the U.S. and Britain. As the chief international economist at the U.S. Treasury in 1942-44, Harry Dexter White drafted the U.S. blueprint for international access to liquidity, which competed with the plan drafted for the British Treasury by Keynes. Overall, White's scheme tended to favor incentives designed to create price stability within the world's economies, while Keynes' wanted a system that encouraged economic growth.

At the time, gaps between the White and Keynes plans seemed enormous. Outlining the difficulty of creating a system that every nation could accept in his speech at the closing plenary session of the Bretton Woods conference on July 22, 1944, Keynes stated:

We, the delegates of this Conference, Mr. President, have been trying to accomplish something very difficult to accomplish.[...] It has been our task to find a common measure, a common standard, a common rule acceptable to each and not irksome to any.

Keynes' proposals would have established a world reserve currency (which he thought might be called "bancor") administered by a central bank vested with the possibility of creating money and with the authority to take actions on a much larger scale (understandable considering deflationary problems in Britain at the time).

In case of balance of payments imbalances, Keynes recommended that both debtors and creditors should change their policies. As outlined by Keynes, countries with payment surpluses should increase their imports from the deficit countries and thereby create a foreign trade equilibrium. Thus, Keynes was sensitive to the problem that placing too much of the burden on the deficit country would be deflationary.

But the U.S., as a likely creditor nation, and eager to take on the role of the world's economic powerhouse, balked at Keynes' plan and did not pay serious attention to it. The U.S. contingent was too concerned about inflationary pressures in the postwar economy, and White saw an imbalance as a problem only of the deficit country. Although compromise was reached on some points, because of the overwhelming economic and military power of the U.S., the participants at Bretton Woods largely agreed on White's plan. As a result, the IMF was born with an economic approach and political ideology that stressed controlling inflation and introducing austerity plans over fighting poverty. This left the IMF severely detached from the realities of Third World countries struggling with underdevelopment from the onset.

Subscriptions and Quotas

What emerged largely reflected U.S. preferences: a system of subscriptions and quotas embedded in the IMF, which itself was to be no more than a fixed pool of national currencies and gold subscribed by each country as opposed to a world central bank capable of creating money. The Fund was charged with managing various nations' trade deficits so that they would not produce currency devaluations that would trigger a decline in imports.

The IMF was provided with a fund, composed of contributions of member countries in gold and their own currencies. The original quotas planned were to total $8.8 billion. When joining the IMF, members were assigned "quotas" reflecting their relative economic power, and, as a sort of credit deposit, were obliged to pay a "subscription" of an amount commensurate to the quota. The subscription was to be paid 25% in gold or currency convertible into gold (effectively the dollar, which was the only currency then still directly gold convertible for central banks) and 75% in the member's own currency. Quota subscriptions were to form the largest source of money at the IMF's disposal. The IMF set out to use this money to grant loans to member countries with financial difficulties. Each member was then entitled to withdraw 25% of its quota immediately in case of payment problems. If this sum was insufficient, each nation in the system was also able to request loans for foreign currency.

Financing Trade Deficits

In the event of a deficit in the current account, Fund members, when short of reserves, would be able to borrow needed foreign currency from this fund in amounts determined by the size of its quota. In other words, the higher the country's contribution was, the higher the sum of money it could borrow from the IMF. Members were obligated to pay back debts within a period of 18 months to five years. In turn, the IMF embarked on setting up rules and procedures to keep a country from going too deeply into debt, year after year. The Fund would exercise "surveillance" over other economies for the U.S. Treasury, in return for its loans to prop up national currencies.

IMF loans were not comparable to loans issued by a conventional credit institution. Instead, it was effectively a chance to purchase a foreign currency with gold or the member's national currency.

The U.S.-backed IMF plan sought to end restrictions on the transfer of goods and services from one country to another, eliminate currency blocs and lift currency exchange controls.

The IMF was designed to advance credits to countries with balance of payments deficits. Short-run balance of payment difficulties would be overcome by IMF loans, which would facilitate stable currency exchange rates. This flexibility meant that member states would not have to induce a depression automatically in order to cut its national income down to such a low level that its imports will finally fall within its means. Thus, countries were to be spared the need to resort to the classical medicine of deflating themselves into drastic unemployment when faced with chronic balance of payments deficits. Before the Second World War, European nations often resorted to this, particularly Britain.

Moreover, the planners at Bretton Woods hoped that this would reduce the temptation of cash-poor nations to reduce capital outflow by restricting imports. In effect, the IMF extended Keynesian measures-government intervention to prop up demand and avoid recession-to protect the U.S. and the stronger economies from disruptions of international trade and growth.

Changing the Par Value

The IMF sought to provide for occasional discontinuous exchange-rate adjustments (changing a member's par value) by international agreement with the IMF. Member nations were permitted first to depreciate (or appreciate in opposite situations) their currencies by 10%. This tends to restore equilibrium in its trade by expanding its exports and contracting imports. This would be allowed only if there was what was called a "fundamental disequilibrium." A decrease in the value of the country's money was called a "devaluation" while an increase in the value of the country's money was called a "revaluation".

It was envisioned that these changes in exchange rates would be quite rare. Regrettably the notion of fundamental disequilibrium, though key to the operation of the par value system, was never spelled out in any detail-an omission that would eventually come back to haunt the regime in later years.

IMF Operations

Never before had international monetary cooperation been attempted on a permanent institutional basis. Even more ground-breaking was the decision to allocate voting rights among governments not on a one-state, one-vote basis but rather in proportion to quotas. Since the U.S. was contributing the most, U.S. leadership was the key implication. Under the system of weighted voting the U.S. was able to exert a preponderant influence on the IMF. With one-third of all IMF quotas at the outset, enough to veto all changes to the IMF Charter on its own. In addition, the IMF was based in Washington, D.C., and staffed mainly by its economists. It regularly exchanged personnel with the U.S. Treasury. When the IMF began operations in 1946, President Harry S. Truman named White as its first U.S. Executive Director. Since no Deputy Managing Director post had yet been created, White served occasionally as Acting Managing Director and generally played a highly influential role during the IMF's first year.

SPECIAL DRAWING RIGHTS

Special Drawing Rights (SDRs) is a potential claim on the freely usable currencies of International Monetary Fund members. It is neither a currency, nor a claim on the IMF.

SDRs are defined in terms of a basket of major currencies used in international trade and finance. At present, the currencies in the basket are the euro, the pound sterling, the Japanese yen and the United States dollar. The amounts of each currency making up one SDR are chosen in accordance with the relative importance of the currency in international trade and finance. The determination of the currencies in the SDR basket and their amounts is made by the IMF Executive Board every five years. The weights of the currencies in the basket in the past were and currently are:

* 1981-1985: USD 42%, DEM 19%, JPY 13%, GBP 13%, FRF 13%
* 1986-1990: USD 42%, DEM 19%, JPY 15%, GBP 12%, FRF 12%
* 1991-1995: USD 40%, DEM 21%, JPY 17%, GBP 11%, FRF 11%
* 1996-2000: USD 39%, DEM 21%, JPY 18%, GBP 11%, FRF 11%
* 2001-2005: USD 45%, EUR 29%, JPY 15%, GBP 11%
* 2006-2010: USD 44%, EUR 34%, JPY 11%, GBP 11%

The value of one SDR in terms of United States dollars is determined daily by the IMF, based on the exchange rates of the currencies making up the basket, as quoted at noon at the London market. (If the London market is closed, New York market rates are used; if both markets are closed, European Central Bank reference rates are used.)

SDRs are used as a unit of account by the IMF and several other international organizations. A few countries peg their currencies against SDRs, and it is also used to denominate some private international financial instruments.

SDRs basically were created to replace gold in large international transactions. Being that under a strict (international) gold standard, the quantity of gold worldwide is relatively fixed, and worldwide the economies of all participating IMF members as an aggregate are growing, a need arose to increase the supply of the basic unit or standard proportionately. Thus SDRs, or "paper gold" are credits that nations with balance of trade surpluses can 'draw' upon nations with balance of trade deficits.

So-called "paper gold" is little more than an accounting transaction within a ledger of accounts, which eliminates the problem of shipping gold back and forth across borders to settle national accounts.

INTERNATIONAL BANK FOR RECONSTRUCTION AND DEVELOPMENT

No provision was made for international creation of reserves. New gold production was assumed sufficient. In the event of structural disequilibria, it was expected that there would be national solutions-a change in the value of the currency or an improvement by other means of a country's competitive position. Few means were given to the IMF, however, to encourage such national solutions. It had been recognized in 1944 that the new system could come into being only after a return to normalcy following the disruption of World War II. It was expected that after a brief transition period-expected to be no more than five years-the international economy would recover and the system would enter into operation.

To promote the growth of world trade and to finance the postwar reconstruction of Europe, the planners at Bretton Woods created another institution, the International Bank for Reconstruction and Development (IBRD)-now the most important agency of the World Bank Group. The IBRD had an authorized capitalization of $10 billion and was expected to make loans of its own funds to underwrite private loans and to issue securities to raise new funds to make possible a speedy postwar recovery. The IBRD was to be a specialized agency of the United Nations charged with making loans for economic development purposes.

READJUSTING THE BRETTON WOODS SYSTEM

The Dollar Shortages and the Marshall Plan

The Bretton Wood arrangements were largely adhered to and ratified by the participating governments. It was expected that national monetary reserves, supplemented with necessary IMF credits, would finance any temporary balance of payments disequilibria. But this did not however prove sufficient to get Europe out of the doldrums.

Postwar world capitalism suffered from a huge dollar shortage. The United States was running huge balance of trade surpluses, and the U.S. reserves were immense and growing. It was necessary to reverse this flow. Dollars had to leave the United States and become available for international use. In other words, the United States would have to reverse the natural economic processes and run a balance of payments deficit.

The modest credit facilities of the IMF were clearly insufficient to deal with Western Europe's huge balance of payments deficits. The problem was further aggravated by the reaffirmation by the IMF Board of Governors in the provision in the Bretton Woods Articles of Agreement that the IMF could make loans only for current account deficits and not for capital and reconstruction purposes. Only the United States contribution of $570 million was actually available for IBRD lending. In addition, because the only available market for IBRD bonds was the conservative Wall Street banking market, the IBRD was forced to adopt a conservative lending policy, granting loans only when repayment was assured. Given these problems, by 1947 the IMF and the IBRD themselves were admitting that they could not deal with the international monetary system's economic problems. Thus, the much looser Marshall Plan-the European Recovery Program-was set up to provide U.S. finance to rebuild Europe largely through grants rather than loans. The Marshall Plan was the program of massive economic aid given by the United States to favored countries in Western Europe for the rebuilding of capitalism. In a speech to Congress on June 5, 1946, U.S. Secretary of State George Marshall stated:

The breakdown of the business structure of Europe during the war was complete. Europe's requirements for the next three or four years of foreign food and other essential products principally from the United States are so much greater than her present ability to pay that she must have substantial help or face economic, social and political deterioration of a very grave character.

From 1947 until 1958, the U.S. deliberately encouraged an outflow of dollars, and, from 1950 on, the United States ran a balance of payments deficit with the intent of providing liquidity for the international economy. Dollars flowed out through various U.S. aid programs: the Truman Doctrine entailing aid to the pro-U.S. Greek and Turkish regimes, which were struggling to suppress socialist revolution, aid to various pro-U.S. regimes in the Third World, and most important, the Marshall Plan. From 1948 to 1954 the United States gave 16

Western European countries $17 billion in grants. To encourage long-term adjustment, the United States promoted European and Japanese trade competitiveness. Policies for economic controls on the defeated former Axis countries were scrapped. Aid to Europe and Japan was designed to rebuild productive and export capacity. In the long run it was expected that such European and Japanese recovery would benefit the United States by widening markets for U.S. exports, and providing locations for U.S. capital expansion.

In 1956, the World Bank created the International Finance Corporation and in 1960 it created the International Development Association (IDA). Both have been controversial. Critics of the IDA argue that it was designed to head off a broader based system headed by the United Nations, and that the IDA lends without consideration for the effectiveness of the program. Critics also point out that the pressure to keep developing economies "open" has lead to their having difficulties obtaining funds through ordinary channels, and a continual cycle of asset buy up by foreign investors and capital flight by locals. Defenders of the IDA pointed to its ability to make large loans for agricultural programs which aided the "Green Revolution" of the 1960s, and its functioning to stabilize and occasionally subsidize Third World governments, particularly in Latin America.

Bretton Woods, then, created a system of triangular trade: the United States would use the convertible financial system to trade at a tremendous profit with developing nations, expanding industry and acquiring raw materials. It would use this surplus to send dollars to Europe, which would then be used to rebuild their economies, and make the United States the market for their products. This would allow the other industrialized nations to purchase products from the Third World, which reinforced the American role as the guarantor of stability. When this triangle became destabilized, Bretton Woods entered a period of crisis which lead ultimately to its collapse.

BRETTON WOODS AND THE COLD WAR

In 1945, Roosevelt and Churchill prepared the postwar era by negotiating with Joseph Stalin at Yalta about respective zones of influence; this same year U.S. and Soviet troops divided

Germany into occupation zones and confronted one another in Korea.

Harry Dexter White succeeded in getting the Soviet Union to participate in the Bretton Woods conference in 1944, but his goal was frustrated when the Soviet Union would not join the IMF. In the past, the reasons why the Soviet Union chose not to subscribe to the articles by December 1945 have been the subject of speculation. But since the release of relevant Soviet archives, it is now clear that the Soviet calculation was based on the behavior of the parties that had actually expressed their assent to the Bretton Woods Agreements. The extended debates about ratification that had taken place both in the UK and the U.S. were read in Moscow as evidence of the quick disintegration of the wartime alliance. Facing the Soviet Union, whose power had also strengthened and whose territorial influence had expanded, the U.S. assumed the role of leader of the capitalist camp. The rise of the postwar U.S. as the world's leading industrial, monetary, and military power was rooted in the impact of the U.S. military victory, in the instability of the national states in postwar Europe, and the wartime devastation of the Soviet economy.

Thus, American power had to be used to rebuild U.S.-friendly regimes and free market capitalism, especially in Europe, and prevent Soviet-backed regimes from spreading across the war-torn countries of Europe. The conflict, however, was that European nations, which still nominally held large colonial possessions overseas, could not simultaneously rebuild their own economies, and hold on to their colonial empires. The fiscal discipline imposed by Bretton Woods made the U.S. the only nation that could afford large-scale foreign deployments within the Western alliance. Over the course of the late 1940s and early 1950s, the United Kingdom and France were gradually forced to accept abandoning colonial outposts, which would in the late 1950s and early 1960s, lead to revolt and finally independence for most of their empires.

The price paid for this position-especially in the Cold War climate-was the militarization of the U.S. economy, what U.S. President Dwight D. Eisenhower called the "armament industry" and "the military-industrial complex," and the related notion that the U.S. should assume a protective role in what was referred to as "the free world." Looking back at the origins of the Cold War, in a paper that Harry Dexter White was writing at the time of his death, he lamented the "tensions between certain of the major powers" that had brought "almost catastrophic" consequences, including an "acute lack of confidence in continued political stability and the crippling fear of war on a scale unprecedented and almost unimaginable in its destructive potentialities."

Despite the economic effort imposed by such a policy, being at the center of the international market gave the U.S. unprecedented freedom of action in pursuing its foreign affairs goals. A trade surplus made it easier to keep armies abroad and to invest outside the U.S. Because other nations could not sustain foreign deployments, U.S. power to decide why, when and how to intervene in global crisis increased. The dollar continued to function as a compass to guide the health of the world economy, and exporting to the U.S. became the primary economic goal of developing or redeveloping economies. This arrangement came to be referred to as the Pax Americana, in analogy to the Pax Britannica of the late 19th century and the Pax Romana of the first.

The late Bretton Woods System

The U.S. balance of payments crisis (1958-68).

After the end of World War II, the U.S. held $26 billion in gold reserves, of an estimated total of $40 billion (approx 65%). As world trade increased rapidly through the 1950s, the size of the gold base increased by only a few percent. In 1958, the U.S. balance of payments swung negative. The first U.S. response to the crisis was in the late 1950s when the Eisenhower administration placed import quotas on oil and other restrictions on trade outflows. More drastic measures were proposed, but not acted on. However, with a mounting recession that began in 1959, this response alone was not sustainable. In 1960, with Kennedy's election, a decade-long effort to maintain the Bretton Woods System at the $35/ounce price was begun.

The design of the Bretton Woods System was that only nations could enforce gold convertibility on the anchor currency- the United States'. Gold convertibility enforcement was not required, but instead, allowed. Nations could forgo converting dollars to gold, and instead hold dollars. Rather than full convertibility, it provided a fixed price for sales between central banks. However, there was still an open gold market, 80% of which was traded through London, which issued a morning "gold fix," which was the price of gold on the open market. For the Bretton Woods system to remain workable, it would either have to alter the peg of the dollar to gold, or it would have to maintain the free market price for gold near the $35 per ounce official price. The greater the gap between free market gold prices and central bank gold prices, the greater the temptation to deal with internal economic issues by buying gold at the Bretton Woods price and selling it on the open market. However, keeping the dollar because of its ability to earn interest was still more desirable than holding gold. In 1960 Robert Triffin noticed that the reason holding dollars was more valuable than gold was because constant U.S. balance of payments deficits helped to keep the system liquid and fuel economic growth. What would be later known as Triffin's Dilemma was predicted when Triffin noted that if the U.S. failed to keep running deficits the system would lose its liquidity, not being able to keep up with the world's economic growth, thus bringing the system to a halt. Yet, continuing to incur such payment deficits also meant that over time the deficits would erode confidence in the dollar as the reserve currency creating instability.

The first effort was the creation of the "London Gold Pool." The theory of the pool was that spikes in the free market price of gold, set by the "morning gold fix" in London, could be controlled by having a pool of gold to sell on the open market, which would then be recovered when the price of gold dropped. Gold's price spiked in response to events such as the Cuban Missile Crisis, and other smaller events, to as high as $40/ ounce. The Kennedy administration began drafting a radical change of the tax system in order to spur more productive capacity, and thus encourage exports. This would culminate with his tax cut program of 1963, designed to maintain the $35 peg.

In 1967 there was an attack on the pound, and a run on gold in the "sterling area," and on November 17, 1967, the British government was forced to devalue the pound. U.S. President Lyndon Baines Johnson was faced with a brutal choice, either he could institute protectionist measures, including travel taxes, export subsidies and slashing the budget-or he could accept the risk of a "run on gold" and the dollar. From Johnson's perspective: "The world supply of gold is insufficient to make the present system workable-particularly as the use of the dollar as a reserve currency is essential to create the required international liquidity to sustain world trade and growth." He believed that the priorities of the United States were correct, and that, while there were internal tensions in the Western alliance, that turning away from open trade would be more costly, economically and politically, than it was worth: "Our role of world leadership in a political and military sense is the only reason for our current embarrassment in an economic sense on the one hand and on the other the correction of the economic embarrassment under present monetary systems will result in an untenable position economically for our allies."

While West Germany agreed not to purchase gold from the U.S., and agreed to hold dollars instead, the pressure on both the Dollar and the Pound Sterling continued. In January 1968 Johnson imposed a series of measures designed to end gold outflow, and to increase American exports. However, to no avail: on March 17, 1968, there was a run on gold, the London Gold Pool was dissolved, and a series of meetings began to rescue or reform the system as it existed. However, as long as the U.S. commitments to foreign deployment continued, particularly to Western Europe, there was little that could be done to maintain the gold peg.

The attempt to maintain that peg collapsed in November 1968, and a new policy program was attempted: to convert Bretton Woods to a system where the enforcement mechanism floated by some means, which would be set by either fiat, or by a restriction to honor foreign accounts.

STRUCTURAL CHANGES UNDERPINNING THE DECLINE OF INTERNATIONAL MONETARY MANAGEMENT

Return to Convertibility

In the 1960s and 70s, important structural changes eventually led to the breakdown of international monetary management. One change was the development of a high level of monetary interdependence. The stage was set for monetary interdependence by the return to convertibility of the Western European currencies at the end of 1958 and of the Japanese yen in 1964. Convertibility facilitated the vast expansion of international financial transactions, which deepened monetary interdependence.

The Growth of International Currency Markets

Another aspect of the internationalization of banking has been the emergence of international banking consortia. Since 1964 various banks had formed international syndicates, and by 1971 over three quarters of the world's largest banks had become shareholders in such syndicates. Multinational banks can and do make huge international transfers of capital not only for investment purposes but also for hedging and speculating against exchange rate fluctuations.

These new forms of monetary interdependence made possible huge capital flows. During the Bretton Woods era countries were reluctant to alter exchange rates formally even in cases of structural disequilibria. Because such changes had a direct impact on certain domestic economic groups, they came to be seen as political risks for leaders. As a result official exchange rates often became unrealistic in market terms, providing a virtually risk-free temptation for speculators. They could move from a weak to a strong currency hoping to reap profits when a revaluation occurred. If, however, monetary authorities managed to avoid revaluation, they could return to other currencies with no loss. The combination of risk-free speculation with the availability of huge sums was highly destabilizing.

The Decline of U.S. Hegemony

A second structural change that undermined monetary management was the decline of U.S. hegemony. The U.S. was no longer the dominant economic power it had been for almost two decades. By the mid-1960s Europe and Japan had become international economic powers in their own right. With total reserves exceeding those of the U.S., with higher levels of growth and trade, and with per capita income approaching that of the U.S., Europe and Japan were narrowing the gap between themselves and the United States. The shift toward a more pluralistic distribution of economic power led to increasing dissatisfaction with the privileged role of the U.S. dollar as the international currency. As in effect the world's central banker, the U.S., through its deficit, determined the level of international liquidity. In an increasingly interdependent world, U.S. policy greatly influenced economic conditions in Europe and Japan. In addition, as long as other countries were willing to hold dollars, the U.S. could carry out massive foreign expenditures for political purposes-military activities and foreign aid-without the threat of balance-of-payments constraints.

Dissatisfaction with the political implications of the dollar system was increased by dantente between the U.S. and the Soviet Union. The Soviet threat had been an important force in cementing the Western capitalist monetary system. The U.S. political and security umbrella helped make American economic domination palatable for Europe and Japan, which had been economically exhausted by the war. As gross domestic production grew in European countries, trade grew. When common security tensions lessened, this loosened the transatlantic dependence on defense concerns, and allowed latent economic tensions to surface.

The decline of the Dollar

Reinforcing the relative decline in U.S. power and the dissatisfaction of Europe and Japan with the system was the continuing decline of the dollar-the foundation that had underpinned the post-1945 global trading system. The Vietnam War and the refusal of the administration of U.S. President Lyndon B. Johnson to pay for it and its Great Society programs through taxation resulted in an increased dollar outflow to pay for the military expenditures and rampant inflation, which led to the deterioration of the U.S. balance of trade position. In the late 1960s, the dollar was overvalued with its current trading position, while the Deutsche Mark and the yen were undervalued; and, naturally, the Germans and the Japanese had no desire to revalue and thereby make their exports more expensive, whereas the U.S. sought to maintain its international credibility by avoiding devaluation. Meanwhile, the pressure on government reserves was intensified by the new international currency markets, with their vast pools of speculative capital moving around in search of quick profits.

In contrast, upon the creation of Bretton Woods, with the U.S. producing half of the world's manufactured goods and holding half its reserves, the twin burdens of international management and the Cold War were possible to meet at first. Throughout the 1950s Washington sustained a balance of payments deficit in order to finance loans, aid, and troops for allied regimes. But during the 1960s the costs of doing so became less tolerable. By 1970 the U.S. held under 16% of international reserves. Adjustment to these changed realities was impeded by the U.S. commitment to fixed exchange rates and by the U.S. obligation to convert dollars into gold on demand.

In sum, monetary interdependence was increasing at a faster pace than international management in the 1960s, leading up to the collapse of the Bretton Woods system. New problems created by interdependence, including huge capital flows, placed stresses on the fixed exchange rate system and impeded national economic management. Amid these problems, economic cooperation decreased, and U.S. leadership declined, and eventually broke down.

THE PARALYSIS OF INTERNATIONAL MONETARY MANAGEMENT

"Floating" Bretton Woods (1968-72)

By 1968, the attempt to defend the dollar at a fixed peg of $35/ounce, the policy of the Eisenhower, Kennedy and Johnson administrations, had become increasingly perishable. Gold outflows from the U.S. accelerated, and despite gaining assurances from Germany and other nations to hold gold, the "dollar shortage" of the 1940s and 1950s had become a dollar glut. In 1967, the IMF agreed in Rio de Janeiro to replace the tranche division set up in 1946. Special Drawing Rights were set as equal to one U.S. dollar, but were not usable for transactions other than between banks and the IMF. Nations were required to accept holding SDRs equal to three times their allotment, and interest would be charged, or credited, to each nation based on their SDR holding. The original interest rate was 1.5%.

The intent of the SDR system was to prevent nations from buying pegged dollars and selling them at the higher free market price, and give nations a reason to hold dollars by crediting interest, at the same time setting a clear limit to the amount of dollars which could be held. The essential conflict was that the American role as military defender of the capitalist world's economic system was recognized, but not given a specific monetary value. In effect, other nations "purchased" American defense policy by taking a loss in holding dollars. They were only willing to do this as long as they supported U.S. military policy, because of the Vietnam war and other unpopular actions, the pro-U.S. consensus began to evaporate. The SDR agreement, in effect, monetized the value of this relationship, but did not create a market for it.

The use of SDRs as "paper gold" seemed to offer a way to balance the system, turning the IMF, rather than the U.S., into the world's central banker. The US tightened controls over foreign investment and currency, including mandatory investment controls in 1968. In 1970, U.S. President Richard Nixon lifted import quotas on oil in an attempt to reduce energy costs; instead, however, this exacerbated dollar flight, and created pressure from petro-dollars. Still, the U.S. continued to draw down reserves. In 1971 it had a reserve deficit of $56 Billion dollars; as well, it had depleted most of its non-gold reserves and had only 22% gold coverage of foreign reserves. In short, the dollar was tremendously overvalued with respect to gold.

THE "NIXON SHOCK"

By the early 1970s, as the Vietnam War accelerated inflation, the United States as a whole began running a trade deficit (for the first time in the twentieth century). The crucial turning point was 1970, which saw U.S. gold coverage deteriorate from 55% to 22%. This, in the view of neoclassical economists, represented the point where holders of the dollar had lost faith in the ability of the U.S. to cut budget and trade deficits.

In 1971 more and more dollars were being printed in Washington, then being pumped overseas, to pay for the government's military expenditures and private investments. In the first six months of 1971, assets for $22 billion fled the U.S. In response, on August 15, 1971 Nixon unilaterally imposed 90-day wage and price controls, a 10% import surcharge, and most importantly "closed the gold window," making the dollar inconvertible to gold directly, except on the open market. Unusually, this decision was made without consulting members of the international monetary system or even his own State Department, and was soon dubbed the "Nixon Shock".

The surcharge was dropped in December 1971 as part of a general revaluation of major currencies, which were henceforth allowed 2.25% devaluations from the agreed exchange rate. But even the more flexible official rates could not be defended against the speculators. By March 1976, all the major currencies were floating in other words, exchange rates were no longer the principal method used by governments to administer monetary policy.

THE SMITHSONIAN AGREEMENT

The shock of August 15 was followed by efforts under U.S. leadership to develop a new system of international monetary management. Throughout the fall of 1971, there was a series of multilateral and bilateral negotiations of the Group of Ten seeking to develop a new multilateral monetary system.

On 17 and 18 December 1971, the Group of Ten, meeting in the Smithsonian Institute in Washington, created the Smithsonian Agreement which devalued the dollar to $38/ounce, with 2.25% trading bands, and attempted to balance the world financial system using SDRs alone. It was criticized at the time, and was by design a "temporary" agreement. It failed to impose discipline on the U.S. government, and with no other credibility mechanism in place, the pressure against the dollar in gold continued.

This resulted in gold becoming a floating asset, and in 1971 it reached $44.20/ounce, in 1972 $70.30/ounce and still climbing. By 1972, currencies began abandoning even this devalued peg against the dollar, though it took a decade for all of the industrialized nations to do so. In February 1973 the Bretton Woods currency exchange markets closed, after a last-gasp devaluation of the dollar to $44/ounce, and reopened in March in a floating currency regime.

BRETTON WOODS II

A number of economists have referred to the system of currency relations which evolved after 2001, in which currencies, particularly the Renminbi, remain fixed to the US Dollar as Bretton Woods II. The argument is that a system of pegged currencies is both stable and desirable, a notion that causes considerable controversy.

CONCLUSIONS

The collapse of the Bretton Woods system is a subject of intense debate. There are a variety of theories as to why it did so, ranging from the budget deficit problems, to the Vietnam War, to marginal tax rates. The fundamental point of agreement is that the U.S. ran an increasing balance of trade deficit, and that, in the end, it could not establish credibility on reining this deficit in. This would lead to the study in economics of credibility as a separate field, and to the prominence of "open" macroeconomic models, such as the Mundell-Fleming model.

4

The Monetary Policy

Monetary policy is the government or central bank process of managing money supply to achieve specific goals-such as constraining inflation, maintaining an exchange rate, achieving full employment or economic growth. Monetary policy can involve changing certain interest rates, either directly or indirectly through open market operations, setting reserve requirements, or trading in foreign exchange markets.

Monetary policy is generally referred to as either being an expansionary policy, or a contractionary policy, where an expansionary policy increases the total supply of money in the economy, and a contractionary policy decreases the total money supply. Expansionary policy is traditionally used to combat unemployment in a recession by lowering interest rates, while contractionary policy has the goal of raising interest rates to combat inflation.

OVERVIEW

Monetary policy rests on the relationship between the rates of interest in an economy, that is the price at which money can be borrowed, and the total supply of money. Monetary policy uses a variety of tools to control one or both of these, to influence outcomes like economic growth, inflation, exchange rates with other currencies and unemployment. Where currency is under a monopoly of issuance, or where there is a regulated system of issuing currency through banks which are tied to a central bank, the monetary authority has the ability to alter the interest rate and the money supply in order to achieve policy goals. The beginning of monetary policy as such comes from the late 19th century, where it was used to maintain the gold standard. A policy is referred to as contractionary if it reduces the size of the money supply or raises the interest rate. An expansionary policy increases the size of the money supply, or decreases the interest rate. Further monetary policies are described as accomodative if the interest set by the central monetary authority is intended to spur economic growth, neutral if it is intended to neither spur growth or combat inflation, or tight if intended to reduce inflation or "cool" an economy. There are several monetary policy tools available to achieve these ends. Increasing interest rates by fiat, reducing the monetary base or increasing reserve requirements all have the effect of contracting the money supply, and, if reversed, expand the money supply. Since the 1970s, monetary policy has generally been formed separately from fiscal policy. And even prior to the 1970s, the Bretton Woods system still ensured that most nations would form the two policies separately.

Within almost all modern nations, special institutions (like the European Central Bank or the Federal Reserve) exist which have the task of executing the monetary policy independently of the executive. In general, these institutions are called central banks and often have other responsibilities such as supervising the smooth operation of the financial system. The primary tool of monetary policy is open market operations. This entails managing the quantity of money in circulation through the buying and selling of various credit instruments, foreign currencies or commodities. All of these purchases or sales result in more or less base currency entering or leaving market circulation. Usually the short term goal of open market operations is to achieve a specific short term interest rate target. In other instances however monetary policy might instead entail the targeting of a specific exchange rate relative to some foreign currency or else relative to gold. For example in the case of the USA the Federal Reserve targets the federal funds rate, the rate at which member banks lend to one another overnight. However the monetary policy of China is to target the exchange rate between the Chinese renminbi and a basket of foreign currencies.

HISTORY OF MONETARY POLICY

Monetary policy is associated with currency and credit. For many centuries there were only two forms of monetary policy:

decisions about coinage, and the decision to print paper money to create credit. Interest rates, while now thought of as part of monetary authority, were not generally coordinated with the other forms of monetary policy. Monetary policy was seen as an executive decision, and was generally in the hands of the authority with seniorage, or the power to coin. With the advent of larger trading networks came the ability to set the price between gold and silver, and the price of the local currency to foreign currencies. This official price could be enforced by law, even if it varied from the market price. With the creation of the Bank of England in 1694, which acquired the responsibility to print notes and back them with gold, the idea of monetary policy as independent of executive action began to be established.

MONEY MARKET

The money market is the financial market for short-term borrowing and lending, typically up to thirteen months. This contrasts with the capital market for longer-term funds. In the money markets, banks lend to and borrow from each other, short-term financial instruments such as certificates of deposit (CDs) or enter into agreements such as repurchase agreements (repos). It provides short to medium term liquidity in the global financial system. Money market derivatives include forward rate agreements (FRAs) and short-term interest rate futures. Trading takes place between banks in the "money centers" (New York and London primarily, also Chicago, Frankfurt, Paris, Singapore, Hong Kong, Tokyo, Toronto, Sydney, San Francisco).

Common Money Market Instruments

* Bankers' acceptance-A draft or bill of exchange accepted by a bank to guarantee payment of the bill.
* Certificate of deposit-A time deposit with a specific maturity date shown on a certificate; large-denomination certificates of deposits can be sold before maturity.
* Commercial paper-An unsecured promissory note with a fixed maturity of one to 270 days; usually it is sold at a discount from face value.
* Eurodollar deposit-Deposits made in U.S. dollars at a bank or bank branch located outside the United States

* Federal Agency Short-Term Securities-(in the US). Short-term securities issued by government sponsored enterprises such as the Farm Credit System, the Federal Home Loan Banks and the Federal National Mortgage Association.
* Federal funds-(in the US). Interest-bearing deposits held by banks and other depository institutions at the Federal Reserve; these are immediately available funds that institutions borrow or lend, usually on an overnight basis. They are lent for the federal funds rate.
* Municipal notes-(in the US). Short-term notes issued by municipalities in anticipation of tax receipts or other revenues.
* Repurchase agreements-Short-term loans-normally for less than two weeks and frequently for one day-arranged by selling securities to an investor with an agreement to repurchase them at a fixed price on a fixed date.
* Treasury bills-Short-term debt obligations of a national government that are issued to mature in 3 to 12 months.

MONEY CREATION

Money creation is the process by which the money supply of a country is increased. There are several ways that a government, in coordination with the country's commercial banks, can increase or decrease the money supply of a country. If a country follows a fractional-reserve banking regime, as virtually all countries do, not all of the money in circulation needs to be backed by other currencies, physical assets such as gold, or government assets. Instead, the country's currency is backed by the economic potential of the country and is based on government fiat, or decree. This perceived potential puts a theoretical limit on the amount of money a country can prudently create.

DEPOSIT CREATION MULTIPLIER

The most common mechanism used to create money is typically called the deposit creation multiplier. It measures the amount by which the commercial banking system increases the money supply. To control the amount of money created by the system, central banks place strict reserve ratios on the commercial banks. For example, central banks generally restrict the proportion of primary deposits that commercial banks can lend out. This is called the cash reserve ratio.

For example, let's assume that a primary deposit of $1000 is made into bank A. If the cash reserve ratio is 12%, then $120 must be kept on hand by the bank and $880 is available to be lent to someone else (called the excess reserve). Now if bank A uses its $880 in excess reserve by lending it out, and that is deposited in bank B, it represents a primary deposit to the second bank. Bank B must keep 12% of $880 on hand but can lend out $774.40. If that $774.40 is eventually deposited in bank C, the third bank must keep $92.93 on hand but can lend out $681.47. The process continues until there is no excess reserve left (For simplicity we will ignore safety reserves.). By adding all the derivative deposits we can calculate the amount of money created. Alternatively we can use the deposit multiplier equation: TD = ID/crr

Where:

*TD = change in Total Deposits

*ID = Initial change in Deposit

*crr = cash reserve ratio

The initial change in deposit of $1000 will increase total deposits by $8333.33 given a reserve ratio of 12% (1000/.12=8333.33).

An Example of the Creation of New Money

The following steps describe one way that new money can be created. It is an example from the US. The government issues a Treasury security. This is simply an IOU, a promise to pay the holder a specified sum of money on a particular date. In this example, let's say the government issues $1,000,000 worth of bonds. Individual investors, pension funds, mutual funds, insurance agencies, banks, foreign government central banks, can all buy the bonds, effectively loaning money to the treasury. They do this to invest their money and receive interest in return. The Federal Reserve prints a check, in the amount of $1,000,000 and makes it payable to the government. This check is the proceeds from the sale of the bonds. The $1,000,000 is recorded as an asset by the Fed. (money owed to the central bank is called an "asset" by the bank) It is assumed the government, with its power to tax, will make good on its debt (this is why the people buying the bonds from the fed consider it a risk-free investment). The government deposits the check in its own account. The government hires employees and buys things with the $1,000,000, and it does so by writing government checks. These government checks are then deposited in commercial banks. For the sake of simplicity, assume it all goes into one commercial bank, which has a zero balance to begin with.

The commercial bank now claims $1,000,000 in new liabilities (the amount on deposit in a bank is called a "liability" by the bank, because the bank has to pay interest to it, amongst other things). In the US, the law allows the bank to lend out 90% of what it has on deposit. This lending of money that it has on deposit is the precise point at which new money is created, because the depositor still has his money, and the person getting the loan now has money too. $900,000 is lent out on Friday for someone to buy a house. This loan is in the form of a check. The home buyer signs the check and gives it to the seller, who deposits it right back into the bank on Monday. Note however, in real life that money would only come from the bank temporarily, which then would issue its own bonds or use a company like Fannie Mae to issue its own bonds, so that again investors can actually lend the money while the bank is simply a middleman, called a "servicer".

The commercial bank now claims $900,000 in new liabilities. 10 percent of that money is put into reserves, and 90% of that, or $810,000 is lent out. As soon as the $810,000 is deposited back into the bank, the cycle repeats and repeats until there is no more money to lend. The total amount lent out to borrowers is $9,000,000. Add that to the $1,000,000 that it still has on deposit and the total is $10,000,000. Commercial banks make profit by charging fees for transactions, and by charging a higher interest rate to those they lend to, than what they pay for the funds. If the commercial bank charges 6% interest on the $9,000,000 it will earn $540,000 per year. If the bank making the loan pays 1% interest to the person who put the money on deposit in the first place it will cost them $100,000 per year. With 90% of that money lent out, if the original depositor wants their money back, the bank has to borrow that money from another bank (or maybe from another source), at rate of interest set by the government (the overnight rate, or the federal funds rate in the US). This is called "asset-liability bouncing", and is a delicate balancing act all banks must work on every day.

A more Realistic Model of Money Creation

In actual fact, the money creation multiplier is more complex than this simple, small description. We must add to the equation the currency drain ratio (the propensity of the public to hold cash rather than deposit it in the banking system), the clearing house drain (the loss of deposits from the system due to interactions between banks), and the safety reserve ratio (excess reserves beyond the legal requirement that commercial banks voluntarily hold-usually a very small amount). Also, most jurisdictions require different levels of reserves for different types of deposits. Foreign currency deposits, domestic time deposits, and government deposits often have different cash reserve ratios.

FEDERAL RESERVE SYSTEM

The Federal Reserve System (also the Federal Reserve; informally The Fed) is the central banking system of the United States.

The Federal Reserve System is a quasi-governmental banking system composed of (1) a presidentially-appointed Board of Governors of the Federal Reserve System in Washington, D.C.; (2) the Federal Open Market Committee; (3) twelve regional Federal Reserve Banks located in major cities throughout the nation; and (4) numerous private member banks, which own varying amounts of stock in the regional Federal Reserve Banks. Ben Bernanke serves as the current Chairman of the Board of Governors of the Federal Reserve System.

Legal Status and Position in Government

The various components of the Federal Reserve System have differing legal statuses.

The Board of Governors of the Federal Reserve System is an independent government agency. The Board is subject to laws like the Freedom of Information Act and the Privacy Act which cover Federal agencies and not private entities. Like most other independent agencies, its decisions do not have to be ratified by the President or anyone else in the executive or legislative branches of government. The Board of Governors does not receive funding from Congress, and the terms of the members of the Board span multiple presidential and congressional terms. Once a member of the Board of Governors is appointed by the president, he or she is relatively independent (although the law provides for the possibility of removal by the President "for cause" under).

The Federal Reserve Banks are nominally "owned" by the private member banks. In Lewis v. United States, 680 F.2d 1239 (9th Cir. 1982), the United States Court of Appeals for the Ninth Circuit stated that the "the Reserve Banks are not federal instrumentalities for purposes of the FTCA [the Federal Tort Claims Act], but are independent, privately owned and locally controlled corporations." The opinion also stated that "the Reserve Banks have properly been held to be federal instrumentalities for some purposes."

The member banks are generally privately-owned corporations. The stocks of many of the member banks are publicly traded.

The Federal Reserve System was created via the Federal Reserve Act of December 23rd, 1913. All national banks were required to join the system and other banks could join. The Reserve Banks opened for business on November 16th, 1914. Federal Reserve Notes were created as part of the legislation, to provide an elastic supply of currency. The notes were to be issued to the Reserve Banks for subsequent transmittal to banking institutions.

History

The first institution with responsibilities of a central bank in the U.S. was the First Bank of the United States, chartered in 1791 by Alexander Hamilton. Thomas Jefferson, in opposition to its proposed charter, wrote the following:

The bill for establishing a national bank, in 1791, undertakes, among other things,

(1) To form the subscribers into a corporation.

(2) To enable them, in their corporate capacities, to receive grants of lands; and, so far, is against the laws of mortmain.

(3) To make alien subscribers capable of holding lands; and so far is against the laws of alienage.

(4) To transmit these lands, on the death of a proprietor, to a certain line of successors; and so far, changes the course of descents.

(5) To put the lands out of the reach of forfeiture, or escheat; and so far, is against the laws of forfeiture and escheat.

(6) To transmit personal chattels to successors, in a certain line; and so far, is against the laws of distribution.

(7) To give them the sole and exclusive right of banking, under the national authority; and, so far, is against the laws of monopoly.

(8) To communicate to them a power to make laws, paramount to the laws of the states; for so they must be construed, to protect the institution from the control of the state legislatures; and so probably they will be construed.

I consider the foundation of the Constitution as laid on this ground--that all powers not delegated to the United States, by the Constitution, nor prohibited by it to the states, are reserved to the states, or to the people (12th amend.). To take a single step beyond the boundaries thus specially drawn around the powers of Congress, is to take possession of a boundless field of power, no longer susceptible of any definition.

The incorporation of a bank, and the powers assumed by this bill, have not, in my opinion, been delegated to the United States by the Constitution. (The Writings of Thomas Jefferson, ed. by H. E. Bergh, Vol. III, p. 145 ff.)

In 1816, the Second Bank of the United States was chartered, later to be dissolved under president Andrew Jackson. From 1837 to 1862, in the Free Banking Era there was no formal central bank, while from 1862 to 1913, a system of national banks was instituted by the 1863 National Banking Act. A series of bank panics, in 1873, 1893, and 1907, caused by market speculation and the actions of international banks, provided public support for the creation of a centralized banking system, which it was thought would provide greater stability. After the Panic of 1907, Congress created the National Monetary Commission to draft a plan for reform of the banking system. Senate Republican leader and financial expert Nelson Aldrich was the head of the Commission. In 1910, Aldrich attended a secret meeting at Jekyll Island, Georgia with leading bankers, including Paul Warburg, Frank Vanderlip of the National City Bank, Henry Davison of J.P. Morgan Company, and Benjamin Strong, also of J.P. Morgan, to draft the Aldrich Plan, which would later become the Federal Reserve Act.

It took the political clout of Woodrow Wilson to get the bankers' plan passed over the objections of agrarian leader William Jennings Bryan. Wilson started with the bankers' plan that had been designed for conservative Republicans by banker Paul Warburg. Wilson had to outmaneuver the agrarian wing of the party, led by William Jennings Bryan, which strenuously denounced banks and Wall Street. They wanted a government-owned central bank which could print paper money whenever Congress wanted; Wilson convinced them that because Federal Reserve notes were obligations of the government, the plan fit their demands. Southerners and westerners learned from Wilson that the system was decentralized into 12 districts and surely would weaken New York and strengthen the hinterlands. One key Congressman, Carter Glass, was given credit for the bill, and his home of Richmond, Virginia, was made a district headquarters. Powerful Senator James A. Reed of Missouri was given two district headquarters in St. Louis and Kansas City. Congress passed the Federal Reserve Act in late 1913. Wilson named Warburg and other prominent bankers to direct the new system, pleasing the bankers. The New York branch dominated the Fed and thus the power of the banking system remained in Wall Street. The new system began operations in 1915 and played a major role in financing the Allied and American war efforts. [Link 1956 pp 199-240]

Roles and Responsibilities

According to the Board of Governors, the main tasks of the Federal Reserve System are:

Conducting the nation's monetary policy by influencing the monetary and credit conditions in the economy in pursuit of maximum employment, stable prices, and moderate long-term interest rates supervising and regulating banking institutions to ensure the safety and soundness of the nation's banking and financial system and to protect the credit rights of consumers maintaining the stability of the financial system and containing systemic risk that may arise in financial markets providing financial services to depository institutions, the U.S. government, and foreign official institutions, including playing a major role in operating the nation's payments system.

ORGANIZATION OF THE FEDERAL RESERVE SYSTEM

The basic structure of the Federal Reserve System includes:

* The Board of Governors
* The Federal Open Market Committee
* The Federal Reserve Banks
* The member banks.

Each privately owned Federal Reserve Bank and each member bank of the Federal Reserve System is subject to oversight by a Board of Governors. The 7 members of the board are appointed by the President and confirmed by the Senate. Members are selected to terms of 14 years (unless removed by the President), with the ability to serve for no more than one term. A governor may serve the remainder of another governor's term in addition to his or her own full term. The current members of the Board of Governors are:

* Ben Bernanke, Chairman
* Donald Kohn, Vice-Chairman
* Susan Bies
* Frederic Mishkin
* Kevin Warsh
* Randall Kroszner.

The Federal Open Market Committee (FOMC) created under comprises the 7 members of the board of governors and 5 representatives selected from the Federal Reserve Banks. The representative from the 2nd District, New York, (currently Timothy Geithner) is a permanent member, while the rest of the banks rotate on two and three year intervals.

CONTROL OF THE MONEY SUPPLY

The Federal Reserve System controls the size of the money supply by conducting open market operations, in which the Federal Reserve engages in the lending or purchasing of specific types of securities with authorized participants, known as primary dealers. All open market operations in the United States are conducted by the Open Market Desk at the Federal Reserve Bank of New York with an aim to making the federal funds rate as close to the target rate as possible. For a detailed look at the process by which changes to a reserve account held at the Fed affect the wider monetary supply of the economy.

The Open Market Desk has two main tools to adjust the monetary supply: repurchase agreements and outright transactions.

To smooth temporary or cyclical changes in the monetary supply, the desk engages in repurchase agreements (repos) with its primary dealers. Repos are essentially secured, short-term lending by the Fed. On the day of the transaction, the Fed deposits money in a primary dealer's reserve account, and receives the promised securities as collateral. When the transaction matures, the process unwinds: the Fed returns the collateral and charges the primary dealer's reserve account for the principal and accrued interest. The term of the repo (the time between settlement and maturity) can vary from 1 day (called an overnight repo) to 65 days, though the Fed will most commonly conduct overnight and 14-day repos.

Since there is an increase of bank reserves during the term of the repo, repos temporarily increase the money supply. The effect is temporary since all repo transactions unwind, with the only lasting net effect being a slight depletion of reserves caused by the accrued interest (think one day of interest at a 4.5% annual yield, which is 0.0121% per day). The Fed has conducted repos almost daily in 2004-2005, but can also conduct reverse repos to temporarily shrink the money supply.

In a reverse repo the Fed will borrow money from the reserve accounts of primary dealers in exchange for Treasury securities as collateral. At maturity, the Fed will return the money to the reserve accounts with the accrued interest, and collect the collateral. Since this drains reserves, reverse repos temporarily contract the monetary supply, except, again, for the extremely small lasting increase caused by the accrued interest. The other main tool available to the Open Market Desk is the outright transaction. Outrights differ from repos in that they permanently alter the money supply. Outright transactions overwhelmingly involve the purchase of Treasury securities in the secondary market.

In an outright purchase, the Fed will buy Treasury securities from primary dealers and finance these purchases by depositing newly created money in the dealer's reserve account at the Fed. Since this operation does not unwind at the end of a set period, the resulting growth in the monetary supply is permanent. The Fed also has the authority to sell Treasuries outright, but this has been exceedingly rare since the 1980s. The sale of Treasury securities results in a permanent decrease in the money supply, as the money used as payment for the securities from the primary dealers is removed from their reserve accounts, thus working the money multiplier process in reverse.

IMPLEMENTATION OF MONETARY POLICY

Buying and selling federal government securities. When the Federal Reserve System buys securities, it in effect puts more money into circulation and takes securities out of circulation. With more money around, interest rates tend to drop, and more money is borrowed and spent. When the Fed sells government securities, it in effect takes money out of circulation, causing interest rates to rise and making borrowing more difficult.

Regulating the amount of money that a member bank must keep in hand as reserves. A member bank lends out most of the money deposited with it. If the Federal Reserve System says that a member bank must keep in reserve a larger fraction of its deposits, then the amount that the member bank can lend drops, loans become harder to obtain, and interest rates rise.

Changing the interest charged to banks that want to borrow money from the federal reserve system. Member banks borrow from the Federal Reserve System to cover short-term needs. The interest that the Fed charges for this is called the discount rate; this will have an effect, though usually rather small, on how much money the member banks will lend.

DISCOUNT RATES

The Federal Reserve System implements monetary policy largely by targeting the federal funds rate. This is the rate that member banks charge each other for overnight loans of federal funds, which are the reserves held by banks at the Fed. The Federal Reserve System also directly sets the discount rate, which is the interest rate that banks pay the Fed to borrow directly from it. However, a bank will prefer to borrow Fed funds from another bank, rather than from the Fed at the normally higher discount rate, which might suggest problems with the bank's credit-worthiness or solvency.

Both of these rates influence the prime rate which is usually about 3 percentage points higher than the federal funds rate. The prime rate is the rate that most banks price their loans at for their best customers. Lower interest rates stimulate economic activity by lowering the cost of borrowing, making it easier for consumers and businesses to buy and build. Higher interest rates slow the economy by increasing the cost of borrowing.

The Federal Reserve System usually adjusts the federal funds rate by 0.25% or 0.50% at a time. From early 2001 to mid 2003 the Federal Reserve lowered its interest rates 13 times, from 6.25 to 1.00%, to fight recession. In November 2002, rates were cut to 1.75, and many interest rates went below the inflation rate. (This is known as a negative real interest rate, because money paid back from a loan with an interest rate less than inflation has lower purchasing power than it had before the loan.) On June 25, 2003, the federal funds rate was lowered to 1.00%, its lowest nominal rate since July, 1958, when the overnight rate averaged 0.68%. Starting at the end of June, 2004, the Federal Reserve System started to raise the target interest rate 17 straight times. The rate is 5.25% as of August 8, 2005; the Fed elected to keep the rate steady on its August 8 meeting after seventeen straight 0.25% increases.

The Federal Reserve System might also attempt to use open market operations to change long-term interest rates, but its "buying power" on the market is significantly smaller than that of private institutions. The Fed can also attempt to "jawbone" the markets into moving towards the Fed's desired rates, but this is not always effective.

THE FEDERAL RESERVE BANKS AND THE MEMBER BANKS

The twelve regional Federal Reserve Banks (not to be confused with the "member banks"), which were established by the Congress as the operating arms of the nation's central banking system, are organized much like private corporations-possibly leading to some confusion about "ownership." For example, the Reserve Banks issue shares of stock to "member banks." However, owning Reserve Bank stock is quite different from owning stock in a private company. The Reserve Banks are not operated for profit, and ownership of a certain amount of stock by a "member bank" is, by law, a condition of membership in the system. The stock may not be sold or traded or pledged as security for a loan; dividends are, by law, limited to 6% per year. The largest of the Reserve Banks, in terms of assets, is the Federal Reserve Bank of New York, which is responsible for the Second District covering the state of New York, the New York City region, Puerto Rico, and the U.S. Virgin Islands.

The dividends paid by the Federal Reserve Banks to member banks are considered partial compensation for the lack of interest paid on member banks' required reserves held at the Federal Reserve Banks. By law, banks in the United States must maintain fractional reserves, most of which are kept on account at the Fed. The Federal Reserve does not pay interest on these funds.

The Federal Reserve Districts are listed below along with their identifying letter and number. These are used on Federal Reserve Notes to identify the issuing bank for each note.: Boston A 1:New York B 2 :Philadelphia C 3 :Cleveland D 4 :Richmond E 5 :Atlanta F 6 :Chicago G 7 :St Louis H 8 :Minneapolis I 9 :Kansas City J 10 :Dallas K 11 :San Francisco L 12.

INFLUENCE OF GOVERNMENT

Central bank independence from political control is a crucial concept in both economic theory and practice. The problem arises as central banks strive to maintain a credible commitment to price stability, when the markets know that there is political pressure to keep interest rates low. Low interest rates tend to keep unemployment below trend, encourage economic growth, and allow for cheap credit and loans. Some models however say such a policy is not sustainable without accelerating inflation in the long term. Thus, a central bank believed to be under political control cannot make a credible commitment to fight inflation, as the markets know that sitting politicians will lobby to keep rates low. This point was one of the major research topics of economist Edward C. Prescott's career. It is in this limited sense that the Federal Reserve System is independent. The members of the FOMC are not elected and do not answer to politicians in making their interest rate decisions.

The Federal Reserve System is financially independent because it runs a surplus, due in part to its ownership of government bonds. In fact, it returns billions of dollars to the government each year. However, the Fed is still subject to oversight by the Congress, which periodically reviews its activities and can alter its responsibilities by statute. To further communication with Congress, the Fed delivers a report to both houses semiannually. Its independence from the executive branch was strengthened by the 1951 Accord. In general, the Federal Reserve System must work within the framework of the overall objectives of economic and financial policy established by the government.

FRACTIONAL-RESERVE BANKING

In its role of setting reserve requirements for the country's banking system, the Fed regulates what is known as fractional-reserve banking. This is the common practice by banks of retaining only a fraction of their deposits to satisfy demands for withdrawals, lending the remainder at interest to obtain income that can be used to pay interest to depositors and provide profits for the banks' owners. Some people also use the term to refer to fiat money, which is money that is not backed by a tangible asset such as gold. The United States' rules and oversight are within limits and guidelines set by the Bank for International Settlements, a banking agency which pre-dates the Bretton Woods financial and monetary system and its institutions.

Criticisms of the Fed

A large and varied group of criticisms are often directed against the Federal Reserve System. Some of these criticisms relate to inflation and fractional reserve banking more generally, and an in-depth treatment of these issues may be found in their respective articles. There were also specific issues relating to the former chairmanship of Alan Greenspan, specifically, that the Fed's credibility is based on a cult of personality around him and his successors. This line of argument is also more thoroughly addressed in this article. Nonetheless, critics still point to a number of specific criticisms about the methods and actions of the Fed; these are treated below.

HISTORICAL CRITICISMS

Criticisms of the Fed are not new, and some historical criticisms are reflective of current concerns.

At one extreme are a few economists from the Austrian School and the Chicago School who want the Fed abolished. They criticize the Fed's expansionary monetary policy in the 1920's, allowing misallocations of capital resources and supporting a massive stock price bubble.

Milton Friedman, leader of the Chicago School, argues that the Fed did not cause the Great Depression but made it worse by contracting the money supply at the very moment that markets needed liquidity. He believes the Fed should be abolished. The Austrian School argues that the expansion of money supply by the Federal Reserve caused malinvestment leading to the Great Depression.

Opacity

Another criticism of the Federal Reserve System is that it is shrouded in secrecy. Meetings of some components of the Fed are held behind closed doors, and the transcripts are released with a lag of five years. Even expert policy analysts are unsure as to the logic behind Fed decisions. Critics argue that such opacity leads to greater market volatility, as the markets must guess, often with only limited information, about how the Fed is likely to change policy in the future.

The jargon-laden fence-sitting opaque style of Fed communication is often called "Fed speak." It has also been known to be standoffish in its relations with the media in an effort to maintain its carefully crafted image and resents any public information that runs contrary to this notion.

For example, Maria Bartiromo reported on CNBC that during a conversation at the White House Correspondents' Dinner in April of 2006, Fed Chairman Ben Bernanke stated investors had misinterpreted his recent congressional remarks as an indication the Fed was nearly done raising rates. This triggered a drop in stock prices just as the market was about to close. Furthermore, the lag in the release of FOMC transcripts, as well as the extremely limited and carefully worded minutes and statement, leads to the public being unaware of the issues of major concern to the Fed, and leaves it with an inadequate understanding of the logic and rationale behind the decisions. Some argue that this is a concerted attempt to keep Congress and the public at arm's length, but this criticism has not gained much widespread acceptance.

OPPOSITION TO FEDERAL RESERVE

In The Creature from Jekyll Island author G. Edward Griffin argues that the Federal Reserve System was planned in secret by several extremely rich and powerful people for the purposes of furthering their family wealth and political power.

Economists of the Austrian School such as Ludwig von Mises contend that it is the Federal Reserve's artificial manipulation of the money supply that leads to the boom/bust business cycle that has occurred over the last century. Many economic libertarians, such as Austrian School economists, believe that the Federal Reserve's manipulation of the money supply to stop "gold flight" from England caused, or was instrumental in causing, the Great Depression.

In general, laissez-faire advocates of free banking argue that there is no better judge of the proper interest rate and money supply than the market. Nobel Economist Milton Friedman says, he "prefer[s] to abolish the federal reserve system altogether. "Friedman and Freedom, Interview with Peter Jaworski. The Journal, Queen's University, March 15, 2002-Issue 37, Volume 129. Ben Bernanke, Chairman of the Board of Governors of Federal Reserve, stated: "Regarding the Great Depression. You're right, we did it. We're very sorry."

The Libertarian Party (United States) platform and the Constitution Party hold positions that the Federal Reserve should be abolished on legal and economic grounds.

OPEN MARKET OPERATION

Open market operations are the means of implementing monetary policy by which a central bank controls its national money supply by buying and selling government securities, or other instruments. Monetary targets, such as interest rates or exchange rates, are used to guide this implementation.

Since most money is now in the form of electronic records, rather than paper records such as banknotes, open market operations are conducted simply by electronically increasing or decreasing the amount of money that a bank has, e.g., in its reserve account at the central bank, in exchange for the bank selling or buying a financial instrument. Newly created money is used by the central bank to buy in the open market a financial asset, such as government bonds, foreign currency, or gold. If the central bank sells these assets in the open market, the amount of money that the bank holds decreases, effectively destroying money.

The process does not literally require the immediate printing of new currency. A central bank account for a member bank can simply be increased electronically. However this will increase the central bank's requirement to print currency when the member bank demands banknotes, in exchange for a decrease in its electronic balance.

Possible Targets of Open Market Operations

Under inflation targeting open market operations target a specific short term interest rate in the debt markets. This target is changed periodically to achieve and maintain an inflation rate within a target band. Many other variants of monetary policy also target interest rates. Both the US Federal Reserve and the ECB use interest rate targets to guide open market operations. Besides interest rate targeting there are other possible targets of open markets operations. A second possible target is the growth of the money supply, as was the case in the U.S. in the late 1970s through the early 1980s under Fed Chairman Paul Volcker.

Under a gold standard open market operations would be used to achieve and maintain a target gold price. The goal would be to keep the value of the currency constant relative to gold.

Under a currency board open market operations would be used to achieve and maintain a fixed exchange rate with relation to some foreign currency.

A central bank can also use a mixture of policy settings that change depending on circumstances. A central bank may peg its exchange rate (like a currency board) with different levels or forms of commitment.

The looser the exchange rate peg, the more latitude the central bank has to target other variables (such as interest rates). It may instead target a basket of foreign currencies rather than a single currency. In some instances it is empowered to use additional means other than open market operations, such as changes in reserve requirements or capital controls, to achieve monetary outcomes.

Economist Robert Mundell has stated that when using open market operations it is only possible to pursue a single target at any given time. You can not use open market operations to target interest rates while being on a gold standard. Likewise if you are targeting interest rates then the exchange rates will fluctuate.

Current Goals and Procedures of Open Market Operations

In the United States, as of 2006 the Fed sets an interest rate target for the Fed funds (overnight bank reserves) market. When the actual Fed funds rate is higher than the target, the desk will usually increase the money supply via a repo (effectively lending). When the actual Fed funds rate is less than the target, the desk will usually decrease the money supply via a reverse repo (effectively borrowing).

The European Central Bank has similar mechanisms for their operations; however, it uses a four-tiered approach with different goals: beside its main goal of steering and smoothing Euroland interest rates while managing the liquidity situation in the market the ECB also has the aim of signalling the stance of monetary policy with its operations.

The regular weekly "main refinancing operations" and the monthly "longer-term refinancing operations" provide liquidity to the financial sector, while ad-hoc "fine-tuning operations" (in the form of reverse or outright transactions, foreign exchange swaps and the collection of fixed-term deposits) aim to smooth interest rates caused by liquidity fluctuations in the market and "structural operations" are used to adjust the central banks' longer-term structural positions vis-a-vis the financial sector.

The Swiss National Bank currently targets the 3 month Swiss franc LIBOR rate, and borrows or lends Swiss francs directly with Swiss banks (in other words, without using repos) on an almost daily basis. These borrowings or loans are typically made for 1 day or 1 week, but may be as long as 1 month.

5

The Policy Tools

MONETARY BASE

Expansionary policy can be implemented by increasing the size of the monetary base. This directly increases the total amount of money circulating in the economy. In the United States, the Federal Reserve can use open market operations to increase the monetary base. The Federal Reserve would buy bonds in exchange for hard currency. When the Federal Reserve disburses this hard currency payment, it adds that amount of currency from the economy, thus increasing the monetary base. Note that open market operations are a relatively small part of the total volume in the bond market, thus the Federal Reserve is not able to influence interest rates through this method.

RESERVE REQUIREMENTS

The monetary authority exerts regulatory control over banks. Expansionary policy can be implemented by requiring banks to hold a lower proportion of their total assets in reserve. Banks only maintain a small portion of their assets as cash available for immediate withdrawal; the rest is invested in illiquid assets like mortgages and loans. By requiring a lower proportion of total assets to be held as liquid cash the Federal Reserve increases the availability of loanable funds. This acts as an increase in the money supply.

DISCOUNT WINDOW LENDING

Many central banks or finance ministries have the authority to lend funds to financial institutions within their country. The lent funds represent an expansion in the monetary base. By extending new loans the monetary authority can directly increase the size of the money supply. By advertising that the discount window will increase future lending, the monetary authority can also indirectly increase the money supply by raising risk-taking by financial institutions.

After the September 11, 2001 attacks in the United States, the Federal Reserve announced that it would extend discount window loans to any and all financial institutions who requested funds. This had the effect of preventing any panics due to fear of insufficient liquidity.

Interest Rates

Monetary authorities in different nations have differing levels of control of economy-wide interest rates. In the United States, the Federal Reserve can only indirectly set the Federal Funds Rate. This rate has some effect on other market interest rates, but there is no direct, definite relationship. In other nations, the monetary authority may be able to mandate specific interest rates on loans, savings accounts or other financial assets. By lowering the interest rate(s) under its control, a monetary authority can expand the money supply, because lower interest rates discourage savings and encourage lending. Both of these effects increase the size of the money supply.

MONETARY POLICY AND THE REAL ECONOMY

The relationship between monetary policy and the real economy is uncertain. It is important to note that expansionary monetary policy should not be confused with economic expansion. The latter being an increase in economic output in the real economy.

Contractionary Monetary Policy

Contractionary monetary policy is monetary policy that seeks to reduce the size of the money supply. In most nations, monetary policy is controlled by either a central bank or a finance ministry. Neoclassical and Keynesian economics significantly differ on the effects and effectiveness of monetary policy on influencing the real economy; there is no clear consensus on how monetary policy effects real economic variables (aggregate output or income, employment). Both economic schools accept that monetary policy affects monetary variables (price levels, interest rates).

Monetary policy relies on a number of tools: monetary base, reserve requirements, discount window lending and interest rates.

Monetary Base

Contractionary policy can be implemented by reducing the size of the monetary base. This directly reduces the total amount of money circulating in the economy. A central bank can use open market operations to reduce the monetary base. The central bank would typically sell bonds in exchange for hard currency. When the central bank collects this hard currency payment, it removes that amount of currency from the economy, thus contracting the monetary base. Note that in the United States open market operations are a relatively small part of the total volume in the bond market, thus the Federal Reserve is not able to influence interest rates through this method.

Reserve Requirements

The monetary authority exerts regulatory control over banks. Contractionary policy can be implemented by requiring banks to hold a higher proportion of their total assets in reserve. Banks only maintain a small portion of their assets as cash available for immediate withdrawal; the rest is invested in illiquid assets like mortgages and loans. By requiring a higher proportion of total assets to be held as liquid cash, the Federal Reserve reduces the availability of loanable funds. This acts as a reduction in the money supply.

Discount Window Lending

Many central banks or finance ministries have the authority to lend funds to financial institutions within their country. The lent funds represent an expansion in the monetary base. By calling in existing loans the monetary authority can directly reduce the size of the money supply. By advertising that the discount window will reduce future lending, the monetary can also indirectly reduce the money supply by reducing risk-taking by financial institutions.

Interest Rates

Monetary authorities in different nations have differing levels of control of economy-wide interest rates. In the United States, the Federal Reserve can only indirectly set the Federal

Funds Rate by open market operations, discount lending, and changes in reserve requirement. This rate has some effect on other market interest rates, but there is no direct, definite relationship. In other nations, the monetary authority may be able to mandate specific interest rates on loans, savings accounts or other financial assets. By raising the interest rate(s) under its control, a monetary authority can contract the money supply, because higher interest rates encourage savings and discourage lending. Both of these effects reduce the size of the money supply.

MONETARY POLICY AND INFLATION

Monetary policy can be used to control inflation. Inflation is defined as continuing increases in price levels. Since price level is a monetary variable, monetary policy can affect it. Contractionary monetary policy has the effect of reducing inflation by reducing upward pressure on price levels.

Note that inflation can also be affected by fiscal policy. However, contractionary fiscal policy is often politically unpopular, because it involves spending cuts and tax increases. Thus, politicians favor the use of monetary policy to control inflation.

Expansionary Monetary Policy vs. Contractionary Monetary Policy

What Effects Does Monetary Policy Have?

Q. I'm having a little trouble trying to understand expansionary monetary policies and contractionary monetary policies. Can you help explain what impact expansionary monetary policies and contractionary monetary policies have on the economy?

A. Thanks for your great question. Students first learning economics often have trouble understanding what contractionary monetary policy and expansionary monetary policy are and why they have the effects they do.

Generally speaking contractionary monetary policies and expansionary monetary policies involve changing the level of the money supply in a country. Expansionary monetary policy is simply a policy which expands (increases) the supply of money, whereas contractionary monetary policy contracts (decreases) the supply of a country's currency.

Expansionary Monetary Policy

In the United States, when the Federal Open Market Committee wishes to increase the money supply, it can do a combination of three things:

1. Purchase securities on the open market, known as Open Market Operations
2. Lower the Federal Discount Rate
3. Lower Reserve Requirements

These all directly impact the interest rate.

When the Fed buys securities on the open market, it causes the price of those securities to rise. In my article on the Dividend Tax Cut we saw that bond prices and interest rates are inversely related. The Federal Discount Rate is an interest rate, so lowering it is essentially lowering interest rates. If the Fed instead decides to lower reserve requirements, this will cause banks to have an increase in the amount of money they can invest. This causes the price of investments such as bonds to rise, so interest rates must fall. No matter what tool the Fed uses to expand the money supply interest rates will decline and bond prices will rise.

Increases in American bond prices will have an effect on the exchange market. Rising American bond prices will cause investors to sell those bonds in exchange for other bonds, such as Canadian ones. So an investor will sell his American bond, exchange his American dollars for Canadian dollars, and buy a Canadian bond.

This causes the supply of American dollars on foreign exchange markets to increase and the supply of Canadian dollars on foreign exchange markets to decrease. As shown in my Beginner's Guide to Exchange Rates this causes the U.S. Dollar to become less valuable relative to the Canadian Dollar. The lower exchange rate makes American produced goods cheaper in Canada and Canadian produced goods more expensive in America, so exports will increase and imports will decrease causing the balance of trade to increase. When interest rates are lower, the cost of financing capital projects is less. So all else being equal, lower interest rates lead to higher rates of investment. What We've Learned About Expansionary Monetary Policy:

1. Expansionary monetary policy causes an increase in bond prices and a reduction in interest rates.
2. Lower interest rates lead to higher levels of capital investment.
3. The lower interest rates make domestic bonds less attractive, so the demand for domestic bonds falls and the demand for foreign bonds rises.
4. The demand for domestic currency falls and the demand for foreign currency rises, causing a decrease in the exchange rate. (The value of the domestic currency is now lower relative to foreign currencies)
5. A lower exchange rate causes exports to increase, imports to decrease and the balance of trade to increase.

WHAT EFFECTS DOES MONETARY POLICY HAVE?

Contractionary Monetary Policy

As you can probably imagine, the effects of a contractionary monetary policy are precisely the opposite of an expansionary monetary policy. In the United States, when the Federal Open Market Committee wishes to decrease the money supply, it can do a combination of three things:

1. Sell securities on the open market, known as Open Market Operations
2. Raise the Federal Discount Rate
3. Raise Reserve Requirements.

These cause interest rates to rise, either directly or through the increase in the supply of bonds on the open market through sales by the Fed or by banks. This increase in supply of bonds reduces the price for bonds. These bonds will be bought up by foreign investors, so the demand for domestic currency will rise and the demand for foreign currency will fall. Thus the domestic currency will appreciate in value relative to the foreign currency. The higher exchange rate makes domestically produced goods more expensive in foreign markets and foreign good cheaper in the domestic market. Since this causes more foreign goods to be sold domestically and less domestic goods sold abroad, the balance of trade decreases. As well, higher interest rates cause the cost of financing capital projects to be higher, so capital investment will be reduced.

What We've Learned About Contractionary Monetary Policy:

1. Contractionary monetary policy causes a decrease in bond prices and an increase in interest rates.
2. Higher interest rates lead to lower levels of capital investment.
3. The higher interest rates make domestic bonds more attractive, so the demand for domestic bonds rises and the demand for foreign bonds falls.
4. The demand for domestic currency rises and the demand for foreign currency falls, causing an increase in the exchange rate. (The value of the domestic currency is now higher relative to foreign currencies)
5. A higher exchange rate causes exports to decrease, imports to increase and the balance of trade to decrease.

WHAT IS DEFLATION AND HOW CAN IT BE PREVENTED?

While I haven't polled every economist who has written an article on deflation this should give you a good idea of what the general consensus on the subject. A psychological factor that has been overlooked is how many workers look at their wages in nominal terms.

The problem with deflation is that the forces causing prices in general to drop should cause wages to drop as well. Wages, however, tend to be rather "sticky" in the downward direction. If prices rise 3% and you give your employees a 3% raise, they're roughly as well off as they were before. This is equivalent to the situation where prices drop 2% and you cut the pay of your employees by 2%. However, if employees are looking at their wages in nominal terms, they'll be much happier with a 3% raise than a 2% pay cut. A low level of inflation makes it easier to adjust wages in an industry whereas deflation causes rigidities in the labor market.

These rigidities lead to an inefficient level of labor usage and slower economic growth.

Now we've seen some of the reasons why deflation is undesirable, we must ask ourselves: "What can be done about deflation?" Of the four factors listed, the easiest one to control is number 1 "The supply of money". By increasing the money supply, we can cause the inflation rate to rise, so we can avoid deflation.

In order to understand how this works, we first need a definition of the money supply. The money supply is more than just the dollar bills in your wallet and the coins in your pocket. Economist Anna J. Schwartz defines the money supply as follows:

> *"The U.S. money supply comprises currency--dollar bills and coins issues by the Federal Reserve System and the Treasury--and various kinds of deposits held by the public at commercial banks and other depository institutions such as savings and loans and credit unions."*

There are three broad measures economists use when looking at the money supply:

> *"M1, a narrow measure of money's function as a medium of exchange; M2, a broader measure that also reflects money's function as a store of value; and M3, a still broader measure that covers items that many regard as close substitutes of money."*

The Federal Reserve has several options at its disposal in order to influence the money supply and thereby raise or lower the inflation rate. The most common way the Federal Reserve changes the inflation rate is by changing the interest rate. The Fed influences interest rates causes the supply of money to change. Suppose the Fed wishes to lower the interest rate. It can do this by buying government securities in exchange for money. By buying up securities on the market, the supply of those securities goes down. This causes the price of those securities to go up and the interest rate to decline. The relationship between the price of a security and interest rates is explained on the third page of my article The Dividend Tax Cut and Interest Rates. When the Fed wants to lower interest rates, it buys a security, and by doing so it injects money into the system because it gives the holder of the bond money in exchange for that security. So the Federal Reserve can increase the money supply by lowering interest rates through buying securities and decrease the money supply by raising the interest rates by selling securities.

Influencing interest rates is a commonly used method of reducing inflation or avoiding deflation. Gongloff at CNN Money sites a Federal Reserve study that says "Japan's deflation could have been dodged, for example, if the Bank of Japan (BOJ) had only cut interest rates by 2 more percentage points between 1991 and 1995." Colin Asher points out that sometimes that if interest rates are too low, this method of controlling deflation is no longer an option, as currently in Japan where interest rates are practically zero. Changing interest rates in some circumstances is an effective way of controlling deflation through controlling the money supply.

WHAT IS DEFLATION?

The Glossary of Economics Terms defines deflation as occurring "when prices are declining over time. This is the opposite of inflation; when the inflation rate (by some measure) is negative, the economy is in a deflationary period."

The article Why Does Money Have Value? explains that inflation occurs when money becomes relatively less valuable than goods. Then deflation is simply the opposite, that over time money is becoming relatively more valuable than the other goods in the economy. Following the logic of that article, deflation can occur because of a combination of four factors:

1. The supply of money goes down.
2. The supply of other goods goes up.
3. Demand for money goes up.
4. Demand for other goods goes down.

Deflation generally occurs when the supply of goods rises faster than the supply of money, which is consistent with these four factors. These factors explain why the price of some goods increase over time while others decline. Personal computers have sharply dropped in price over the last fifteen years. This is because technological improvements have allowed the supply of computers to increase at a much faster rate than demand or the supply of money. During the 1980's there was a sharp increase in the price of 1950's baseball cards, due to a huge increase in demand and a basically fixed amount of supply of both cards and money. So your suggestion to increase the money supply if we're worried about deflation is a good one.

Before we decide that the Fed should increase the money supply, we have to determine how much of a problem deflation really is and how the Fed can influence the money supply. First we'll look at the problems caused by deflation.

Why is Deflation Bad?

Most economists agree that deflation is both a disease and a symptom of other problems in the economy. In Deflation: The Good, The Bad and the Ugly Don Luskin at Capitalism Magazine examines James Paulsen's differentiation of "good deflation" and "bad deflation". Paulsen's definitions are clearly looking at deflation as a symptom of other changes in the economy. He describes "good deflation" as occuring when businesses are "able to constantly produce goods at lower and lower prices due to cost-cutting initiatives and efficiency gains". This is simply factor 2 "The supply of other goods goes up" on our list of the four factors which cause deflation.

Paulsen refers to this as "good deflation" since it allows "GDP growth to remain strong, profit growth to surge and unemployment to fall without inflationary consequence." "Bad deflation" is a more difficult concept to define. Paulsen simply states that "bad deflation has emerged because even though selling price inflation is still trending lower, corporations can no longer keep up with cost reductions and/or efficiency gains." Both Luskin and I have difficulty with that answer, as it seems like half an explanation. Luskin concludes that bad deflation is actually caused by "the revaluation of a country's monetary unit of account by that country's central bank". In essence this is really factor 1 "The supply of money goes down" from our list. So "bad deflation" is caused by a relative decline in the money supply and "good deflation" is caused by a relative increase in the supply of goods.

These definitions are inherently flawed because deflation is caused by relative changes. If the supply of goods in a year increases by 10% and the supply of money in that year increases by 3% causing deflation, is this "good deflation" or "bad deflation"? Since the supply of goods has increased, we have "good deflation", but since the central bank hasn't increased the money supply fast enough we should also have "bad deflation". Asking whether "goods" or "money" caused deflation is like asking "When you clap your hands, is the left hand or the right hand responsible for the sound?". Saying that "goods grew too fast" or "money grew too slowly" is inherently saying the same thing since we're comparing goods to money, so "good deflation" and "bad deflation" are terms that probably should be retired.

Looking at deflation as a disease tends to get more agreement among economists. Luskin says that the true problem with deflation is that it causes problems in business relationships: "If you are a borrower, you are contractually committed to making loan payments that represent more and more purchasing power--while at the same time the asset you bought with the loan to begin with is declining in nominal price. If you are a lender, chances are that your borrower will default on your loan to him under such conditions."

Colin Asher, an economist at Nomura Securities, told Radio Free Europe that the problem with deflation is that "in deflation [there's] a declining spiral. Businesses make less profits so they cut back [on] employment. People feel less like spending money. Businesses then don't make any profits and everything works itself into a declining spiral." Deflation also has a psychological element as it "becomes rooted in peoples' psychologies and becomes self-perpetuating. Consumers are discouraged from buying expensive items like automobiles or homes because they know those things will be cheaper in the future."

Mark Gongloff at CNN Money agrees with these opinions. Gongloff explains that "when prices fall simply because people have no desire to buy--leading to a vicious cycle of consumers postponing spending because they believe prices will fall further--then businesses can't make a profit or pay off their debts, leading them to cut production and workers, leading to lower demand for goods, which leads to even lower prices."

Curing Deflation by Printing Money

We finally get to the original question: "Is the problem that there is more to printing money than printing money? Is in fact the way printed money gets into circulation, that the fed buys bonds, and thus gets money into the economy?". That's precisely what happens. The money the Fed gets to buy government securities has to come from somewhere. Generally it is just created in order for the Fed to carry out its open market operations. So in most instances, when economists talk about "printing more money" and "the Fed lowering interest rates" they're talking about the same thing. If interest rates are already zero, as in Japan, there is little room to lower them further, so using this policy to fight deflation will not work well. Fortunately interest rates in the U.S. have not yet reached the lows of those in Japan.

The Federal Reserve and Interest Rates

The Federal Reserve is responsible for maintaining full employment (generally considered to be around 4 to 5 percent unemployment) while keeping inflation low. This task may sound simple but, in reality, it's a delicate balancing act.

The most powerful weapon in the Fed's arsenal is the ability to influence the direction of interest rates. When interest rates are low, capital is easier to acquire. This can spur economic development because, human nature being what it is, the more cash you have available, the more you are likely to pay for something you want-whether it is a car or that new plasma screen television. Left unchecked, however, and the result is "too much money chasing too few goods," as the saying goes.

This leads to inflation as businesses realize they can charge higher prices for their goods and services. Suddenly, it costs you more to fill up your gas tank and refrigerator. If interest rates are too high, however, the result can be a recession and, in extreme cases, deflation; the result of which can be economically devastating-imagine going to pay off your mortgage and realizing that, although the balance has not increased, it's going to cost you more dollars in terms of purchasing power than it did before! How can the Federal Reserve influence the direction of interest rates? In one of two ways:

1. By raising or lowering the discount rate.
2. By indirectly influencing the direction of the Federal funds rate.

The Discount Rate

The discount rate is the interest rate banks are charged when they borrows funds overnight directly from one of the

Federal Reserve Banks. When the cost of money increases for your bank, they are going to charge you more as a result. This makes capital more expensive and results in less borrowing. Spending decreases, causing it to become more difficult for prices to rise; the opposite being true when capital becomes less expensive due to a decrease in the discount rate.

The Federal Funds Rate

The Federal funds rate is the rate that banks charge each other for overnight loans. "Why would one bank borrow cash from another?" you ask. The Fed can require banks to keep a certain percentage of assets in the form of cash on hand or deposited in one of the Federal Reserve banks. From time to time, it will establish a required ratio of reserves to deposits; when this ratio is increased, more cash must be kept in the vault at night, making it more difficult (and expensive) for funds to be acquired. When the reserve requirement is lowered, the money supply is loosened; because less cash has to be kept on hand it becomes easier to acquire capital.

The increased (or decreased) cost of acquiring funds is passed on to consumers as banks adjust their prime lending rate (the rate banks charge their best customers) to compensate. The prime lending rate is not uniform; Bank of America may have one rate while U.S. Bank has another. As a result, the most widely quoted prime rate figure in the United States is the one found in the Wall Street Journal. It represents a polling of the nation's thirty largest banks; when twenty-three of those institutions have changed their prime rates, the WSJ responds by updating the published rate. This ultimately affects your bottom line because many credit cards, for example, base the interest rate you pay on a premium above the WSJ prime rate.

Federal Reserve Board

Definition: The Federal Reserve Board, also know as the "Fed," controls the nation's interests rates by setting the key rates. Alan Greenspan has headed the Fed for many years. When he sneezes the market gets a cold, is an old Wall Street saying. Any change in interest rates will have a dramatic effect on the markets if it was not anticipated. Raising and lowering interest rates is analogous to turning up or down the heat while cooking.

Primary Dealers

Primary dealers are banks or brokerage firms who may trade directly with the Federal Reserve System of the United States. They are required to make bids or offers when the Fed conducts open market operations, provide information to the Fed's open market trading desk, and to actively participate in U.S. Treasury securities auctions. They consult with both the U.S. Treasury and the Fed about funding the budget deficit and implementing monetary policy. Many former employees of primary dealers work at the Treasury, because of their expertise in the government debt markets, though the Fed avoids a similar revolving door policy.

Between them, these dealers purchase the vast majority of the U.S. Treasury securities (T-bills, T-notes, and T-bonds) sold at auction, and resell them to the public. Their activities extend well beyond the Treasury market, for example, according to the Wall Street Journal Europe (2/9/06 p. 20), all of the top ten dealers in the foreign exchange market are also primary dealers, and between them account for almost 73% of forex trading volume. Arguably, this group's members are the most influential and powerful non-governmental institutions in world financial markets. Group membership changes slowly, with the current list available from the New York Fed.

The primary dealers form a worldwide network that is needed to distribute the huge amount of new U.S. government debt. For example, Daiwa Securities, Mizuho Securities, and Nomura Securities distribute the debt to Japanese buyers. BNP Paribas, Barclays, Deutsche Bank, and Greenwich Capital (a division of the Royal Bank of Scotland) distribute the debt to European buyers. Goldman Sachs, Lehman Brothers, and Citigroup account for many American buyers. Nevertheless, most of these firms compete internationally and in all major financial centers.

The newest primary dealer (effective on August 1, 2006) is Cantor Fitzgerald. The previous last major change to the list (excluding name changes and mergers) was Countrywide Securities, which joined in 1999. It is an American firm which focuses on mortgage markets and electronic or internet securities sales.

Repurchase Agreement

Repurchase agreements (RPs or Repos) are financial instruments used in the money markets. A more accurate and descriptive term is Sale and Repurchase Agreement, since what transpires is sale of securities now for cash by party A (the cash borrower) to party B (the cash lender), with the promise made by A to B of repurchasing those securities later (with A paying the requisite implicit interest to B at the time of repurchase- the implicit interest rate is known as the repo rate). There is little that prevents any security from being employed in a repo; so, Treasury or Government bills, corporate and Treasury/ Government bonds, and stocks/shares, may all be used as securities involved in a repo. "' A Reverse Repo is the repo as seen from the point of view of the cash lender, since the cash lender does not repurchase, but rather has securities repurchased from (i.e. the cash lender is the passive party in the act of securities repurchasing).

Normally, both parties view the transaction from the trader's perspective. A trader looking to borrow money is transacting a repo, while a trader looking to obtain securities is executing a reverse repo. When a customer provides money to a trader in return for securities, the transaction is often termed a repo by both parties.

A repo is similar to a secured loan, with the lender of money receiving securities as collateral to protect against default. The legal title to securities passes from the seller to the investor. The one providing the cash is referred to as an "investor"; the provider of the collateral is the "seller". Coupons that are paid out on the securities during the life of the loan are generally passed directly onto the seller of the Repo. It is possible to instead pass on the coupon by altering the cash paid at the end of the agreement, though this is more typical of Sell/Buy Backs.

Typically, repos are short-term, either overnight, or with a maturity of few days. However, repo agreements up to 3 months are not uncommon; these can be used to cover futures contracts, and are commonly called term repos.

Motivations for Repos

For the customer, a repo is an opportunity to invest cash for a custom period of time (other investments typically involve whole numbers of months). It is a short-term and secure investment; in return for investing, the customer receives collateral. Market liquidity for repos is good and yields are competitive for investors.

For the trader, repos are used to finance long positions and reduce funding costs of other speculative investments.

There is a small credit risk with using repos. It is essentially a collateralized borrowing; but it is possible that the borrower of cash may fail to repurchase the securities sold at the promised date (in other words, default). In this case the lender may keep the security, but it may have lost value since the original transaction date. To prevent this minor amount of credit risk, some repos are over-collateralized. The credit risk is directly associated with the maturity of the repo: the longer the maturity, the greater the credit risk coming with the repo.

In addition to using repo as a vehicle to obtain cheap funding cost using secured financing, the best traders are also able to gain by making markets in repo using matched traders. The concept of a matched trade follows closely to that of a broker that takes both sides of an active trade, essentially having no risk. In the case of a matched repo trade, the trader engages in both a repo and a reverse repo within a short period of time. Profits can be obtained by traders who can take both sides of the market, but still leave themselves with a positive spread between the two repo rates. There are three types of repo maturities: overnight, term, and open repo. Overnight refers to a one-day maturity transaction. Term refers to a repo with a specified end date. Open simply has no end date.

Repo transactions occur in three forms: specified delivery, Triparty, and held in custody. The third form is quite rare. The first form requires the delivery of a pre-specified bond at the onset and maturity of the contractual period. Triparty allows for a wide range of instruments to satisfy a general pool in the repo contract.

Repo transactions came into focus within the financial press due to the technicalities of settlements following the collapse of Refco. Occasionally, a party involved in a repo transaction may not have a specific bond at the end of the repo contract. This may cause a string of failures from one party to the next, for as long as different parties have transacted for the same underlying instrument. The focus of the media attention centers on attempts to mitigate these failures.

Federal Reserve use of Repos

Repurchase agreements when transacted by the Federal Open Market Committee of the Federal Reserve in open market operations initially add reserves to the banking system and then withdraw them; reverse repos initially drain reserves and later add them back.

Under a repurchase agreement ("RP" or "repo"), the Federal Reserve (Fed) buys US Treasury securities, U.S. agency securities, or mortgage backed securities from a primary dealer who agrees to buy them back, typically within one to seven days; a reverse repo is the opposite. Thus the Fed describes these transactions from the counter-party's viewpoint rather than from their own viewpoint.

If the Fed is one of the transacting parties, the RP is called a "system repo," but if they are trading on behalf of a customer (e.g. a foreign central bank) it is called a "customer repo." Until 2003 the Fed did not use the term "reverse repo"-which it believed implied that it was borrowing money (counter to its charter)-but used the term "matched sale" instead.

Types of Repo and Related Products

Due Bill/Hold in Custody Repo: In a Due Bill repo, the collateral pledged by the (cash) borrower is not actually delivered to the cash lender. Rather, it is placed in an internal account ("held in custody") by the borrower, for the lender, throughout the duration of the trade. This has become less common as the Repo market has grown, particularly owing to the creation of centralized counterparties. Due to the high risk to the security lender, these are generally only transacted with large, financially stable institutions.

Tri-Party Repo: The distinguishing feature of a Tri-Party Repo is that a custodian bank or international clearing organization acts as an intermediary between the two parties to the Repo. The tri-party agent is responsible for the administration of the transaction including collateral allocation, marking to market and substitution of collateral. Both the lender and borrower of cash in transaction enter into these transactions to avoid the administrative burden of bi-lateral Repos. A Tri-Party repo may be seen as the outgrowth of the Due Bill repo, in which the collateral is held by a neutral third party.

Whole Loan Repo: A Whole Loan Repo is a form of Repo where the transaction is collateralized by a loan or other form of obligation (e.g. mortgage receivables) rather than a security.

Equity Repo: The underlying security for most Repo transactions are government or corporate bonds. Equity Repos are simply repos on Equity securities such as common (or ordinary) shares. Some complications can arise because of greater complexity in the tax rules for dividends as opposed to coupons.

Sell/Buy Backs and Buy/Sell Backs A Sell/Buy Back is the spot sale and a forward repurchase of a Security. The basic motivation of Sell/Buy Backs is generally same as for a Classic Repo i.e. attempting to benefit from the lower financing rates generally available for collateralized as opposed to non-secured borrowing. The economics of the transaction are also similar with the interest on the cash borrowed through the sell/buy back being implicit in the difference between the sale price and the purchase price.

There are a number of differences between the two structures. A Repo is technically a single transaction while a Sell/Buy Back is a pair of transactions (a sell and a buy). A Sell/Buy back does not require any special legal documentation while a Repo generally requires a master agreement to be in place between the buyer and seller (typically a GMRA/ISMA or PSA/ISMA).

Any coupon payment on the underlying security during the life of the Sell/Buy Back will generally be passed back to the seller of the security by adjusting the cash paid at the termination of the Sell/Buy Back. In a Repo the coupon will be passed on immediately to the seller of the security.

A Buy/Sell Back is the equivalent of a Reverse Repo.

Securities Lending: The general motivation of Repo is the borrowing or lending of cash. In securities lending, the purpose is to temporarily obtain the security for other purposes, such as covering short positions or for use in complex financial structures. Securities are generally lent out for a fee. Securities lending trades are governed by different types of legal agreements than Repos.

The size of the Repo Market: The US Federal Reserve and the European Repo Council (a body of the International Securities Market Association) both try to estimate the size of their respective repo markets. At the end of 2004, the US repo market reached USD 5 trillion and the European one passed EUR 5 trillion in outstandings. Both are growing at two-digit pace.

FACTOR PRICE EQUALIZATION

Factor price equalization is an economic theory, which states that the relative prices for two identical factors of production in the same market will eventually equal each other because of competition. The price for each single factor need not become equal, but relative factors will. Whichever factor receives the lowest price before two countries integrate economically and effectively become one market will therefore tend to become more expensive relative to other factors in the economy, while those with the highest price will tend to become cheaper.

An often-cited example of factor price equalization is wages. When two countries enter a free trade agreement, wages for identical jobs in both countries tend to approach each other. After NAFTA was signed, for instance, unskilled labor wages gradually fell in the United States, at the same time as they gradually rose in Mexico. The same force has applied more recently to the various countries of the European Union.

The result was first proven mathematically as an outcome of the Heckscher-Ohlin model assumptions.

6

Fair Trade Movements

MEANING

The Fair Trade movement promotes international labour, environmental and social standards for the production of labelled and unlabelled goods ranging from handicrafts to agricultural commodities. The movement focuses in particular on exports from developing countries to developed countries.

The most widely recognized definition of fair trade was created by FINE, an informal Association of the four main Fair Trade networks (Fair-trade Labelling Organizations International, International Fair Trade Association, Network of European Worldshops and European Fair Trade Association): European Fair Trade Association. (2006). Definition of Fair Trade URL accessed on August 2, 2006.: "Fair Trade is a trading partnership, based on dialogue, transparency and respect, that seeks greater equity in international trade.

It contributes to sustainable development by offering better trading conditions to, and securing the rights of, marginalized producers and workers-especially in the South. Fair Trade organisations (backed by consumers) are engaged actively in supporting producers, awareness raising and in campaigning for changes in the rules and practice of conventional international trade. Fair Trade's strategic intent is:

* deliberately to work with marginalised producers and workers in order to help them move from a position of vulnerability to security and economic self-sufficiency
* to empower producers and workers as stakeholders in their own organisations

* to actively to play a wider role in the global arena to achieve greater equity in international trade."

Implicit and often explicit in fair trade is a criticism of the current organisation of international trade as being "unfair". When developing countries export to Northern markets, they often face tariff barriers that can be as much as four times higher than those encountered by Northern countries. Poverty advocates claim that those barriers cost poor countries $100 billion a year-twice as much as they receive in aid. Oxfam International. (n.d.) Rigged Rules and Double Standards URL accessed on August 2, 2006. Advocates of fair trade practices also hold that the fluctuation of commodity prices does not guarantee a living wage for many producers in developing countries, forcing many into crippling debt. The Fair-trade Foundation. (n.d.) What is Fair-trade? URL accessed on August 2, 2006. Market prices may not properly reflect the true costs associated with producing the product due to economic externalities such as environmental and social costs.

HISTORY

Origins

The first attempts to commercialize fair trade goods in Northern markets were initiated in the 1940s and 1950s by religious groups and various politically-oriented non-governmental organizations (NGOs). The Mennonite Central Committee (MCC) and the Church of the Brethren were the first, in 1946 and 1949 respectively, to develop fair trade supply chains in Third World countries. International Fair Trade Association. (2005). Crafts and Food. URL accessed on August 2, 2006. The products, almost exclusively handicrafts ranging from jute goods to cross-stitch work, were mostly sold in World Shops. The goods themselves had often no other function than to indicate that a donation had been made. Hockerts, K. (2005).

SOLIDARITY TRADE

The Fair Trade movement as we know today was however shaped in Europe in the 1960s. Fair trade during that period was often seen as a political gesture against neo-imperialism: radical student movements began targeting multinational corporations and concerns that traditional business models were fundamentally flawed started to emerge. The global free market economic model came under attack during that period and fair trade ideals, built on a post-Keynesian approach to economics where price is directly linked to the actual production costs and where all producers are given fair and equal access to the markets, gained in popularity. Redfern A. & Snedker P. (2002) Creating Market Opportunities for Small Enterprises: Experiences of the Fair Trade Movement. International Labor Office. p4 The slogan at the time, "Trade not Aid", gained international recognition in 1968 when it was adopted by the UNCTAD (United Nations Conference on Trade and Development) to put the emphasis on the establishment of fair trade relations with the developing world. International Fair Trade Association. (2005). Where did it all begin? URL accessed on August 2, 2006.

Throughout the 1960s and 1970s, important segments of the Fair Trade movement worked to find markets for products from countries that were excluded from the mainstream trading channels for political reasons. The work conditions of the producers were then rarely emphasized. The first fair trade effort to import fair trade coffee to Northern markets, for example, was a solidarity initiative with the Sandinista government in Nicaragua. Renard, M.-C., (2003). Fair Trade: quality, market and conventions. Journal of Rural Studies, 19, 87-96. At the time however, the overwhelming majority of fair trade goods sold in World Shops remained handicrafts.

Handicrafts vs. Agricultural Goods

In the early 1980s, alternative trading organizations faced a major challenge: the novelty of their fair trade products started wearing off, demand reached a plateau and the handicrafts began to look "tired and old fashioned" in the marketplace. Redfern A. & Snedker P. (2002) Creating Market Opportunities for Small Enterprises: Experiences of the Fair Trade Movement. International Labor Office. p6 The decline of the handicrafts market forced fair trade supporters to rethink their business model and find innovative remedies to the ongoing crisis in the industry.

Agricultural commodities provided alternative trading organizations the perfect substitute to the declining handicrafts market: they offered a renewable source of income while being easily marketable as virtually every single consumer can become a potential buyer. The first traded agricultural products were tea and coffee, quickly followed by dried fruits, cocoa, sugar, fruit juices, rice, spices and nuts. Coffee quickly became the main growth engine behind Fair Trade: between 25 to 50 % of the total alternative trading organization turnover in 2005 came from coffee sales. International Fair Trade Association. (2005). Market Access and Fair Trade Labeling. URL accessed on August 2, 2006.

Rise of Labelling Initiatives

Sales of fair trade products however only really took off with the arrival of the first Fair-trade labelling initiatives. Although buoyed by ever growing sales, fair trade had been generally contained to relatively small World shops scattered across Europe and to a lesser extent, North America. Many felt that these shops were too disconnected from the rhythm and the life-style of contemporary developed societies.

The inconvenience of going to them to buy only a product or two was too high even for the most militant customers. The only way to increase sale opportunities was to start offering fair trade products where consumers normally shop, in large distribution channels. Renard, M.-C., (2003). Fair Trade: quality, market and conventions. Journal of Rural Studies, 19, 87-96. The problem was to find a way to expand distribution without compromising consumer trust in fair trade products and in their origins. Following long debates within Fair Trade circles, the first Fair-trade label, Max Havelaar, was created in 1988 by the Dutch ATO Solidaridad. The independent certification allowed the goods to be sold outside the World shops and into the mainstream, reaching a larger consumer segment and boosting fair trade sales significantly. The labeling initiative also allowed customers and distributors alike to track the origin of the goods to confirm that the products were really benefiting the farmers at the end of the supply chain. Redfern A. & Snedker P. (2002) Creating Market Opportunities for Small Enterprises: Experiences of the Fair Trade Movement. International Labor Office. The concept caught on: within years, similar Fair-trade labelling organizations such as the Fair-trade Foundation, Trans Fair and Rate wise market, emerged across Europe and North America in an effort to follow Max Havelaar's footsteps and boost Fair-trade sales. The organizations originally operated independently and launched their own campaigns and certification marks.

In 1997, these organizations created Fair-trade Labelling Organizations International (FLO), an umbrella organization whose mission is to set the Fair-trade standards, support, inspect and certify disadvantaged producers and harmonize the Fair-trade message across the movement. In 2002, FLO launched a new International Fair-trade Certification Mark. The goals of the launch were to improve the visibility of the Mark on supermarket shelves, convey a dynamic, forward-looking image for Fair-trade, facilitate cross border trade and simplify procedures for importers.

PRESENT STATUS OF FAIR TRADE

Global Fair Trade sales have boomed over the past decade. FINE estimated that in 2000, sales of Fair Trade products (labelled and non-labelled) in Europe amounted to approximately ,260 million; in 2005, the figure was estimated at ,660 million, a 154% jump, representing a sustained annual increase of about 20% a year. FINE. (2005) Fair Trade in Europe 2005: Facts and Figures on Fair Trade in 25 European countries. Brussels: Fair Trade Advocacy Office. p7 Similar sales patterns have emerged in the Americas and the Pacific Rim, as Fair Trade sales in both regions have jumped from $291 million in 2003 to $376 million in 2004. Fair Trade Federation. (2005). Fair Trade Trends in the Americas and the Pacific Rim.

Key Fair-trade Principles

Fair-trade advocates generally support the following principles and practices in trading relationships: International Fair Trade Association (2006). Key Principles of Fair Trade URL accessed on August 2, 2006. Creating opportunities for economically disadvantaged producers: Fair trade is a strategy for poverty alleviation and sustainable development. Its purpose is to create opportunities for producers who have been economically disadvantaged or marginalized by the conventional trading system.Transparency and accountability: Fair trade involves transparent management and commercial relations to deal fairly and respectfully with trading partners. Capacity building: Fair trade is a means to develop producers' independence.

Fair-trade relationships provide continuity, during which producers and their marketing organizations can improve their management skills and their access to new markets. Payment of a fair price: A fair price in the regional or local context is one that has been agreed through dialogue and participation. It covers not only the costs of production but enables production which is socially just and environmentally sound. It provides fair pay to the producers and takes into account the principle of equal pay for equal work by women and men.

Fair-traders ensure prompt payment to their partners and, whenever possible, help producers with access to pre-harvest or pre-production financing. Gender equity: Fair trade means that women's work is properly valued and rewarded. Women are always paid for their contribution to the production process and are empowered in their organizations. Working conditions: Fair trade means a safe and healthy working environment for producers. The participation of children (if any) does not adversely affect their well-being, security, educational requirements and need for play and conforms to the UN Convention on the Rights of the Child as well as the law and norms in the local context. Environment: Fair trade actively encourages better environmental practices and the application of responsible methods of production.

FAIR-TRADE CERTIFICATION AND LABELLING

Fair-trade labelling (usually simply Fair-trade or Fair Trade Certified) is a Certification system designed to allow consumers to identify goods which meet agreed standards. Overseen by an international umbrella organisation, the Fair-trade Labelling Organizations International (FLO), the system involves independent auditing of producers to ensure the agreed standards are met.

For a product to carry the International Fair-trade Certification Mark, it must come from FLO inspected and certified producer organizations. The crops must be grown and harvested in accordance with the International Fair-trade standards set by FLO e.V. The supply chain is monitored by FLO-Cert to ensure the integrity of labelled products.

Fair-trade certification guarantees not only fair prices, but also the principles of ethical purchasing. These principles include adherence to ILO agreements such as those banning child and slave labour, guaranteeing a safe workplace and the right to unionise, adherence to the United Nations charter of human rights, a fair price that covers the cost of production and facilitates social development, and protection and conservation of the environment. The Fair-trade certification system also promotes long-term business relationships between buyers and sellers, and greater transparency throughout the supply chain.

The FLO Fair-trade certification system covers a growing range of products, including bananas, honey, coffee, oranges, cocoa, cotton, dried and fresh fruits and vegetables, juices, nuts and oil seeds, quinoa, rice, spices, sugar, tea and wine. Companies offering products that meet the Fair-trade standards may apply for licences to use the International Fair-trade Certification Mark for those products.

The current international Fair-trade Mark was launched in 2002 by FLO. The goals of the launch were to improve the visibility of the Mark on supermarket shelves, convey a dynamic, forward-looking image for Fair-trade, facilitate cross border trade and simplify procedures for importers and traders. The Fair-trade Certification Mark harmonization process is still under way â" as of August 2006, all but three Labelling Initiatives (namely Trans Fair USA, Trans Fair Canada and Max Havelaar Switzerland) have adopted the new International Fair-trade Certification Mark. Full transition to the new Mark should become reality as it gradually replaces the old Certification Marks at various speeds in various countries. Fair-trade Labelling Organizations International (2006). About Fair Trade URL accessed on August 4, 2006. The Mark is currently used in over 16 countries: Australia, Austria, Belgium, Denmark, Finland, France, Germany, Ireland, Italy, Luxembourg, the Netherlands, New Zealand, Norway, Spain, Sweden and the United Kingdom. In 2005, FLO labelled Fair-trade sales amounted to approximately, 1.1 billion worldwide, a 37 % year-to-year increase. As per December 2005, 508 certified producer organizations in 58 developing countries were Fair-trade certified. Fair-trade Labelling Organizations International. (2005) FLO Annual Report 2005. URL accessed on August 4, 2006.

FAIR TRADE IMPACT STUDIES

Several independent studies have recently measured the impact of Fair trade on disadvantaged farmers and workers.

In 2002, Loraine Ronchi of the Poverty Research Unit at the University of Sussex studied the impact of Fair Trade on the Coocafe cooperative in Costa Rica. Ronchi found that Fair Trade strengthened producer organizations and concluded that "in light of the coffee crisis of the early 1990s, Fair Trade can be said to have accomplished its goal of improving the returns to small producers and positively affecting their quality of life and the health of the organisations that represent them locally, nationally and beyond". Ronchi, L. (2002). The Impact of Fair Trade on Producers and their Organizations: A Case Study with Coocafe in Costa Rica. University of Sussex. p25-26.

In 2003, the Fair Trade Research Group at Colorado State University conducted seven case studies of Latin American Fair-trade coffee producers (UCIRI, CEPCO, Majomut, Las Colinas & El SincuyoLa Selva, Tzotzilotic and La Voz) and concluded that Fair Trade has "in a short time greatly improved the well-being of small-scale coffee farmers and their families" Murray D., Raynolds L. & Taylor P. (2003). One Cup at a time: Poverty Alleviation and Fair Trade coffee in Latin America. Colorado State University, p28 The various case studies most notably found that producers had under Fair Trade greater access to credit and external development funding. Taylor, Pete Leigh (2002). Poverty Alleviation Through Participation in Fair Trade Coffee Networks, Colorado State University, p18. The studies also found that Fair Trade producers had, compared to conventional coffee producers, greater access to training and enhanced ability to improve the quality of their coffee. Murray D., Raynolds L. & Taylor P. (2003). One Cup at a time: Poverty Alleviation and Fair Trade coffee in Latin America. Colorado State University, p8. Families of Fair Trade producers were also said to be more stable and children had better access to education than in families growing conventional coffee. Murray D., Raynolds L. & Taylor P. (2003). One Cup at a time:

Poverty Alleviation and Fair Trade coffee in Latin America. Colorado State University, p10-11

FAIR TRADE AND POLITICS

European Politics

In June 2006, Green MEP Frithjof Schmidt submitted the report Fair Trade and Development to the European Parliament Development Committee.

The report stresses that the most significant part of the increase in Fair Trade sales has been achieved with respect to labelled products and that Fair Trade labelling initiatives have been developed in most European countries.

The Report was followed by a resolution which urged the Commission to issue a Recommendation on Fair Trade recognising its role in the pursuit of the EU's Development and Trade policy. The resolution also recommended to set up minimum criteria a certain product needs to comply with in order to be considered 'Fair Trade', in order to reduce the risk of abuse. European Parliament (2006). Fair Trade and Development-call for the Commission to act. URL accessed on August 5, 2006.

"This resolution responds to the impressive growth of Fair Trade, showing the increasing interest of European consumers in responsible purchasing," said Green MEP Frithjof Schmidt during the plenary debate. Peter Mandelson, EU Commissioner for External Trade, responded that the resolution will be well-received at the Commission. "Fair Trade makes the consumers think and therefore it is even more valuable. We need to develop a coherent policy framework and this resolution will help us. "Frithjof Schmidt MEP (2006). Parliament in support of Fair Trade URL accessed on August 2, 2006.

The resolution was unanimously adopted on July 6, 2006.

WORLD BANK

The World Bank has taken a positive stance on fair trade. According to the Bank's 2003 Study of Sustainable Coffee Markets, sustainable coffees (both fair trade and organic) "can provide such benefits as improved natural resource management; fewer agrochemicals used in production, which decreases costs and health risks; and increased use of rural labour, which provides more jobs for those in desperate need. "The World Bank Group. (2003). The State of Sustainable Coffee: A Study of Twelve Major Markets.

FOREIGN DIRECT INVESTMENT

Foreign direct investment (FDI) is defined as a long term investment by a foreign direct investor in an enterprise resident in an economy other than that in which the foreign direct investor is based. The FDI relationship, consists of a parent enterprise and a foreign affiliate which together form a Transnational Corporation (TNC). In order to qualify as FDI the investment must afford the parent enterprise control over its foreign affiliate. The UN defines control in this case as owning 10% or more of the ordinary shares or voting power of an incorporated firm or its equivalent for an unincorporated firm.

In the years after the Second World War global FDI was dominated by the United States, as much of the world recovered from the destruction wrought by the conflict. The U.S. accounted for around three-quarters of new FDI (including reinvested profits) between 1945 and 1960. Since that time FDI has spread to become a truly global phenomenon, no longer the exclusive preserve of OECD countries.

FDI has grown in importance in the global economy with FDI stocks now constituting over 20% of global GDP. In the last few years, the emerging market countries such as China and India have become the most favoured destinations for FDI and investor confidence in these countries has soared. As per the FDI Confidence Index compiled by A.T. Kearney for 2005, China and India hold the first and second position respectively, whereas United States has slipped to the third position.

Types of FDI

* *Greenfield Investment*: Direct investment in new facilities or the expansion of existing facilities. Greenfield investments are the primary target of a host nation's promotional efforts because they create new production capacity and jobs, transfer technology and know-how, and can lead to linkages to the global marketplace.

However, it often does this by crowding out local industry; multinationals are able to produce goods more cheaply (because of advanced technology and efficient processes) and uses up resources (labor, intermediate goods, etc). Another downside of greenfield investment is that profits from production do not feed back into the local economy, but instead to the multinational's home economy. This is in contrast to local industries whose profits flow back into the domestic economy to promote growth.

* *Mergers and Acquisitions*: Occur when a transfer of existing assets from local firms to foreign firms takes place, this is the primary type of FDI. Cross-border mergers occur when the assets and operation of firms from different countries are combined to establish a new legal entity. Cross-border acquisitions occur when the control of assets and operations is transferred from a local to a foreign company, with the local company becoming an affiliate of the foreign company. Unlike greenfield investment, acquisitions provide no long term benefits to the local economy--even in most deals the owners of the local firm are paid in stock from the acquiring firm, meaning that the money from the sale could never reach the local economy. Nevertheless, mergers and acquisitions are a significant form of FDI and until around 1997, accounted for nearly 90% of the FDI flow into the United States.
* Horizontal Foreign Direct Investment is investment in the same industry abroad as a firm operates in at home.
* *Vertical Foreign Direct Investment*: Takes two forms (1) backward vertical FDI: where an industry abroad provides inputs for a firm's domestic production process (2) forward verticle FDI: in which an industry abroad sells the outputs of a firm's domestic production processes.

Gresham's Law

Gresham's law is commonly stated as: "Bad money drives good money out of circulation". A more correct rendering of Gresham's Law is that "Bad money drives out good if they exchange for the same price." This law was first formulated by Nicolaus Copernicus. Gresham's law applies specifically when there are two forms of commodity money in circulation which are forced, by the application of legal tender laws, to be respected as having the same face value in the marketplace. It is named after Sir Thomas Gresham, an English financier in Tudor times.

GOOD MONEY AND BAD MONEY

The terms "good" and "bad" money are used in a technical sense, and with regard to exchange values imposed by legal tender legislation, as follows:

Good Money

Good money is money that has little difference between its exchange value and its commodity value. In the original discussions of Gresham's law, money was conceived of entirely as metallic coins, so the commodity value is the market value of the coined bullion of which the coins are made.

An example is the US dollar, which, prior to the 1900s was equal to 1/20.67 ounce (1.5048 g) of gold, and carried an exchange value roughly equal to its coined gold market value.

It is worth noting that in the absence of legal tender laws, metal coin money will freely exchange at somewhat above bullion market value. (This is not a purely theoretical result, but rather can be observed today in bullion coins such as the Krugerrand (South Africa) and the American Gold Eagle (United States). Honestly coined money is of a known purity, and in a convenient form to handle. People prefer to trade in coins than in anonymous hunks of bullion, so they attribute more value to the coins. Thus, coining is frequently profitable.

Bad Money

Bad money is money that has a substantial difference between its commodity value and its market value, where market value is lower than exchange value.

In Gresham's day, bad money included any coin that had been "debased". Debasement was often done by members of the public, cutting or scraping off some of the metal. Coinage could also be debased by the issuing body, whereby less than the officially mandated amount of precious metal is contained in an issue of coinage, usually by alloying it with base metal.

Other examples of "bad" money include counterfeit coins made from base metal. In all of these examples, the market value was the supposed value of the coin in the market.

In the case of clipped, scraped or counterfeit coins, the market value has been reduced by fraud, while the exchange value remains at the higher value. On the other hand, with coinage debased by a government issuer the market value of the coinage was often reduced quite openly, but the exchange value of the debased coins was held at the higher level by legal tender laws.

All modern money is "bad money" in this sense, since fiat money has entirely replaced the commodity money to which Gresham's law applies. The ubiquity of fiat money could indeed be taken as evidence for the truth of Gresham's law.

THEORY

Gresham's law says that any circulating currency consisting of both "good" and "bad" money, where both forms are required to be accepted at equal value under legal tender law, quickly becomes dominated by the "bad" money. This is because people spending money will hand over the "bad" coins rather than the "good" ones, keeping the "good" ones for themselves.

Consider a customer purchasing an item which costs five pence, who has in their possession several silver sixpence coins. Some of these coins are more debased, while others are less so â□" but legally, they are all mandated to be of equal value. The customer would prefer to retain the better coins, and so offers the shopkeeper the most debased one. In turn, the shopkeeper must give one penny in change â□" and has every reason to give the most debased penny. Thus, the coins that circulate in the transaction will tend to be of the most debased sort available to the parties.

If "good" coins have a face value below that of their metallic content, individuals may melt them down and sell the metal for its higher bullion value. For an example of this, consider the 1965 US Half-dollars which were made from only 40% silver. The previous year the half-dollar was 90% silver. With the release of the 1965 half, which was legally required to be accepted at the same value as the previous year's 90% halves, the older 90% silver coinage of the US quickly disappeared from circulation, and the debased money was allowed to circulate in its stead. As the price of bullion silver rose above the face value of the coins, many of those old half-dollars were melted down. In addition to being melted down for its bullion value, money that is considered to be "good" tends to leave an economy through international trade. International traders are not bound by legal tender laws the way citizens of the country are, so they will offer higher value for good coins than bad ones, and thus higher value than can be obtained within the country. The good coins may leave their country of origin to become part of international trade. Thus, the good money is driven out of the country of issue, escaping that country's legal tender laws and leaving the "bad" money behind. This occurred in Britain during the period of the Gold Exchange Standard.

ORIGIN OF THE TITLE

George Selgin in his paper "Gresham's Law" offers the following comments: The expression "Gresham's Law" dates back only to 1858, when British economist Henry Dunning Macleod (1858, p. 476-8) decided to name the tendency for bad money to drive good money out of circulation after Sir Thomas Gresham (1519-1579). However, references to such a tendency, sometimes accompanied by discussion of conditions promoting it, occur in various medieval writings, most notably Nicholas Oresme's (c. 1357) Treatise on money, and can even be found in much earlier works, including Aristophanes' The Frogs, where the prevalence of bad politicians is attributed to forces similar to those favoring bad money over good.

The passage from The Frogs referred to is as follows; it is usually dated at 405 B.C.:: The course our city runs is the same towards men and money.: She has true and worthy sons.: She has fine new gold and ancient silver,: coins untouched with alloys, gold or silver,: each well minted, tested each and ringing clear.: Yet we never use them!: Others pass from hand to hand,: sorry brass just struck last week and branded with a wretched brand.: So with men we know for upright, blameless lives and noble names.: These we spurn for men of brass....

"Gresham's Law" was also earlier described by the astronomer Nicolaus Copernicus, in the year that Gresham was born in a treatise named Monetae cudendae ratio.

Gresham's Context

According to George Selgin in his paper "Gresham's Law": As for Gresham himself, he observed "that good and bad coin cannot circulate together" in a letter written to Queen Elizabeth on the occasion of her accession in 1558. The statement was part of Gresham's explanation for the "unexampled state of badness" England's coinage had been left in following the "Great Debasements" of Henry VIII and Edward VI, which reduced the metallic value of English silver coins to a small fraction of what that value had been at the time of Henry VII. It was owing to these debasements, Gresham observed to the Queen, that "all your fine gold was conveyed out of this your realm."

Gresham made his observations of good and bad money while in the service of Queen Elizabeth, with respect only to the observed poor quality of the British coinage. The previous monarchs, Henry VIII and Edward VI, forced the people to accept debased coinage by means of their legal tender laws. Gresham also made his comparison of good and bad money where the precious metal in the money was the same. He did not compare silver to gold, or gold to paper.

Gresham's Law in Reverse

In an influential theoretical article, Rolnick and Weber (1986) argued that bad money would drive good money to a premium rather than driving it out of circulation. However their research did not take into account the context in which Gresham made his observation. Rolnick and Weber ignored the influence of legal tender legislation which requires people to accept both good and bad money as if they were of equal value. They also focussed mainly on the interaction between different metallic moneys, comparing the relative "goodness" of silver to that of gold, which is not what Gresham was speaking of.

The experiences of dollarization in countries with weak economies and currencies (for example Israel in the 1980s, the Eastern European countries in the period immediately after the collapse of the Soviet bloc, or South American countries throughout the late twentieth and early twenty-first century) may be seen as Gresham's Law operating in its reverse form (Guidotti & Rodriguez, 1992), since in general the dollar has not been legal tender in such situations, and in some cases its use has been illegal. These examples show that in the absence of legal tender laws, Gresham's law works in reverse. If given the choice of what money to accept, people will transact with money they believe to be of highest long-term value. However, if not given the choice, and required to accept all money, good and bad, they will tend to keep the money of greater perceived value in their possession, and pass on the bad money to someone else. Said in another way, in the absence of legal tender laws, the seller will not accept anything but money of real worth (good money), while the existence of legal tender laws will force the seller to accept money with no commodity value (bad money). Thus, the buyer will always try to spend his bad money first, but in the absence of legal tender laws, the seller will not accept money with no real worth.

Analogical Extensions of Gresham's Law

The Gresham's Law principle has been applied, by analogy, to many different fields.

For example, movie critics have invoked Gresham's law to explain why movies with innovative visuals and writing are rare but, once created, are much copied or made into sequels. The claim is that production companies and theaters see all movies as virtually interchangeable product, and prefer ones which are cheaper to make or that have less risk to promote.

In higher education, "diploma mills" have come into existence producing low-cost qualifications which are often of little or no market value. It may seem that according to Gresham's law these "bad" diplomas ought to drive out the "good diplomas". However, unlike money, there is no law requiring employers to accept all diplomas as being of equal value and each employer is free to assess the value of qualifications as they see fit. Therefore Gresham's law does not apply.

In business, bad managers and employees can drive out good ones.

In democracy, a less intelligent majority may be able to outvote an exceptionally intelligent minority, effectively driving out the most intelligent voters by guaranteeing that their votes will be defeated.

In schools, curriculum is prone to "dumbing down" to make it accessible to the least academically prepared students, thereby leaving no meaningful academic challenges for the better prepared students, or even students of average academic preparedness.

In the market for second hand cars, lemon automobiles (analogous to bad currency) will drive out the good cars. This is because the seller of good cars will find that the "average" price of both lemons and good cars is less than the fair price of the good car.

In morality, a version exists positing that "the evil acts of bad men illicit from good men acts which, under better circumstances, would also be called evil".

7

The International Law and its Significance

International Law also called public international law to distinguish from "private international law", i.e. resolution for conflict of laws in its most general sense, "consists of rules and principles of general application dealing with the conduct of states and of international organizations and with their relations inter se, as well as with some of their relations with persons, whether natural or juridical." Columbia Law School, McKeever, 2003-Definition of International Law International law concerns the structure and conduct of states, international organizations, and, to a certain degree, also multinational corporations and individuals.

While both are supranational systems of law, the term "public international law" should be distinguished from "private international law". Public international law regulates the relationship between states and international entities, regulates competing demands, and establishes the framework for predictable and agreed behaviour among parties. Private international law selects between conflicting municipal systems of law to regulate the relationship between persons, as defined both legally and naturally. Columbia Law School, McKeever, 2003-Institutions Involved in the Process

The necessity for international law arose in the context of increased international communication, trade, and conflict.

According to the President of the International Court of Justice, Rosalyn Higgins, international law is a normative system "harnessed to the achievement of common values-values that speak to us all, whether we are rich or poor, black or white, of any religion or none, or come from countries that are industrialized or developing". Higgins R, Problems and process: international law and how we use it (Oxford: Clarendon Press, 1994) at 16.

THE SCOPE OF INTERNATIONAL LAW

International law establishes the framework and the criteria for identifying states as the principal actors in the international legal system. As the existence of a state presupposes control and jurisdiction over territory, international law deals with the acquisition of territory, state immunity and the legal responsibility of states in their conduct with each other. The law is similarly concerned with the treatment of individuals within state boundaries.

There is thus a comprehensive regime dealing with group rights, the treatment of aliens, the rights of refugees, international crimes, nationality problems and human rights generally. It further includes the important functions of the maintenance of international peace and security, arms control, the pacific settlement of disputes and the regulation of the use of force in international relations. Even when the law is not able to stop the outbreak of war, it has developed principles to govern the conduct of hostilities and the treatment of prisoners. International law is also used to govern issues relating to the global environment, the global commons such as international waters and outer space, global communications, and world trade.

Whilst municipal law is hierarchical or vertical, with the legislature enacting binding legislation, international law is horizontal, with all states being sovereign and theoretically equal. Because of this, the value and authority of international law is dependent upon the voluntary participation of states in its formulation, observance, and enforcement. Although there may be exceptions, most states enter into legal commitments to other states out of enlightened self-interest rather than adherence to a body of law that is higher than their own. As D. W. Greig notes, "international law cannot exist in isolation from the political factors operating in the sphere of international relations". Greig, D. W., International Law, 2nd edn (Butterworths: London, 1976)

Where there are breaches of the law, international law has no established compulsory judicial system for the settlement of disputes or coercive penal system. That is not to say that there are no judicial or quasi-judicial tribunals in international law. The formation of the United Nations, for example, created a means for the world community to enforce international law upon members that violate its charter. Traditionally, states were the sole subjects of international law. With the proliferation of international organizations over the last century, they have in some cases been recognized as relevant parties as well. Recent interpretations of international human rights law, international humanitarian law, and international trade law have been inclusive of corporations, and even individuals.

FUNDAMENTAL CONFLICTS OVER INTERNATIONAL LAW

The 17th, 18th and 19th centuries saw the growth of the concept of a "nation-state", which comprised nations controlled by a centralized system of government. The concept of nationalism became increasingly important as people began to see themselves as citizens of a particular nation with a distinct national identity. Until the beginning of the 20th century, relations between nation-states were dictated by Treaty, unenforceable agreements to behave in a certain way towards another state. Many people now view the nation-state as the primary unit of international affairs.

States may choose to voluntarily enter into commitments under international law, but they will often follow their own counsel when it comes to interpretation of their commitments. As the 20th century progressed, a number of violent armed conflicts, including WWI and WWII, exposed the weaknesses of a voluntary system of international treaties. In an attempt to create a stronger system of laws to prevent future conflicts, a vehicle for the application of international law was found in the creation of the United Nations, an international law making body, and new international criminal laws were applied at the Nuremberg trials. Over the past fifty years, more international laws and law making bodies have been created. Many people feel that these modern developments endanger nation states by taking power away from state governments and ceding it to international bodies such as the U.N. and the World Bank.

Some scholars and political leaders have recently argued that international law has evolved to a point where it exists separately from the mere consent of states. There is a growing trend toward judging a state's domestic actions in the light of international law and standards. A number of states, notably the United States vehemently oppose this interpretation, maintaining that sovereignty is the only true international law and that states have free reign over their own affairs. Similarly, a number of scholars now discern a legislative and judicial process to international law that parallels such processes within domestic law. Opponents to this point of view maintain that states only commit to international law with express consent and have the right to make their own interpretations of its meaning; and that international courts only function with the consent of states. Because international law is a relatively new area of law its development is uncertain and its relevance and propriety is hotly disputed.

SOURCES OF INTERNATIONAL LAW

International law has three primary sources: international treaties, custom, and general principles of law (cf. Art. 38 of the Statute of the International Court of Justice). International treaty law is comprised of obligations states expressly and voluntarily accept between themselves in treaties. Customary international law is derived from the consistent practice of States accompanied by opinio juris, i.e. the conviction of States that the consistent practice is required by a legal obligation. Judgments of international tribunals as well as scholarly works have traditionally been looked to as persuasive sources for custom in addition to direct evidence of state behavior. Attempts to codify customary international law picked up momentum after the Second World War with the formation of the International Law Commission (ILC). Codified customary law is made the binding interpretation of the underlying custom by agreement through treaty. For states not party to such treaties, the work of the ILC may still be accepted as custom applying to those states. General principles of law are those commonly recognized by the major legal systems of the world. Certain norms of international law achieve the binding force of peremptory norms (jus cogens) as to include all states with no permissible derogations. Legal principles common to major legal systems may also be invoked to supplement international law when necessary.

INTERPRETATION OF INTERNATIONAL LAW

Where there are disputes about the exact meaning and application of national laws, it is the responsibility of the courts to decide what the law means. In international law as a whole, there are no courts which have the authority to do this. It is generally the responsibility of states to interpret the law for themselves. Unsurprisingly, this means that there is rarely agreement in cases of dispute. Insofar as treaties are concerned, the Vienna Convention on the Law of Treaties writes on the topic of interpretation that:: "A treaty shall be interpreted in good faith in accordance with the ordinary meaning to be given to the terms of the treaty in their context and in the light of its object and purpose." (article 31(1) This is actually a compromise between three different theories of interpretation:

* The textual approach is a restrictive interpretation which bases itself on the "ordinary meaning" of the text, the actual text has considerable weight.
* A subjective approach considers the idea behind the treaty, treaties "in their context", what the writers intended when they wrote the text.
* A third approach bases itself on interpretation "in the light of its object and purpose", i.e. the interpretation that best suits the goal of the treaty, also called "effective interpretation". These are general rules of interpretation; specific rules might exist in specific areas of international law.

Enforcement by States

Apart from a state's natural inclination to uphold certain norms, the force of international law has always come from the pressure that states put upon one another to behave consistently and to honor their obligations. As with any system of law, many violations of international law obligations are overlooked. If addressed, it is almost always purely through diplomacy and the consequences upon an offending state's reputation. Though violations may be common in fact, states try to avoid the appearance of having disregarded international obligations.

States may also unilaterally adopt sanctions against one another such as the severance of economic or diplomatic ties, or through reciprocal action. In some cases, domestic courts may render judgment against a foreign state (the realm of private international law) for an injury, though this is a complicated area of law where international law intersects with domestic law. States have the right to employ force in self-defense against an offending state that has used force to attack its territory or political independence. States may also use force in collective self-defense, where force is used against another state. The state that force is used against must authorize the participation of third-states in its self-defense. This right is recognized in the United Nations Charter.

Enforcement by International Bodies

Violations of the UN Charter by members of the United Nations may be raised by the aggrieved state in the General Assembly for debate. The General Assembly cannot make binding resolutions, but under the "Uniting for Peace" resolution (GA/RES/0377) it declared it could authorize the use of force if there had been Breaches of the Peace or Acts of Aggression, provided that the Security Council due to a negative vote of a permanent member failed to act. It could call for other collective measures (such as economic sanctions) given a situation constituted the milder "threat to the Peace". The legal significance of such a resolution is unclear, as the General Assembly cannot issue binding resolutions.

They can also be raised in the Security Council. The Security Council can pass resolutions of the UN Charter to recommend "Pacific Resolution of Disputes." Such resolutions are not binding under international law, though they usually are expressive of the council's convictions. In rare cases, the Security Council can pass resolutions of the UN Charter related to "threats to Peace, Breaches of the Peace and Acts of Aggression," and these are legally binding under international law, and can be followed up with economic sanctions, military action, and similar uses of force through the auspices of the United Nations. It has been argued that resolutions passed outside can also be binding; the legal basis for that is the Council's broad powers under Article 24(2), which states that "in discharging these duties (exercise of primary responsibility in international peace and security), it shall act in accordance with the Purposes and Principles of the United Nations". The mandatory nature of such resolutions was upheld by the International Court of Justice in its advisory opinion on Namibia. The binding nature of such resolutions can be deduced from an interpretation of their language and intent.

States can also, upon mutual consent, submit disputes for arbitration by the International Court of Justice (ICJ), located in The Hague, Netherlands. The judgments given by the Court in these cases are binding, although it possesses no means to enforce its rulings. The Court may give an advisory opinion on any legal question at the request of whatever body may be authorized by or in accordance with the Charter of the United Nations to make such a request. Some of the advisory cases brought before the court have been controversial with respect to the courts competence and jurisdiction.

Often enormously complicated matters, ICJ cases (of which there have been less than 150 since the court was created from the Permanent Court of International Justice in 1945) can stretch on for years and generally involve thousands of pages of pleadings, evidence, and the world's leading specialist public international lawyers. As of 2005, there are twelve cases pending at the ICJ. Decisions made through other means of arbitration may be binding or non-binding depending on the nature of the arbitration agreement, whereas decisions resulting from contentious cases argued before the ICJ are always binding on the involved states. Though states (or increasingly, international organizations) are usually the only ones with standing to address a violation of international law, some treaties, such as the International Covenant on Civil and Political Rights have an optional protocol that allows individuals who have had their rights violated by member states to petition the international Human Rights Committee.

THE BACKDROP

Through the ages a code developed for the relations and conduct between nations. Even when nations were at war, envoys were often considered immune to violence. The first formal attempts in this direction, which over time have developed into the current international law, stem from the era of the Renaissance in Europe. In the Middle Ages, it had been considered the obligation of the Church to mediate in international disputes. During the Council of Constance (1414) Pawel Wlodkowic, rector of Jagiellonian University (Krakaw, Poland), theologian, lawyer and diplomat, presented the theory that all, including pagan, nations have right to self-govern and to live in peace and possess their land.

At the beginning of the 17th century, several generalizations could be made about the political situation. Self-governing, autonomous states existed. Almost all of them were governed by monarchs. The Peace of Westphalia is often cited as being the birth of the modern nation-states, establishing states as sovereigns answering to no-one within its own borders. Land, wealth, and trading rights were often the topics of wars between states. Some people assert that international law developed to deal with the new states arising, others claim that the lack of influence of the Pope and the Catholic church gave rise to the need for new generally-accepted codes in Europe.

The French monk Emeric Cruce (1590-1648) came up with the idea of having representatives of all countries meeting in one place to discuss their conflicts so as to avoid war and create more peace. He suggested this in his The New Cyneas (1623), choosing Venice to be the selected city for all of the representatives to meet, and suggested that the Pope should preside over the meeting. Of course, during the Thirty Years' War (1618-1648), this was not acceptable to the Protestant nations. He also said that armies should be abolished and called for a world court. Though his call to abolish armies was not taken seriously, Emeric Cruce does deserve his place in history through his foresight that international organizations are crucial to solve international disputes. The statesmen of the time believed no nation could escape war, so they prepared for it. King Henry IV's Chief Minister, the Duke of Sully, proposed the founding of an alliance of the European nations that was to meet to arbitrate issues and wage war not between themselves but collectively on the Ottoman Turks, and he called it the Grand Design, but was never established.

After World War I, the nations of the world decided to form an international body. U.S. President Woodrow Wilson came up with the idea of a "League of Nations". However, due to political wrangling in the U.S. Congress, the United States did not join the League of Nations, which was one of the causes of its demise. When World War II broke out, the League of Nations was finished. Yet at the same time, the United Nations was being formed. On January 1, 1942, US President Franklin D. Roosevelt issued the "Declaration by United Nations" on behalf of 26 nations who had pledged to fight against the Axis powers. Even before the end of the war, representatives of 50 nations met in San Francisco to draw up the charter for an international body to replace the League of Nations. On October 24, 1945, the United Nations officially came into existence, setting a basis for much international law to follow. Modern international law is often affirmed as the product of modern European civilization. The seafaring principalities of India established legal rules for ocean navigation and regional commerce.

The Greek system of independent city-states bore a close resemblance to contemporary nation-state system. The Aetolian and Achaean leagues of the 3rd century BC represented early organisational efforts at international cooperation and facilitated the development of arbitration as a dispute settlement technique.

INTERNATIONAL LEGAL THEORY

The intellectual seeds of modern international law germinated in the 16th and 17th centuries, when the influence of the Roman Catholic Church in international affairs gradually weakened. Many early international legal theorists were concerned with axiomatic truths thought to be reposed in natural law. Among the early natural law writers, Francisco de Victoria, Dominican professor of theology at the University of Salamanca, examined the question of just war and Spanish authority in the Americas. He did so while Spain was at the height of its power, after the violent Spanish conquest of Peru in 1536.

Eclectic School

Central in the development of modern international law was Hugo Grotius a Dutch theologian, humanist and jurist. In his principal work De jure Belli ac Pacis Libri Tres ("Three Books on the Law of War and Peace"; 1625), Grotius claimed that nations as well as persons ought to be governed by universal principle based on morality and divine justice. Much of Grotius's content drew from the Bible and from classical history (just war theory of Augustine of Hippo). Drawing also from domestic contract law, he also noted that relations between polities were governed by jus gentium, the law of peoples, which had been established by the consent of the community of nations.

The fundamental facets of the Grotian or eclectic school, especially the doctrines of legal equality, territorial sovereignty, and independence of states, became definitive to international law in Europe. These principals were recognised in the Peace of Westphalia and became the foundation for the treaties of Osnabrack and Manster. Another eclectic thinker, German philosopher Christian von Wolff, contended that the foundation for international community should come as a world superstate (civitas maxima), having authority over the component member states. This view was rejected by the Swiss diplomat Emmerich de Vattel, who favoured a rationale of equality of states as articulated by 18th century natural law. Vattel suggested in his major work Le droit des gens that the law of nations was comprised of custom and law on the one hand, and natural law on the other.

Legal Positivism

The early positive school emphasized the importance of custom and treaties as sources of international law. Among the early positivists was Alberico Gentilis, a professor of civil law at Oxford who used historical examples to posit that positive law (jus voluntarium) was determined by general consent. Another professor at Oxford, Richard Zouche, published the first manual of international law in 1650.

In the 18th century legal positivism became popular and found its way into international legal philosophy. The principal figure among 18th century positivists was Cornelius van Bynkershoek, a celebrated Dutch jurist who asserted that the bases of international law were customs and treaties commonly consented to by various states. A second positivist, John Jacob Moser was a prolific German scholar who emphasized the importance of state practice in international law. A contemporary German scholar, Georg Friedrich von Martens, published the first systematic manual on positive international law, Precis du droit des gens moderne de l'Europe. The growth of nationalism and Hegelian philosophy in the 19th century pushed natural law farther from the legal realm. Commercial law became nationalized into private international law, distinct from public international law. Positivism narrowed the range of international practice that might qualify as law, favouring rationality to morality and ethics. The Congress of Vienna in 1815 marked formal recognition of the political and international legal system based on the conditions of Europe.

BRANCHES OF INTERNATIONAL LAW

* International criminal law
* The law pertaining to use of force
* International human rights law
* International humanitarian law
* Law of the sea
* Diplomatic law
* Consular law
* Law of State Responsibility
* International environmental law
* International trade law.

The Bretton Woods Conference of 1944 proposed the creation of an International Trade Organization (ITO) to establish rules and regulations for trade between countries. The ITO would have complemented the other two Bretton Woods Institutions: The International Monetary Fund (IMF) and the World Bank.

The ITO charter was agreed at the UN Conference on Trade and Employment in Havana in March 1948, but was blocked by the U.S. Senate. As a result, the ITO never came into existence. It has been suggested that the failure may have resulted from fears within the American business community that the International Trade Organization could be used to regulate European cartels rather than to break them up. Only one element of the ITO survived: the General Agreement on Tariffs and Trade (GATT). Seven rounds of negotiations occurred under GATT before the eighth round-the Uruguay Round-concluded in 1995 with the establishment of the World Trade Organisation (WTO) as the GATT's replacement. The GATT principles and agreements were adopted by the WTO, which was charged with administering and extending them.

NEW TRADE THEORY

New Trade Theory (NTT) is the economic critique of international free trade from the perspective of increasing returns to scale and the network effect. Beginning in the 1970s some economists asked whether it might be effective for a nation to shelter infant industries until they had grown to sufficient size to compete internationally.

The Theory

New Trade theorists challenge the assumption of diminishing returns to scale, and some argue that using protectionist measures to build up a huge industrial base in certain industries will then allow those sectors to dominate the world market (via a Network effect).

They wondered whether free trade would have prevented the development of the Japanese auto industries in the 1950s, when quotas and regulations prevented import competition. Japanese companies were encouraged to import foreign production technology but were required to produce 90 per cent of parts domestically within five years. It is said that the short-term hardship of Japanese consumers (who were unable to buy the superior vehicles produced by the world market) was more than compensated for by the long-term benefits to producers, who gained time to out-compete their international rivals.

Less quantitative forms of this "infant industry" argument against totally free trade have been advanced by trade theorists since at least 1848.

Impact of the Theory

Although there was nothing particularly 'new' about the idea of protecting 'infant industries' (an idea offered in theory since the 18th century, and in trade policy since the 1880s) what was new in "New Trade Theory" was the rigour of the mathematical economics used to model the increasing returns to scale, and especially the use of the network effect to argue that the formation of important industries was path dependent in a way which industrial planning and judicious tariffs might control. The model they developed was highly technical, and predicted the possibilities of national specialization-by-industry observed in the industrial world (movies in Hollywood, watches in Switzerland, etc). The story of path-dependent industrial concentrations sometimes leads to monopolistic competition.

Econometric Testing

The econometric evidence for NTT was mixed, and again; highly technical. Due to the time-scales required and the particular nature of production in each 'monopolizable' sector, statistical judgements have been hard to make. In many ways, there is too limited a data-set to produce a reliable test of the hypothesis which doesn't require arbitrary judgements from the researchers. Japan is cited as evidence of the benefits of "intelligent" protectionism, but critics of NTT have argued that the empirical support post-war Japan offers for beneficial protectionism is unusual, and that the NTT argument is based on a selective sample of historical cases. Although many examples (like Japanese cars) can be cited where a 'protected' industry subsequently grew to world status, regressions on the outcomes of such "industrial policies" (including the failures) have been less conclusive.

History of the Theory's Development

The theory was initially associated with Paul Krugman and the MIT economists of the early 1970s. Looking back in 1996 Krugman wrote that International economics a generation earlier had completely ignored returns to scale::"The idea that trade might reflect an overlay of increasing-returns specialization on comparative advantage was not there at all: instead, the ruling idea was that increasing returns would simply alter the pattern of comparative advantage."

OPEC

The Organization of the Petroleum Exporting Countries (OPEC) is made up of Algeria, Indonesia, Iran, Iraq, Kuwait, Libya, Nigeria, Qatar, Saudi Arabia, the United Arab Emirates, and Venezuela; since 1965 its international headquarters have been in Vienna, Austria. The principal aim of the Organization, according to its Statute, is "the coordination and unification of the petroleum policies of its member countries and the determination of the best means for safeguarding their interests, individually and collectively; devising ways and means of ensuring the stabilization of prices in international oil markets with a view to eliminating harmful and unnecessary fluctuations; giving due regard at all times to the interests of the producing nations and to the necessity of securing a steady income to the producing countries; an efficient, economic and regular supply of petroleum to consuming nations, and a fair return on their capital to those investing in the petroleum industry." OPEC's influence on the market has not always been a stabilizing one, however. It alarmed the world and triggered high inflation across both the developing and developed world through its use of the oil weapon in the 1973 oil crisis. Its ability to control the price of oil has diminished greatly since its heyday, following the much-expanded development of the Gulf of Mexico, the North Sea, and the growing fluidity of the market. However, OPEC still has considerable impact on the price of oil. It is still commonly used as a textbook example of a cartel.

MEMBERSHIP

The Organization now has 11 member states. They are listed below with their affiliation dates.

Africa:

* (July 1969)
* (December 1962)
* (July 1971)

Middle East:

* (September 1960)
* (September 1960)
* (September, 1960)
* (December 1961)
* (September 1960)
* (November 1967)

South America:

* (September 1960)

Southeast Asia:

* (December 1962. Membership currently under review as Indonesia is no longer considered by OPEC as a net oil exporter. See also current acting OPEC secretaries general)

Former Members:

* (Full member from 1975 to 1995)

* (Full member from 1963 to 1993)

OPEC's official language is English, although the official language of a majority of OPEC member-states is Arabic, as seven current members are Arab states. Only one member nation (Nigeria) has English as an official language.

History

Venezuela was the first country to move towards the establishment of the Organization of the Petroleum Exporting Countries (OPEC) by approaching Iran, Iraq, Kuwait and Saudi Arabia, in 1949, and suggesting that they exchange views and explore avenues for regular and closer communications between them. In September 1960, government of Iraq invited Iran, Kuwait, Saudi Arabia and Venezuela to meet in Baghdad, to discuss the reduction in prices of crudes produced by their respective countries. As a result OPEC was founded to unify and coordinate members' petroleum policies. Original OPEC members include Iran, Iraq, Kuwait, Saudi Arabia, and Venezuela. Between 1960 and 1975, the organization expanded to include Qatar (1961), Indonesia (1962), Libya (1962), the United Arab Emirates (1967), Algeria (1969), and Nigeria (1971). Ecuador and Gabon were members of OPEC, but Ecuador withdrew in December 1992, and Gabon followed suit in January 1995. Although Iraq remains a member of OPEC, Iraqi production has not been a part of any OPEC quota agreements since March 1998. EIA estimates that the current eleven OPEC members account for about 40% of world oil production, and about 2/3 of the world's proven oil reserves.

The Yom Kippur War

The persistence of the Arab-Israeli conflict finally triggered a response that transformed OPEC from a mere cartel into a formidable political force. After the Six Day War of 1967, the Arab members of OPEC formed a separate, overlapping group, the Organization of Arab Petroleum Exporting Countries, for the purpose of centering policy and exerting pressure on the West over its support of Israel. Egypt and Syria, though not major oil-exporting countries, joined the latter grouping to help articulate its objectives. Later, the Yom Kippur War of 1973 galvanized Arab opinion. Furious at the emergency re-supply effort that had enabled Israel to withstand Egyptian and Syrian forces, the Arab world imposed the 1973 oil embargo against the United States and Western Europe. In the 1970s, the great Western oil conglomerates suddenly faced a unified block of producers.

This Arab-Israeli conflict triggered a crisis already in the making. They consistently drew the oil away from non-Arab nations. The West could not continue to increase its energy use 5% annually, pay low oil prices, yet sell inflation-priced goods to the petroleum producers in the Third World. This was stressed by the Shah of Iran, whose nation was the world's second-largest exporter of oil, and the closest ally of the United States in the Middle East at the time. "Of course [the world price of oil] is going to rise," the Shah told the New York Times in 1973. "Certainly! And how...; You [Western nations] increased the price of wheat you sell us by 300%, and the same for sugar and cement...; You buy our crude oil and sell it back to us, redefined as petrochemicals, at a hundred times the price you've paid to us...; It's only fair that, from now on, you should pay more for oil. Let's say 10 times more." Quoted in Walter LaFeber, Russia, America, and the Cold War (New York, 2002), p. 292.

Operations

OPEC's member countries hold about two-thirds of the world's oil reserves. They supply 40% of the world's oil production and half of the exports.

Since worldwide oil sales are denominated in U.S. dollars, changes in the value of the dollar against other world currencies affect OPEC's decisions on how much oil to produce. For example, when the dollar falls relative to the other currencies, OPEC-member states receive smaller revenues in other currencies for their oil, causing substantial cuts in their purchasing power, because they continue to sell oil in the U.S. dollar. After the introduction of the euro, Iraq decided it wanted to be paid for its oil in euros instead of US dollars.

OPEC decisions have considerable influence on international oil prices. For example, in the 1973 energy crisis OPEC refused to ship oil to western countries that had supported Israel in the Yom Kippur War or October War, which they fought against

Egypt and Syria. This refusal caused a fourfold increase in the price of oil, which lasted five months, starting on October 17, 1973, and ending on March 18, 1974. OPEC nations then agreed, on January 7, 1975, to raise crude oil prices by 10%. At that time, OPEC nations-including many who had recently nationalized their oil industries-joined the call for a new international economic order to be initiated by coalitions of primary producers. Concluding the First OPEC Summit in Algiers they called for stable and just commodity prices, an international food and agriculture program, technology transfer from North to South, and the democratization of the economic system. The policy has been successful, causing the price of crude oil to rise to levels that had, at one time, been reached only by refined products. However, OPEC's ability to raise prices does have some limits. An increase in oil price decreases consumption, and could cause a net decrease in revenue. Furthermore, an extended rise in price could encourage systematic behavior change, such as alternative energy utilization, or increased conservation.

Leading up to the 1990-91 Gulf War, Iraqi President Saddam Hussein advocated that OPEC push world oil prices up, thereby helping Iraq, and other member states, service debts. But the division of OPEC countries occasioned by the Iraq-Iran War and the Iraqi invasion of Kuwait marked a low point in the cohesion of OPEC. Once supply disruption fears that accompanied these conflicts dissipated, oil prices began to slide dramatically. After oil prices slumped at around $10 a barrel, concerted diplomacy, sometimes attributed to Venezuela's president Hugo Chajvez, achieved a coordinated scaling back of oil production beginning in 1998. In 2000, Chajvez hosted the first summit of heads of state of OPEC in 25 years. In August 2004, OPEC began communicating that its members had little excess pumping capacity, indicating that the cartel was losing influence over crude oil prices. Indonesia is reconsidering its membership having become a net importer and being unable to meet its production quota.

8

Recent Trends in Trade Policies

It is the stated policy of most First World countries to eliminate protectionism through free trade policies enforced by international treaties and organizations such as the World Trade Organization. Despite this, many of these countries still place protective and/or revenue tariffs on foreign products to protect some favored or politically influential industries, or to reduce the taxation demands on their internal domestic manufacturing, making their products more competitive. The elimination of these tariffs remains a contentious peg their currencies to the dollar and, thus, set prices of their exports lower than they would be if the market determined the relative prices of each currency.

Protectionist quotas can cause foreign producers to become more profitable, mitigating their desired effect. This happens because quotas artificially restrict supply, so it is unable to meet demand; as a result the foreign producer can command a premium price for its products. These increased profits are known as quota rents.

For example, in the United States (1981-1994), Japanese automobile companies were held to voluntary export quotas. These quotas limited the supply of Japanese automobiles desired by consumers in the United States (1.68 million, raised to 1.85 million in 1984, and raised again to 2.30 million in 1985), increasing the profit margin on each automobile more than enough (14% or about $1200 in 1983 dollars, about $2300 in 2005 dollars) to cover the reduction in the number of automobiles that they sold, leading to greater overall profits for Japanese automobile manufacturers in the United States export market (Berry et al. 1999).

INTRODUCTION

Banking, the business of providing financial services to consumers and businesses. The basic services a bank provides are checking accounts, which can be used like money to make payments and purchase goods and services; savings accounts and time deposits that can be used to save money for future use; loans that consumers and businesses can use to purchase goods and services; and basic cash management services such as check cashing and foreign currency exchange. Four types of banks specialize in offering these basic banking services: commercial banks, savings and loan associations, savings banks, and credit unions.

A broader definition of a bank is any financial institution that receives, collects, transfers, pays, exchanges, lends, invests, or safeguards money for its customers. This broader definition includes many other financial institutions that are not usually thought of as banks but which nevertheless provide one or more of these broadly defined banking services. These institutions include finance companies, investment companies, investment banks, insurance companies, pension funds, security brokers and dealers, mortgage companies, and real estate investment trusts. This article, however, focuses on the narrower definition of a bank and the services provided by banks in Canada and the United States.

Banking services are extremely important in a free market economy such as that found in Canada and the United States. Banking services serve two primary purposes. First, by supplying customers with the basic mediums-of-exchange (cash, checking accounts, and credit cards), banks play a key role in the way goods and services are purchased. Without these familiar methods of payment, goods could only be exchanged by barter (trading one good for another), which is extremely time-consuming and inefficient. Second, by accepting money deposits from savers and then lending the money to borrowers, banks encourage the flow of money to productive use and investments. This in turn allows the economy to grow. Without this flow, savings would sit idle in someone's safe or pocket, money would not be available to borrow, people would not be able to purchase cars or houses, and businesses would not be able to build the new factories the economy needs to produce more goods and grow. Enabling the flow of money from savers to investors is called financial intermediation, and it is extremely important to a free market economy.

BANKING INSTITUTIONS

Banking institutions include commercial banks, savings and loan associations (SLAs), savings banks, and credit unions. The major differences between these types of banks involve how they are owned and how they manage their assets and liabilities. Assets of banks are typically cash, loans, securities (bonds, but not stocks), and property in which the bank has invested. Liabilities are primarily the deposits received from the bank's customers. They are known as liabilities because they are still owned by, and can be withdrawn by, the depositors of the financial institution.

Until the early 1980s, the assets and liabilities of banks were tightly regulated. As a result, clear distinctions existed between the activities and types of services offered by these different types of banks. Although subsequent deregulation in the 1990s blurred these distinctions, differences do remain.

Commercial Banks

Commercial banks are so named because they specialize in loans to commercial and industrial businesses. Commercial banks are owned by private investors, called stockholders, or by companies called bank holding companies. The vast majority of commercial banks are owned by bank holding companies. (A holding company is a corporation that exists only to hold shares in another company.) In 1984, 62 percent of banks were owned by holding companies. In 2000, 76 percent of banks were owned by holding companies. The bank holding company form of ownership became increasingly attractive for several reasons. First, holding companies could engage in activities not permitted in the bank itself-for example, offering investment advice, underwriting securities, and engaging in other investment banking activities. But these activities were permitted in the bank if the holding company owned separate companies that offer these services.

Using the holding company form of organization, bankers could then diversify their product lines and offer services requested by their customers and provided by their European counterparts. Second, many states had laws that restricted a bank from opening branches to within a certain number of miles from the bank's main branch. By setting up a holding company, a banking firm could locate new banks around the state and therefore put branches in locations not previously available.

Commercial banks are "for profit" organizations. Their objective is to make a profit. The profits either can be paid out to bank stockholders or to the holding company in the form of dividends, or the profits can be retained to build capital (net worth). Commercial banks traditionally have the broadest variety of assets and liabilities.

Their historical specialties have been commercial lending to businesses on the asset side and checking accounts for businesses and individuals on the liability side. However, commercial banks also make consumer loans for automobiles and other consumer goods as well as real estate (mortgage) loans for both consumers and businesses.

Savings and Loan Associations

Savings and loan associations (SLAs) are usually owned by stockholders, but they can be owned by depositors as well. (If owned by depositors, they are called "mutuals.") If stock owned, the goal is to earn a profit that can either be paid out as a dividend or retained to increase capital. If owned by depositors, the objective is to earn a profit that can be used either to build capital or lower future loan rates or to raise future deposit rates for the depositor-owners. Until the early 1980s, regulations restricted SLAs to investing in real estate mortgage loans and accepting savings accounts and time deposits (savings accounts that exist for a specified period of time). As a result, historically SLAs have specialized in savings deposits and mortgage lending.

Savings Banks

Traditional savings banks, also known as mutual savings banks (MSBs), have no stockholders, and their assets are administered for the sole benefit of depositors. Earnings are paid to depositors after expenses are met and reserves are set aside to insure the deposits. During the 1980s savings banks were in a great state of flux, and many began to provide the same kinds of services as commercial banks.

Since 1982 savings banks have been permitted to convert to SLAs. SLAs also may convert to savings banks. Both SLAs and MSBs can now offer a full range of financial services, including multiple savings instruments; checking accounts; consumer, commercial, and agricultural loans; and trust and credit card services.

Credit Unions

Credit unions are not-for-profit, cooperative organizations that are owned by their members. Their goal is to minimize the rate members pay on loans and maximize the rate paid to members on deposits. Whatever surplus is earned is retained to build the capital of the credit union. Members must share a common bond. That bond is typically employment (members all work for the same employers) or geography (members all live in the same geographic area). Historically, credit unions specialized in providing automobile and other personal loans and savings deposits for their members. However, more recently credit unions have offered mortgage loans, credit card loans, and some commercial loans in addition to checking accounts and time deposits.

Credit unions, SLAs, and savings banks help encourage thriftiness by paying interest to consumers who put their money in savings deposits. Consequently, credit unions, SLAs, and savings banks are often referred to as thrift institutions.

Of the various types of banks in the United States, commercial banks account for the greatest single source of the financial industry's assets. In 2000 the 8,528 commercial banks in the United States controlled 24 percent of the financial industry's total assets. Commercial banks, however, have seen their share of financial-industry assets erode over time, as more money has shifted to money market and other mutual funds. In the mid-1990s, for example, the approximately 11,000 commercial banks then in existence controlled 27 percent of assets. In 1950 they controlled nearly 50 percent of financial assets. Savings institutions' share of financial assets has also dropped from roughly 13 percent in 1950 to 5 percent in 2000. Credit unions' share has remained fairly constant at 2 percent.

BANKING SERVICES

Commercial banks and thrifts offer various services to their customers. These services fall into three major categories: deposits, loans, and cash management services.

Deposits

There are four major types of deposits: demand deposits, savings deposits, hybrid checking/savings deposits, and time deposits. What distinguishes one type from another are the conditions under which the deposited funds may be withdrawn.

A demand deposit is a deposit that can be withdrawn on demand at any time and in any amount up to the full amount of the deposit. The most common example of a demand deposit is a checking account. Money orders and traveler's checks are also technically demand deposits. Checking accounts are also considered transaction accounts in that payments can be made to third parties-that is, to someone other than the depositor or the bank itself-via check, telephone, or other authorized transfer instruction. Checking accounts are popular because as demand deposits they provide perfect liquidity (immediate access to cash) and as transaction accounts they can be transferred to a third party as payment for goods or services. As such, they function like money.

Savings accounts pay interest to the depositor, but have no specific maturity date on which the funds need to be withdrawn or reinvested. Any amount can be withdrawn from a savings account up to the amount deposited. Under normal circumstances, customers can withdraw their money from a savings account simply by presenting their "passbook" or by using their automated teller machine (ATM) card. Savings accounts are highly liquid. They are different from demand deposits, however, because depositors cannot write checks against regular savings accounts. Savings accounts cannot be used directly as money to purchase goods or services.

The hybrid savings and checking account allows customers to earn interest on the account and write checks against the account. These are called either negotiable order of withdrawal (NOW) accounts, or money market deposit accounts, which are savings accounts that allow a maximum of three third-party transfers each month.

Time deposits are deposits on which the depositor and the bank have agreed that the money will not be withdrawn without substantial penalty to the depositor before a specific date. These are frequently called certificates of deposits (CDs). Because of a substantial early withdrawal penalty, time deposits are not as liquid as demand or savings deposits nor can depositors write checks against them. Time deposits also typically require a minimum deposit amount.

Loans

Banks and thrifts make three types of loans: commercial and industrial loans, consumer loans, and mortgage loans. Commercial and industrial loans are loans to businesses or industrial firms. These are primarily short-term working capital loans (loans to finance the purchase of material or labor) or transaction or longer-term loans (loans to purchase machines and equipment). Most commercial banks offer a variable rate on these loans, which means that the interest rate can change over the course of the loan. Whether a bank will make a loan or not depends on the credit and loan history of the borrower, the borrower's ability to make scheduled loan payments, the amount of capital the borrower has invested in the business, the condition of the economy, and the value of the collateral the borrower pledges to give the bank if the loan payments are not made.

Consumer loans are loans for consumers to purchase goods or services. There are two types of consumer loans: closed-end credit and open-end credit.

Closed-end credit loans are loans for a fixed amount of money, for a fixed period of time (usually not more than five years), and for a fixed purpose (for example, to buy a car). Most closed-end loans are called installment loans because they must be repaid in equal monthly installments. The item purchased by the consumer serves as collateral for the loan. For example, if the consumer fails to make payments on an automobile, the bank can recoup the cost of its loan by taking ownership of the car.

Open-end credit loans are loans for variable amounts of money up to a set limit. Unlike closed-end loans, open-end credit does not require a borrower to specify the purpose of the loan and the lender cannot foreclose on the loan. Credit cards are an example of open-end credit. Most open-end loans carry fixed interest rates-that is, the rate does not vary over the term of the loan. Open-end loans require no collateral, but interest rates or other penalties or fees may be charged-for example, if credit card charges are not paid in full, interest is charged, or if payment is late, a fee is charged to the borrower. Open-end credit interest rates usually exceed closed-end rates because open-end loans are not backed by collateral.

Mortgage loans or real estate loans are loans used to purchase land or buildings such as houses or factories. These are typically long-term loans and the interest rate charged can be either a variable or a fixed rate for the term of the loan, which often ranges from 15 to 30 years. The land and buildings purchased serve as the collateral for the loan.

Cash Management and Other Services

Although deposits and loans are the basic banking services provided by banks and thrifts, these institutions provide a wide variety of other services to customers. For consumers, these include check cashing, foreign currency exchange, safety deposit boxes in which consumers can store valuables, electronic wire transfer through which consumers can transfer money and securities from one financial institution to another, and credit life insurance which automatically pays off loans in the event of the borrower's death or disability.

In recent years, banks have made their services increasingly convenient through electronic banking. Electronic banking uses computers to carry out transfers of money. For example, automated teller machines (ATMs) enable bank customers to withdraw money from their checking or savings accounts by inserting an ATM card and a private electronic code into an ATM. The ATMs enable bank customers to access their money 24 hours a day and seven days a week wherever ATMs are located, including in foreign countries. Banks also offer debit cards that directly withdraw funds from a customer's account for the amount of a purchase, much like writing a check. Banks also use electronic transfers to deposit payroll checks directly into a customer's account and to automatically pay a customer's bills when they are due. Many banks also use the Internet to enable customers to pay bills, move money between accounts, and perform other banking functions.

For businesses, commercial banks also provide specialized cash management and credit enhancement services. Cash management services are designed to allow businesses to make efficient use of their cash. For example, under normal circumstances a business would sell its product to a customer and send the customer a bill. The customer would then send a check to the business, and the business would then deposit the check in the bank. The time between the date the business receives the check and deposits the check in the bank could be several days or a week. To eliminate this delay and allow the business to earn interest on its money sooner, commercial banks offer services to businesses whereby customers send checks directly to the bank, not the business. This practice is referred to as "lock box" services because the payments are mailed to a secure post office box where they are picked up by bank couriers for immediate deposit.

Another important business service performed by banks is a credit enhancement. Commercial banks back up the performance of businesses by promising to pay the debts of the business if the business itself cannot pay. This service substitutes the credit of the bank for the credit of the business. This is valuable, for example, in international trade where the exporting firm is unfamiliar with the importing firm in another country and is, therefore, reluctant to ship goods without knowing for certain that the importer will pay for them. By substituting the credit of a foreign bank known to the exporter's bank, the exporter knows payment will be made and will ship the goods. Credit enhancements are frequently called standby letters of credit or commercial letters of credit.

BENEFITS FOR THE ECONOMY

The deposit and loan services provided by banks benefit an economy in many ways. First, checking accounts, because they act like cash, make it much easier to buy goods and services and therefore help both consumers and businesses, who would find it inconvenient to carry or send through the mail huge amounts of cash. Second, loans enable consumers to improve their standard of living by borrowing money to purchase cars, houses, and other expensive consumer goods that they otherwise could not afford. Third, loans help businesses finance plant expansion and production of new goods, and therefore increase employment and economic growth. Finally, since banks want loans repaid, banks choose borrowers carefully and monitor performance of a company's managers very closely. This helps ensure that only the best projects get financed and that companies are run efficiently. This creates a healthy, efficient economy. In addition, since the owners (stockholders) of a company receiving a loan want their company to be profitable and managed efficiently, bankers act as surrogate monitors for stockholders who cannot be present on a regular basis to watch the company's managers.

The checking account services offered by banks provide an additional benefit to the economy. Because checks are widely accepted as payment for goods and services, the checking accounts offered by banks are functionally equivalent to real money-that is, currency and coin. When banks issue checking accounts they, in effect, create money without the federal government having to print more currency. Under government regulations in many countries, banks must hold a reserve of paper currency and coin equal to at least 10 percent of their checking account deposits. In the United States banks keep these reserves in their own vaults or on deposit with the U.S. government's central bank known as the Federal Reserve, or the Fed. If someone wants a $10 loan, the bank can give that person a $10 checking account with only $1 of currency in its vault. As a result U.S. banks can create at least $10 of checking account money for every $1 of real money (currency or coin) actually printed by the federal government. This arrangement, which allows extra deposit money to be created by banks, is referred to as a fractional reserve banking system.

Because banks attract large amounts of savings from depositors, banks can make many loans to many different customers in various amounts and for various maturities (dates when loans are due). Banks can thereby diversify their loans, and this in turn means that a bank is at less risk if one of its customers fails to repay a loan. The lowering of risk makes bank deposits safer for depositors. Safety encourages even more bank deposits and therefore even more loans. This flow of money from savers through banks to the ultimate borrower is called financial intermediation because money flows through an intermediary-that is, the bank.

BANKING REGULATION

Banking is one of the most heavily regulated industries in the United States, and the regulatory structure is quite complex. This owes in part to the fact that the United States has a dual banking system. A dual banking system means that banks and thrifts can be chartered and therefore regulated either by the state in which they operate or by a national chartering agency.

The Office of the Comptroller of the Currency (OCC) in the U.S. Department of Treasury is the federal chartering agency for national banks. The Office of the Comptroller of the Currency provides general supervision of national banks, including periodic bank examinations to determine compliance with rules and regulations and the soundness of bank operations. The Office of Thrift Supervision (OTS) in the Treasury Department charters national savings and loans (SLAs) and savings banks.

The agencies that insure deposits in banks and thrifts also have a role in regulating them. Almost all banks and thrifts are federally insured by the Federal Deposit Insurance Corporation (FDIC). The FDIC insures each depositor (not each separate deposit) for up to $100,000 in each bank or thrift in which the depositor has deposits and up to $250,000 for individual retirement accounts (IRAs) held in a bank or savings association. The Bank Insurance Fund (BIF) in the FDIC insures commercial bank and savings bank deposits. The Savings Association Insurance Fund (SAIF) in the FDIC insures savings and loan deposits. The National Credit Union Share Insurance Fund (NCUSIF) in the National Credit Union Administration (NCUA) insures credit union deposits.

The Federal Reserve is also responsible for regulating commercial banks that are members of the Federal Reserve System and bank holding companies. As a result, a nationally chartered, federally insured, Federal Reserve member bank is subject to the regulations of the OCC, BIF, and the Federal Reserve.

The regulatory landscape is complicated further by the fact that state banking authorities regulate state-chartered banks and frequently conduct their own examinations of state banks. To help sort out the maze of potential regulators, banks are assigned one regulator with primary responsibility for examining the bank. The primary regulator of nationally chartered banks and thrifts is the OCC. The primary regulator of state-chartered banks that belong to the Federal Reserve is the Federal Reserve. The primary regulator of state-chartered banks that are not Fed members but are FDIC insured is the FDIC, while the primary regulator of state-chartered, non-insured banks is the state.

The regulatory agencies also enforce legislation passed by the U.S. Congress. Such legislation attempts to ensure that lending institutions act fairly and that bank customers are well informed about banking services and practices. For example, the Truth-in-Lending Act (1968) and the Fair Credit and Charge Card Disclosure Act (1988) require lenders to disclose the true interest rate on loans on a uniform basis so that borrowers know the true cost of credit.

The Fair Housing Act (1968) and the Equal Credit Opportunity Act (1976) prohibit discrimination against borrowers on the basis of race, color, religion, national origin, sex, marital status, age, or receipt of public assistance. The Community Reinvestment Act (1977) requires banks, savings and loans, and savings banks to meet the credit needs of their local communities. This act was intended to prevent banks located in low-income areas from refusing loans to local residents, who were often members of minority groups. The Truth-in-Savings Act (1991) mandates uniform disclosure of the terms and conditions that banking institutions impose on their deposit accounts so that depositors know the true interest rate they receive on their deposits.

CENTRAL BANKING

Governments create central banks to perform a variety of functions. The functions actually performed vary considerably from country to country. Broadly speaking, central banks serve as the government's banker, as the banker to the banking system, and as the policymaker for monetary and financial matters. As the government's banker, the central bank can act as the repository for government receipts, as the collection agent for taxes, and as the auctioneer for government debt. It can also act as a lender to the government and as the government's advisor on financial matters. As the banker for the country's banks, the central bank can act as the repository for bank reserves, as the supervisor and regulator of banks, as the facilitator of interbank services such as check clearing and money transfers, and as a lender when banks need money to honor deposit withdrawals or other needs for liquidity.

As the country's monetary policymaker, the central bank controls the amount of credit and money available, the level of interest rates, and the exchange rate (the rate at which one nation's currency can be exchanged for another nation's). To achieve its monetary policy objectives, central bankers use a combination of policy tools. For example, the central bank may increase or decrease the amount of money (coin and currency) in circulation by buying or selling government debt instruments, such as bonds, on the open market. This policy tool is known as open market operations. Since interest rates are usually related to how much money and credit are available in the economy, the central bank can usually lower interest rates by buying bonds from the public with money. This increases the amount of money in the economy and lowers interest rates. To raise rates, the authority would sell bonds, thereby reducing the amount of money available to the public. The central bank could also cause a lowering or raising of interest rates by increasing or decreasing the amount of money banks must hold as a reserve against their deposits. By increasing reserves, the central bank forces banks to hold more money in their vaults, which means they can lend less money. Less money available for loans makes loans harder to get which, in turn, causes banks and other lenders to raise interest rates on loans.

Central banks can be either privately owned or owned by the government. In Europe, central banks are owned and operated by the government. In the United States, commercial banks own the central bank, which is called the Federal Reserve. The Federal Reserve, established in 1913, consists of a seven-person Board of Governors located in Washington, D.C., and the presidents of 12 regional Federal Reserve Banks. Each member of the Board of Governors is appointed by the U.S. president and confirmed by the U.S. Senate for staggered 14-

year terms. From among the seven governors, the president also designates and the Senate confirms a chairman of the board for a four-year term. The Federal Reserve's primary policy group is called the Federal Open Market Committee (FOMC). It consists of the seven governors plus five regional Federal Reserve Bank presidents. The FOMC is responsible for controlling the money supply and interest rates in the United States.

Because central banks control the money supply, there is always the danger that central banks will simply create more money and then lend it to the government to finance its expenditures. This often leads to excessive money creation and inflation (a continuous increase in the prices of goods), which can be caused by having too much money available to purchase goods. Inflation occurred in the United States when the government printed Continental dollars to pay for the Revolutionary War. So many were printed that they became worthless, and a popular slogan of the day was "It's not worth a Continental." The danger of inflation is particularly acute in countries where the government owns the central bank. Government ownership of the central bank is illegal in the United States, except in national emergencies. European countries agreed in the Maastricht Treaty of 1992 not to allow central banks to lend money to their governments.

BANKING IN OTHER COUNTRIES

Canada

Because of Canada's close historical relationship with the United States and the United Kingdom, development of the Canadian banking system has been influenced by both countries. Unlike the United States, however, Canada always had a branch-banking system. Until 1994 banks in the United States were restricted to opening branches only in the city or state where they were incorporated. One of the first laws passed by Canada's Parliament after confederation, in 1867, allowed any Canadian-chartered bank to operate in any part of the dominion. This law encouraged the growth of Canada's branch-banking system, in which a few large banks operate all the country's banking offices. In 2000 there were only 13 domestic banks in Canada, and the six largest controlled more than 90 percent of all bank assets in Canada. The remaining seven domestic banks accounted for about 2 percent of bank assets, and foreign banks accounted for about 7 percent of bank assets.

The largest commercial banks of Canada operate extensively in foreign countries, particularly in the West Indies, Asia, and the United States. In addition to the usual business of commercial loans, Canadian banks operating in foreign countries have specialized in investment banking and wealth-management activities. The regulator of federally chartered Canadian banks and financial institutions is the Office of the Superintendent of Financial Institutions (OSFI), which was established in 1987. Since 1967 deposit insurance has been provided by the Canada Deposit Insurance Corporation (CBIC), which insures up to $60,000 Canadian per depositor per institution. Both the OSFI and the CBIC are Crown Corporations owned by the government.

The central bank of Canada is the Bank of Canada. Created in 1935, it is owned by the Ministry of Finance and is responsible for Canadian monetary policy. Unlike the U.S. Federal Reserve, the Bank of Canada is also responsible for issuing and managing the national debt. In the United States, this function is performed by the Department of the Treasury. The primary policy group of the Bank of Canada is called the Governing Council. This group consists of the governor of the Bank of Canada, the senior deputy governor, and four deputy governors. The Bank of Canada is less independent of the government than is the U.S. Federal Reserve because it must consult with the minister of finance on policy matters.

The European Continent

Until recently, European banking was very different from banking in the United States. European banks were frequently owned by the government and could engage in activities that were prohibited to banks in the United States. Most of these prohibited activities involved investment banking such as security underwriting (selling a firm's stock or bonds at a guaranteed price) or security placement (finding buyers for a firm's stock or bonds). These services are important to businesses and being able to provide them gave European banks an advantage over U.S. banks. These differences are rapidly disappearing. Most European banks are now privately owned and recent U.S. legislation has allowed U.S. banks to engage in investment-banking activities through the bank holding company form of organization.

Two differences remain between U.S. and European banking. The first is that many European banks can own nonbank commercial and industrial businesses. Such ownership is still prohibited, for the most part, for U.S. banks and holding companies. As a result, banks in Europe tend to be more business oriented and much more involved with corporate governance (corporate decision-making) than their U.S. counterparts. This also explains why most European companies rely more heavily on bank loans to finance their activities than do U.S. companies which rely more on funds raised by selling stocks and bonds in financial markets.

The second difference is that banking is much more concentrated in Europe. In other words, banking markets are dominated by a few large banks whereas in the United States many banks compete for a customer's deposits and loans. This stems from the fact that European countries have had very liberal branching laws allowing banks to have extensive deposit-gathering networks in their home country and also from the fact that most European countries are not as concerned about monopolies as are U.S. regulators. It is not clear how long this difference will last, however, as legislation in the United States in 1994 allowed banks to establish banks and branches in other states.The establishment of the Economic and Monetary Union (EMU) in 1992 created a new banking system in Europe that parallels that of the United States in many ways. The EMU created a new European Central Bank (ECB) that will coordinate monetary policy throughout most of continental Europe. It also established a uniform currency in Europe called the euro that beginning in 2002 was the currency used throughout Western Europe, except in Denmark, Sweden, and the United Kingdom. The EMU also allowed banks to branch throughout Europe and not just in their home country.

United Kingdom

Since the 17th century Britain has been known for its prominence in banking. The capital, London, still remains a major financial center, and virtually all the world's leading commercial banks are represented there.

Aside from the central Bank of England, which was incorporated, early English banks were privately owned rather than stock-issuing firms. Bank failures were common; so in the early 19th century, stock-issuing banks, with a larger capital base, were encouraged as a means of stabilizing the industry. By 1833 these corporate banks were permitted to accept and transfer deposits in London, although they were prohibited from issuing money, a prerogative monopolized by the Bank of England. Corporate banking flourished after legislation in 1858 approved limited liability for stock-issuing banks. The banking system, however, failed to preserve the large number of institutions typical of U.S. banking. At the turn of the 20th century, a wave of bank mergers reduced both the number of private and stock-issuing banks.

The present structure of British commercial banking was substantially in place by the 1930s, with the Bank of England, then privately owned, at the apex, and 11 London clearing banks ranked below the Bank of England. Clearing banks sort and then forward checks to the bank from which they were originally drawn for payment. Two changes have occurred since then: The Bank of England was nationalized (became government-owned) in 1946 by the postwar Labour government; and in 1968 a merger among the largest five clearing banks left the industry in the hands of four: Barclays, Lloyds (now Lloyds TSB Group), Midland (now part of HSBC Holdings), and National Westminster (taken over by the Royal Bank of Scotland in 2000).

The larger clearing banks, with their national branch networks, dominate British banking. They are the key links in the transfer of business payments through the checking system, as well as the primary source of short-term business finance. Moreover, through their ownership and control over subsidiaries, the big British banks influence other financial markets such as consumer and housing finance and merchant banking. The dominance of the clearing banks was challenged in recent years by the rise of "parallel markets," encompassing financial activities by smaller banking houses, building societies (banking institutions similar to SLAs in the United States), and other financial concerns, as well as local government authorities. The major banks responded to this competition by offering new services and competitive terms.

A restructuring in the banking industry took place in the late 1970s. The Banking Act of 1979 formalized Bank of England control over the British banking system, which was previously supervised on an informal basis. Only institutions approved by the Bank of England as "recognized banks" or "licensed deposit-taking institutions" are permitted to accept deposits from the public. The act also extended Bank of England control over the new financial intermediaries that have flourished since 1960.

Developing Countries

The type of national economic system that characterizes developing countries plays a crucial role in determining the nature of the banking system in those countries. In capitalist countries a system of private enterprise in banking prevails. In state-managed economies, banks have been nationalized. Other countries have patterned themselves after the social-democracies of Europe; in Egypt, Peru, and Kenya, for instance, government-owned and privately owned banks coexist. In many countries, the banking system developed under colonialism, with banks owned by institutions in the parent country. In some, such as Zambia and Cameroon, this heritage continued, although modified, after decolonization.

In other nations, such as Nigeria and Saudi Arabia, the rise of nationalism led to mandates for majority ownership by the indigenous population. Banks in developing countries are similar to their counterparts in developed nations. Commercial banks accept and transfer deposits and are active lenders, especially for short-term purposes. Other financial intermediaries, particularly government-owned development banks, arrange long-term loans. Banks are often used to finance government expenditures. The banking system may also play a major role in financing exports.

9

International Banks and Banking

The expansion of trade in recent decades has been paralleled by the growth of multinational banking. Banks have historically financed international trade, but a notable recent development has been the expansion of branches and subsidiaries that are physically located abroad, as well as the increased volume of loans to foreign borrowers. In 1960 only eight U.S. banks had foreign offices with a total of 131 branches. By 1998 about 82 U.S. banks had about 935 foreign branches.

Similarly, the number of foreign banks with offices in the United States has increased dramatically. In 1975, 79 foreign banks were chartered in the United States, accounting for 5 percent of U.S. bank assets. In 1998, 243 foreign banks had U.S. offices, accounting for 23 percent of U.S. bank assets. Most of these banks are business-oriented banks, but some have also engaged in retail banking. In 1978 the U.S. Congress passed the International Banking Act, which imposed constraints on the activities of foreign banks in the United States, removing some of the advantages they had acquired in relation to U.S. banks.

As banks make more international loans, many experts believe that there must be greater international cooperation regarding standards and regulations to lower the risk of bank failure and international financial collapse. In 1988 the Basel Committee on Banking Supervision, an international organization of bank regulators based in Basel, Switzerland, took the first steps in this direction with the Basel Capital Accord. The accord established a global standard for assessing the financial soundness of banks and required banks to maintain a minimum ratio of capital to risky assets. Many banking experts believe this accord became the primary tool for strengthening the safety of international banking. The accord was eventually adopted by 100 countries. In 2001 the Basel Committee recommended a new set of regulations known as the New Basel Capital Accord to replace the 1988 agreement.

HISTORY OF BANKING

Origins of Banking

Many of today's banking services were first practiced in ancient Lydia, Phoenicia, China, and Greece, where trade and commerce flourished. The temples in Babylonia made loans from their treasuries as early as 2000 BC. The temples of ancient Greece served as safe-deposit vaults for the valuables of worshipers. The Greeks also coined money and developed a system of credit. The Roman Empire had a highly developed banking system, and its bankers accepted deposits of money, made loans, and purchased mortgages. Shortly after the fall of Rome in AD 476, banking declined in Europe.

The increase of trade in 13th-century Italy prompted the revival of banking. The money-changers of the Italian states developed facilities for exchanging local and foreign currency. Soon merchants demanded other services, such as lending money, and gradually bank services were expanded.

The first bank to offer most of the basic banking functions known today was the Bank of Barcelona in Spain. Founded by merchants in 1401, this bank held deposits, exchanged currency, and carried out lending operations. It also is believed to have introduced the bank check. Three other early banks, each managed by a committee of city officials, were the Bank of Amsterdam (1609), the Bank of Venice (1587), and the Bank of Hamburg (1619). These institutions laid the foundation for modern banks of deposit and transaction.

For more than 300 years, banking on the European continent was in the hands of powerful statesmen and wealthy private bankers, such as the Medici family in Florence and the Fuggers in Germany. During the 19th century, members of the Rothschild family became the most influential bankers in all Europe and probably in the world. This international banking family was founded by German financier Mayer Amschel Rothschild (1743-1812), but it soon spread to all the major European financial capitals. The Bank of France was organized in 1800 by Napoleon. The bank had become the dominant financial institution in France by the mid-1800s. In Germany, banking experienced a rapid development about the middle of the 19th century with the establishment of several strong stock-issuing, or publicly owned, banks.

Banking in the British Isles originated with the London goldsmiths of the 16th century. These men made loans and held valuables for safekeeping. By the 17th century English goldsmiths created the model for today's modern fractional reserve banking-that is, the practice of keeping a fraction of depositors' money in reserve while extending the remainder to borrowers in the form of loans. Customers deposited gold and silver with the goldsmiths for safekeeping and were given deposit receipts verifying their ownership of the gold deposited with the goldsmith. These receipts could be used as money because they were backed by gold. But the goldsmiths soon discovered that they could take a chance and issue additional receipts against the gold to other people who needed to borrow money. This worked as long as the original depositors did not withdraw all their gold at one time. Hence, the amount of receipts or claims on the gold frequently exceeded the actual amount of the gold, and the idea that bankers could create money was born.

Bank of North America

The first important bank in the United States was the Bank of North America, established in 1781 by the Second Continental Congress. It was the first bank chartered by the U.S. government. Other banks existed in the colonies prior to this, most notably the Bank of Pennsylvania, but these banks were chartered by individual states. In 1787 the Bank of North America changed to a Pennsylvania charter following controversy about the legality of a congressional charter. Other large banks were chartered in the early 1780s by the various states, primarily to issue paper money called bank notes. These notes supplemented the coins then in circulation and assisted greatly in business expansion. The banks were also permitted to accept deposits and to make loans. Because there were no minimum reserve requirements on deposits, bank notes were secured by the assets of the issuing banks. Most assets took the form of business loans. The only restraint on a bank's ability to extend loans was the public's unwillingness to accept its notes. Acceptance of a bank's notes usually was determined by the bank's record in exchanging the notes for coins when called upon to do so. Since most of them were able to do this, the early banks enjoyed wide latitude in granting loans.

In 1791 the federal government chartered the Bank of the United States, commonly referred to as the "First" Bank of the United States, to serve both the government and the public. One-fifth of the bank's capital was supplied by the federal government. The bank was a repository of government funds and a source of loans for individuals and the federal and state governments. The charter of the "First" Bank of the United States was allowed to lapse in 1811, in part because half of its stock was owned by foreigners but also because of opposition to the bank by more than 80 state-chartered banks. The main reason for the conflict between state banks and the "First" Bank of the United States was that the public preferred the notes of the Bank of the United States because of the bank's excellent reputation. This made it difficult for state banks to attract customers.

Second Bank of the United States

During the War of 1812, hard currency (coins) became scarce and many state banks stopped redeeming their notes for coins. This brought into question the underlying value of bank notes and limited their use as money. At the same time, however, banks began increasing the amount of notes they issued. This rapid increase in paper money caused prices to rise and created inflation. These developments created a demand for establishing the "Second" Bank of the United States, which was chartered in 1816. The bank had a stormy career. Many local bankers who had to compete with this government-sponsored bank opposed it, as did President Andrew Jackson. As a result of Jackson's opposition, the federal government withdrew its deposits in 1833, and three years later, when the bank's charter was not renewed, it went out of existence.

FREE BANKING AND THE SAFETY FUND SYSTEM

In 1838 New York State passed a free banking law. Before this date all incorporated banks had been chartered by states and had been granted the note-issuing privilege. Under free banking, charters could be obtained without a special act of the state legislature. The main requirement for new banks was that they post collateral of government bonds equal in value to the notes to be issued. In principle, noteholders were protected because, if the bank failed, proceeds from the sale of the collateral would be used to reimburse them. Free banking was soon adopted by other states. Because there was little regulation of new banks, many banks failed and bank fraud occurred. The free-banking years of 1837 to 1863 are also known as the Wildcat Banking era.

In New England, however, the Suffolk Bank in Boston, Massachusetts, had redeemed bank notes of out-of-town banks only if they kept on deposit amounts large enough to cover the redemptions. Since Boston was a trade center, the pressure was great on all New England banks to accept this system, known as the Suffolk banking system. Practically all New England banks had joined the system by 1825.

In the early 1800s New York State also developed the safety fund system, under which each member bank contributed a small percentage of its capital annually to a state-managed fund. The purpose of the fund was to protect noteholders in the event of bank failure. In 1842 Louisiana enacted legislation to limit the number of banks and to require them to maintain one-third of their assets in cash and two-thirds in short-term obligations.

THE NATIONAL BANKING ACT OF 1863

The Civil War (1861-1865) brought about the National Banking Act of 1863, and with it a fundamental change in the structure of commercial banking in the United States. Originally named the National Currency Act, but later amended and renamed, the National Banking Act created the system known as dual banking, in which banks could have either a state or federal charter. This system still exists in the United States. The act established the Office of the Comptroller of the Currency in the Department of the Treasury and gave it the power to issue national bank charters to any bank that met minimum requirements. The philosophy of relatively "free banking" continued until 1935 when Congress made it more difficult to obtain a bank charter. The 1863 act allowed nationally chartered banks to issue a uniform bank note backed by U.S. government bonds. The amount of the notes was not to exceed 90 percent of the value of the bonds. Officials hoped that the issuance of uniform bank notes backed by the U.S. government would guarantee the value of bank notes and thereby produce a useful nationwide currency, while also inducing state banks to take out national charters.

However, because the regulations accompanying a national charter were much stricter than state charters, a movement toward federal charters did not happen as planned. In 1865 the U.S. Congress enacted a 10 percent tax on any bank or individual paying out or using state bank notes. As a result of the tax, many banks converted to national charters, but many others simply stopped issuing their own notes. Instead, these state banks began to issue their customers demand deposit money-that is, checking accounts, instead of bank notes.

By the 1870's, deposits were well established as a substitute for paper or coin currency, and state banks experienced a revival. State charters contained several advantages over federal charters. State-chartered banks were allowed to hold lower cash reserves relative to deposits, and less capital. State-chartered banks had more flexible branching opportunities and fewer restrictions on the types of loans that could be made.

The National Banking Act was successful in correcting some failings of the pre-Civil War commercial banking system. It produced a unified national paper currency consisting primarily of national bank notes. Bank crises, however, did not disappear. Panics occurred in 1873, 1884, 1893, and 1907, although the causes of these crises varied. Between 1873 and 1907, demand deposits far outweighed bank note circulation. At times some banks were unable to make immediate payment of demands on these deposits. Consequently these banks failed, and their depositors suffered losses of all or part of the money in their accounts.

FEDERAL RESERVE ACT OF 1913

The financial panic of 1907 resulted in the Federal Reserve Act of 1913. This act went further than any earlier legislation in recognizing the importance of stable money and credit conditions to the health of the national economy. Under the Federal Reserve Act, a central bank was reestablished for the United States, the first since the "Second" Bank of the United States. The new bank was charged with maintaining sound credit conditions. To achieve this goal, the Federal Reserve System was given control over the minimum amount of reserves that member banks must hold for each dollar of deposits. It also obtained the power to lend money to member banks and regulate the types of assets they can hold. Members of the Federal Reserve System include national banks, whose membership is required, and state banks, whose membership is optional. Membership requires a bank to buy stock in the Federal Reserve System. Most large banks under state charter have joined the system. World War I (1914-1918) brought about inflation and a sharp postwar recession (economic slowdown). Although the banks had bought large quantities of U.S. government bonds during the war, they also lent large amounts of money to individuals engaged in stock market speculation. By investing in bonds, banks helped finance government expenditures during the war and the attendant expansion of American productive resources in the decade following World War I. By lending money to speculators, they became a major factor in the climb of stock prices and the wave of speculation that resulted in the crash of 1929.

BANKING DURING THE GREAT DEPRESSION

The Great Depression of the 1930s dealt a severe blow to the commercial banking industry. Many banks failed (went out of business) when their loans could not be repaid. The number of commercial banks declined from 26,000 in 1928 to about 14,000 in 1933. Total deposits in these banks declined by about 35 percent. Depositors rushed to retrieve their money, a process known as a run on the banks, and the federal government was forced to close all the banks for four days in 1933 to stem the panic. It became apparent to observers that the Federal Reserve System had not solved all the problems of bank stability.

Consequently, during the Great Depression, Congress recognized the importance of a sound banking system and created a number of agencies to restore public confidence in the banking system. Among the first of these was the Federal

Housing Administration, which was created in 1934 to insure payment on home loans made by private lending institutions. The guarantee helped preserve the value of bank loans and enabled banks to continue to lend money to home-buyers.

The Banking Act of 1933, also known as the Glass-Steagall Act, created the Federal Deposit Insurance Corporation (FDIC) to insure bank deposits, increase the confidence of depositors, and therefore prevent bank runs. Federal Reserve member banks were required to join the FDIC. Membership was optional for other banks. The Glass-Steagall Act also set interest rate ceilings on deposits to reduce competition among banks, which was considered a cause of bank failures during the Great Depression. It also prevented banks from becoming too involved in investment-banking activities, such as underwriting stocks or bonds for companies. Underwriting, which typically involves selling stocks or bonds at a guaranteed price, can be risky and can cause banks to fail. The act also prevented banks from buying stock, which is a risky activity if the stock market crashes. This prohibition on investment-banking activities lasted until the 1980s.

The banking system began to recover in 1934. By 1937 deposits had reached pre-Depression levels. During World War II (1939-1945), deposits increased rapidly and more than doubled from 1941 to 1946. For the next 40 years the U.S. banking system went through a continuous expansion and modernization. In particular, there was an enormous increase in lending to consumers, through installment loans (loans for a fixed amount repaid in equal monthly payments) and credit card loans (loans for a varied amount repaid more flexibly).

BANKING AFTER WORLD WAR II

Some of the legislation enacted during the Great Depression and in the immediate postwar period began to have negative repercussions on the banking industry by the 1970s, according to some experts. Interest ceilings on deposits, which were required by the Glass-Steagall Act, prevented banks from competing with unregulated money market funds or even bonds issued by the U.S. Treasury. As people withdrew deposits to earn higher interest elsewhere (a process known as disintermediation), SLAs found it increasingly difficult to raise funds to make mortgage loans. Many SLAs went out of business. Disintermediation was not the only problem SLAs faced, however. Many SLAs decided to venture into business lending in the early 1980s with drastic consequences as commercial real estate markets collapsed. Many business loans went bad and forced even more SLAs out of business. In 1980, 3,998 SLAs existed in the United States. By 1992 the number had dwindled to only 2,039. There were 672 SLA failures from 1989 to 1992 alone and over 1,200 overall. The SLA crisis ultimately led to the collapse of the Federal Savings and Loan Insurance Corporation. It necessitated a restructuring of deposit insurance in the United States and a government bailout of the SLA industry that cost taxpayers an estimated $200 billion.

Restrictions on how banks could expand geographically also affected the industry. The Bank Holding Company Act of 1956 prohibited bank holding companies from acquiring banks across state lines. As a result of geographic limitations on expansions, banks were forced to operate primarily in local markets, which made banks particularly susceptible to local economic downturns. This act also restricted the activities of bank holding companies, limiting them to only those activities that were closely related to banking.

Legislation enacted in the 1980s and 1990s began to address these issues. The Depository Deregulation and Monetary Control Act of 1980 eliminated ceilings on interest rates. The 1994 Riegle-Neal Interstate Banking and Branching Efficiency Act legalized interstate banking, allowing banks to diversify geographically.

The most sweeping legislation, however, took place in 1999 when Congress removed most of the remaining provisions of the Glass-Steagall Act and replaced it with the Gramm-Leach-Bliley Act, named after Republican Party sponsors Phil Gramm, Jim Leach, and Thomas Bliley, Jr. The act also removed some of the restrictions of the Bank Holding Company Act of 1956 by permitting bank holding companies to engage in the full range of financial services, including lending, deposit taking, investment advising, insurance, stock and bond underwriting, and other investment banking services. The act did not, however, allow bank holding companies to own nonfinancial businesses. Many observers believe that the new law will increase the dominance of bank holding companies and lead to the establishment of so-called universal banks that offer a full array of financial services, including traditional banking services, insurance, investment advice, and stock and bond brokerage services. Critics of the law, however, caution that the new law, combined with the provisions of the 1994 act that ended restrictions on branching and allowed nationwide banking, may ultimately diminish competition for financial services in the United States.

E-BANKING: INTRODUCTION

This booklet, one of several comprising the FFIEC Information Technology Examination Handbook (IT Handbook), provides guidance to examiners and financial institutions on identifying and controlling the risks associated with electronic banking (e-banking) activities. The booklet primarily discusses e-banking risks from the perspective of the services or products provided to customers. This approach differs from other booklets that discuss risks from the perspective of the technology and systems that support automated information processing. To avoid duplication of material, this booklet refers the reader to other IT Handbook booklets for detailed explanations of technology-specific issues or controls.

Examiners may use the examination procedures and request letter items included in this booklet in appendix A to review risks in the electronic delivery of financial products and services. These procedures address services and products of varied complexity. Examiners should adjust the procedures, as appropriate, for the scope of the examination and the risk profile of the institution. The procedures may be used independently or in combination with procedures from other IT Handbook booklets or from agency handbooks covering non-IT areas.

Definition of e-banking

For this booklet, e-banking is defined as the automated delivery of new and traditional banking products and services directly to customers through electronic, interactive communication channels. E-banking includes the systems that enable financial institution customers, individuals or businesses, to access accounts, transact business, or obtain information on financial products and services through a public or private network, including the Internet. Customers access e-banking services using an intelligent electronic device, such as a personal computer (PC), personal digital assistant (PDA), automated teller machine (ATM), kiosk, or Touch Tone telephone. While the risks and controls are similar for the various e-banking access channels, this booklet focuses specifically on Internet-based services due to the Internet's widely accessible public network. Accordingly, this booklet begins with a discussion of the two primary types of Internet websites: informational and transactional.

Informational Websites

Informational websites provide customers access to general information about the financial institution and its products or services. Risk issues examiners should consider when reviewing informational websites include:

Potential liability and consumer violations for inaccurate or incomplete information about products, services, and pricing presented on the website;

Potential access to confidential financial institution or customer information if the website is not properly isolated from the financial institution's internal network;

Potential liability for spreading viruses and other malicious code to computers communicating with the institution's website; and Negative public perception if the institution's on-line services are disrupted or if its website is defaced or otherwise presents inappropriate or offensive material.

Transactional Websites

Transactional websites provide customers with the ability to conduct transactions through the financial institution's website by initiating banking transactions or buying products and services. Banking transactions can range from something as basic as a retail account balance inquiry to a large business-to-business funds transfer. E-banking services, like those delivered through other delivery channels, are typically classified based on the type of customer they support. The following table lists some of the common retail and wholesale e-banking services offered by financial institutions.

Table : Common E-Banking Services

Retail Services	Wholesale Services
Account management	Account management
Bill payment and presentment	Cash management
New account opening	Small business loan applications, approvals, or advances
Consumer wire transfers	
Investment/Brokerage services	Commercial wire transfers
Loan application and approval	Business-to-business payments
Account aggregation	Employee benefits/pension administration

Since transactional websites typically enable the electronic exchange of confidential customer information and the transfer of funds, services provided through these websites expose a financial institution to higher risk than basic informational websites. Wholesale e-banking systems typically expose financial institutions to the highest risk per transaction, since commercial transactions usually involve larger dollar amounts. In addition to the risk issues associated with informational websites, examiners reviewing transactional e-banking services should consider the following issues:

Security controls for safeguarding customer information;

Authentication processes necessary to initially verify the identity of new customers and authenticate existing customers who access e-banking services;

Liability for unauthorized transactions;

Losses from fraud if the institution fails to verify the identity of individuals or businesses applying for new accounts or credit on-line;

Possible violations of laws or regulations pertaining to consumer privacy, anti-money laundering, anti-terrorism, or the content, timing, or delivery of required consumer disclosures; and

Negative public perception, customer dissatisfaction, and potential liability resulting from failure to process third-party payments as directed or within specified time frames, lack of availability of on-line services, or unauthorized access to confidential customer information during transmission or storage.

E-banking Components

E-banking systems can vary significantly in their configuration depending on a number of factors. Financial institutions should choose their e-banking system configuration, including outsourcing relationships, based on four factors:

Strategic objectives for e-banking;

Scope, scale, and complexity of equipment, systems, and activities;

Technology expertise; and

Security and internal control requirements.

Financial institutions may choose to support their e-banking services internally. Alternatively, financial institutions can outsource any aspect of their e-banking systems to third parties. The following entities could provide or host (i.e., allow applications to reside on their servers) e-banking-related services for financial institutions:

Another financial institution,

Internet service provider,

Internet banking software vendor or processor,

Core banking vendor or processor,

Managed security service provider,

Bill payment provider,

Credit bureau, and

Credit scoring company.

E-banking systems rely on a number of common components or processes. The following list includes many of the potential components and processes seen in a typical institution:

Website design and hosting,

Firewall configuration and management,

Intrusion detection system or IDS (network and host-based),

Network administration,

Security management,

Internet banking server,

E-commerce applications (e.g., bill payment, lending, brokerage),

Internal network servers,

Core processing system,

Programming support, and

Automated decision support systems.

These components work together to deliver e-banking services. Each component represents a control point to consider.

Through a combination of internal and outsourced solutions, management has many alternatives when determining the overall system configuration for the various components of an e-banking system. However, for the sake of simplicity, this booklet presents only two basic variations. First, one or more technology service providers can host the e-banking application and numerous network components as illustrated in the following diagram.

In this configuration, the institution's service provider hosts the institution's website, Internet banking server, firewall, and intrusion detection system. While the institution does not have to manage the daily administration of these component systems, its management and board remain responsible for the content, performance, and security of the e-banking system.

Second, the institution can host all or a large portion of its e-banking systems internally. A typical configuration for in-house hosted, e-banking services is illustrated below. In this case, a provider is not between the Internet access and the financial institution's core processing system. Thus, the institution has day-to-day responsibility for system administration.

E-banking Support Services

In addition to traditional banking products and services, financial institutions can provide a variety of services that have been designed or adapted to support e-commerce. Management should understand these services and the risks they pose to the institution. This section discusses some of the most common support services: weblinking, account aggregation, electronic authentication, website hosting, payments for e-commerce, and wireless banking activities.

Weblinking

A large number of financial institutions maintain sites on the World Wide Web. Some websites are strictly informational, while others also offer customers the ability to perform financial transactions, such as paying bills or transferring funds between accounts.

Virtually every website contains "weblinks." A weblink is a word, phrase, or image on a webpage that contains coding that will transport the viewer to a different part of the website or a completely different website by just clicking the mouse. While weblinks are a convenient and accepted tool in website design, their use can present certain risks. Generally, the primary risk posed by weblinking is that viewers can become confused about whose website they are viewing and who is responsible for the information, products, and services available through that website. There are a variety of risk management techniques institutions should consider using to mitigate these risks. These risk management techniques are for those institutions that develop and maintain their own websites, as well as institutions that use third-party service providers for this function. The agencies have issued guidance on weblinking that provides details on risks and risk management techniques financial institutions should consider.

Account Aggregation

Account aggregation is a service that gathers information from many websites, presents that information to the customer in a consolidated format, and, in some cases, may allow the customer to initiate activity on the aggregated accounts. The information gathered or aggregated can range from publicly available information to personal account information (e.g., credit card, brokerage, and banking data). Aggregation services can improve customer convenience by avoiding multiple log-ins and providing access to tools that help customers analyze and manage their various account portfolios. Some aggregators use the customer-provided user IDs and passwords to sign in as the customer. Once the customer's account is accessed, the aggregator copies the personal account information from the website for representation on the aggregator's site (i.e., "screen scraping"). Other aggregators use direct data-feed arrangements with website operators or other firms to obtain the customer's information. Generally, direct data feeds are thought to provide greater legal protection to the aggregator than does screen scraping. Financial institutions are involved in account aggregation both as aggregators and as aggregation targets. Risk management issues examiners should consider when reviewing aggregation services include:

Protection of customer passwords and user IDs-both those used to access the institution's aggregation services and those the aggregator uses to retrieve customer information from aggregated third parties-to assure the confidentiality of customer information and to prevent unauthorized activity,

Disclosure of potential customer liability if customers share their authentication information (i.e., IDs and passwords) with third parties, and

Assurance of the accuracy and completeness of information retrieved from the aggregated parties' sites, including required disclosures Additional information regarding management of risks in aggregation services can be found in appendix D.

Electronic Authentication

Verifying the identities of customers and authorizing e-banking activities are integral parts of e-banking financial services. Since traditional paper-based and in-person identity authentication methods reduce the speed and efficiency of electronic transactions, financial institutions have adopted alternative authentication methods, including:

Passwords and personal identification numbers (PINs),

Digital certificates using a public key infrastructure (PKI),

Microchip-based devices such as smart cards or other types of tokens,

Database comparisons (e.g., fraud-screening applications), and

Biometric identifiers.

The authentication methods listed above vary in the level of security and reliability they provide and in the cost and complexity of their underlying infrastructures. As such, the choice of which technique(s) to use should be commensurate with the risks in the products and services for which they control access. Additional information on customer authentication techniques can be found in this booklet under the heading "Authenticating E-Banking Customers."

The Electronic Signatures in Global and National Commerce (E-Sign) Act establishes some uniform federal rules concerning the legal status of electronic signatures and records in commercial and consumer transactions so as to provide more legal certainty and promote the growth of electronic commerce. The development of secure digital signatures continues to evolve with some financial institutions either acting as the certification authority for digital signatures or providing repository services for digital certificates.

Website Hosting

Some financial institutions host websites for both themselves as well as for other businesses. Financial institutions that host a business customer's website usually store, or arrange for the storage of, the electronic files that make up the website. These files are stored on one or more servers that may be located on the hosting financial institution's premises. Website hosting services require strong skills in networking, security, and programming. The technology and software change rapidly. Institutions developing websites should monitor the need to adopt new interoperability standards and protocols such as Extensible Mark-Up Language (XML) to facilitate data exchange among the diverse population of Internet users.

Risk issues examiners should consider when reviewing website hosting services include damage to reputation, loss of customers, or potential liability resulting from:

Downtime (i.e., times when website is not available) or inability to meet service levels specified in the contract,

Inaccurate website content (e.g., products, pricing) resulting from actions of the institution's staff or unauthorized changes by third parties (e.g., hackers),

Unauthorized disclosure of confidential information stemming from security breaches, and

Damage to computer systems of website visitors due to malicious code (e.g., virus, worm, active content) spread through institution-hosted sites.

Payments for E-commerce

Many businesses accept various forms of electronic payments for their products and services. Financial institutions play an important role in electronic payment systems by creating and distributing a variety of electronic payment instruments, accepting a similar variety of instruments, processing those payments, and participating in clearing and settlement systems. However, increasingly, financial institutions are competing with third parties to provide support services for e-commerce payment systems. Among the electronic payments mechanisms that financial institutions provide for e-commerce are automated clearing house (ACH) debits and credits through the Internet, electronic bill payment and presentment, electronic checks, e-mail money, and electronic credit card payments. Additional information on payments systems can be found in other sections of the IT Handbook.

Most financial institutions permit intrabank transfers between a customer's accounts as part of their basic transactional e-banking services. However, third-party transfers-with their heightened risk for fraud-often require additional security safeguards in the form of additional authentication and payment confirmation.

Bill Payment and Presentment

Bill payment services permit customers to electronically instruct their financial institution to transfer funds to a business's account at some future specified date. Customers can make payments on a one-time or recurring basis, with fees typically assessed as a "per item" or monthly charge. In response to the customer's electronic payment instructions, the financial institution (or its bill payment provider) generates an electronic transaction-usually an automated clearinghouse (ACH) credit-or mails a paper check to the business on the customer's behalf. To allow for the possibility of a paper-based transfer, financial institutions typically advise customers to make payments effective 3-7 days before the bill's due date.

Internet-based cash management is the commercial version of retail bill payment. Business customers use the system to initiate third-party payments or to transfer money between company accounts. Cash management services also include minimum balance maintenance, recurring transfers between accounts and on-line account reconciliation. Businesses typically require stronger controls, including the ability to administer security and transaction controls among several users within the business.

This booklet discusses the front-end controls related to the initiation, storage, and transmission of bill payment transactions prior to their entry into the industry's retail payment systems (e.g., ACH, check processing, etc.). The IT Handbook's "Retail Payments Systems Booklet" provides additional information regarding the various electronic transactions that comprise the back end for bill payment processing.

The extent of front-end operating controls directly under the financial institution's control varies with the system configuration. Some examples of typical configurations are listed below in order of increasing complexity, along with potential control considerations.

Financial institutions that do not provide bill payment services, but may direct customers to select from several unaffiliated bill payment providers.

Caution customers regarding security and privacy issues through the use of on-line disclosures or, more conservatively, e-banking agreements.

Financial institutions that rely on a third-party bill payment provider including Internet banking providers that subcontract to third parties.

Set dollar and volume thresholds and review bill payment transactions for suspicious activity.

Gain independent audit assurance over the bill payment provider's processing controls.

Restrict employees' administrative access to ensure that the internal controls limiting their capabilities to originate, modify, or delete bill payment transactions are at least as strong as those applicable to the underlying retail payment system ultimately transmitting the transaction.

Restrict by vendor contract and identify the use of any subcontractors associated with the bill payment application to ensure adequate oversight of underlying bill payment system performance and availability.

Evaluate the adequacy of authentication methods given the higher risk associated with funds transfer capabilities rather than with basic account access.

Consider the additional guidance contained in the IT Handbook's "Information Security," "Retail Payment Systems," and "Outsourcing Technology Services" booklets.

Financial institutions that use third-party software to host a bill payment application internally.

Determine the extent of any independent assessments or certification of the security of application source code.

Ensure software is adequately tested prior to installation on the live system.

Ensure vendor access for software maintenance is controlled and monitored.

Financial institutions that develop, maintain, and host their own bill payment system.

Consider additional guidance in the IT Handbook's "Development and Acquisition Booklet."

Financial institutions can offer bill payment as a stand-alone service or in combination with bill presentment. Bill presentment arrangements permit a business to submit a customer's bill in electronic form to the customer's financial institution. Customers can view their bills by clicking on links on their account's e-banking screen or menu. After viewing a bill, the customer can initiate bill payment instructions or elect to pay the bill through a different payment channel.

In addition, some businesses have begun offering electronic bill presentment directly from their own websites rather than through links on the e-banking screens of a financial institution. Under such arrangements, customers can log on to the business's website to view their periodic bills. Then, if so desired, they can electronically authorize the business to "take" the payment from their account.

The payment then occurs as an ACH debit originated by the business's financial institution as compared to the ACH credit originated by the customer's financial institution in the bill payment scenario described above. Institutions should ensure proper approval of businesses allowed to use ACH payment technology to initiate payments from customer accounts.

Cash management applications would include the same control considerations described above, but the institution should consider additional controls because of the higher risk associated with commercial transactions. The adequacy of authentication methods becomes a higher priority and requires greater assurance due to the larger average dollar size of transactions. Institutions should also establish additional controls to ensure binding agreements-consistent with any existing ACH or wire transfer agreements-exist with commercial customers. Additionally, cash management systems should provide adequate security administration capabilities to enable the business owners to restrict access rights and dollar limits associated with multiple-user access to their accounts.

Person-to-Person Payments

Electronic person-to-person payments, also known as e-mail money, permit consumers to send "money" to any person or business with an e-mail address. Under this scenario, a consumer electronically instructs the person-to-person payment service to transfer funds to another individual. The payment service then sends an e-mail notifying the individual that the funds are available and informs him or her of the methods available to access the funds including requesting a check, transferring the funds to an account at an insured financial institution, or retransmitting the funds to someone else. Person-to-person payments are typically funded by credit card charges or by an ACH transfer from the consumer's account at a financial institution. Since neither the payee nor the payer in the transaction has to have an account with the payment service, such services may be offered by an insured financial institution, but are frequently offered by other businesses as well.

Some of the risk issues examiners should consider when reviewing bill payment, presentment, and e-mail money services include:

Potential liability for late payments due to service disruptions,

Liability for bill payment instructions originating from someone other than the deposit account holder,

Losses from person-to-person payments funded by transfers from credit cards or deposit accounts over which the payee does not have signature authority,

Losses from employee misappropriation of funds held pending access instructions from the payer, and

Potential liability directing payment availability information to the wrong e-mail or for releasing funds in response to e-mail from someone other than the intended payee.

Wireless E-banking

Wireless banking is a delivery channel that can extend the reach and enhance the convenience of Internet banking products and services. Wireless banking occurs when customers access a financial institution's network(s) using cellular phones, pagers, and personal digital assistants (or similar devices) through telecommunication companies' wireless networks. Wireless banking services in the United States typically supplement a financial institution's e-banking products and services.

Wireless devices have limitations that increase the security risks of wireless-based transactions and that may adversely affect customer acceptance rates. Device limitations include reduced processing speeds, limited battery life, smaller screen sizes, different data entry formats, and limited capabilities to transfer stored records.

These limitations combine to make the most recognized Internet language, Hypertext Markup Language (HTML), ineffective for delivering content to wireless devices. Wireless Markup Language (WML) has emerged as one of a few common language standards for developing wireless device content. Wireless Application Protocol (WAP) has emerged as a data transmission standard to deliver WML content.

Manufacturers of wireless devices are working to improve device usability and to take advantage of enhanced "third-generation" (3G) services. Device improvements are anticipated to include bigger screens, color displays, voice recognition applications, location identification technology (e.g., Federal Communications Commission (FCC) Enhanced 911), and increased battery capacity. These improvements are geared towards increasing customer acceptance and usage. Increased communication speeds and improvements in devices during the next few years should lead to continued increases in wireless subscriptions.

As institutions begin to offer wireless banking services to customers, they should consider the risks and necessary risk management controls to address security, authentication, and compliance issues.

10

Bank Operations in India

INTRODUCTION

The Indian banking can be broadly categorized into nationalized (government owned), private banks and specialized banking institutions. The Reserve Bank of India acts a centralized body monitoring any discrepancies and shortcoming in the system. Since the nationalization of banks in 1969, the public sector banks or the nationalized banks have acquired a place of prominence and has since then seen tremendous progress. The need to become highly customer focused has forced the slow-moving public sector banks to adopt a fast track approach.

The unleashing of products and services through the net has galvanized players at all levels of the banking and financial institutions market grid to look anew at their existing portfolio offering. Conservative banking practices allowed Indian banks to be insulated partially from the Asian currency crisis. Indian banks are now quoting al higher valuation when compared to banks in other Asian countries (viz. Hong Kong, Singapore, Philippines etc.) that have major problems linked to huge Non Performing Assets (NPAs) and payment defaults. Co-operative banks are nimble footed in approach and armed with efficient branch networks focus primarily on the 'high revenue' niche retail segments.

The Indian banking has finally worked up to the competitive dynamics of the 'new' Indian market and is addressing the relevant issues to take on the multifarious challenges of globalization. Banks that employ IT solutions are perceived to be 'futuristic' and proactive players capable of meeting the multifarious requirements of the large customers base. Private banks have been fast on the uptake and are reorienting their strategies using the internet as a medium The Internet has emerged as the new and challenging frontier of marketing with the conventional physical world tenets being just as applicable like in any other marketing medium.

The Indian banking has come from a long way from being a sleepy business institution to a highly proactive and dynamic entity. This transformation has been largely brought about by the large dose of liberalization and economic reforms that allowed banks to explore new business opportunities rather than generating revenues from conventional streams (i.e. borrowing and lending). The banking in India is highly fragmented with 30 banking units contributing to almost 50% of deposits and 60% of advances. Indian nationalized banks (banks owned by the government) continue to be the major lenders in the economy due to their sheer size and penetrative networks which assures them high deposit mobilization. The Indian banking can be broadly categorized into nationalized, private banks and specialized banking institutions.

The Reserve Bank of India act as a centralized body monitoring any discrepancies and shortcoming in the system. It is the foremost monitoring body in the Indian financial sector. The nationalized banks (i.e. government-owned banks) continue to dominate the Indian banking arena. Industry estimates indicate that out of 274 commercial banks operating in India, 223 banks are in the public sector and 51 are in the private sector. The private sector bank grid also includes 24 foreign banks that have started their operations here. Under the ambit of the nationalized banks come the specialized banking institutions. These co-operatives, rural banks focus on areas of agriculture, rural development etc.,

Capital Market

Stock market volatility touches every participant directly/ indirectly in the capital market. General feeling is that the stock markets worldwide have become very fragile in the recent past on account of various developments such as Asian crisis. Brazil Real fall and Russian debacle. Many far-reaching stock reforms have been introduced in the Indian market for the last few years. These reforms, in turn, changed market structure. Changing market structure influences nature of stock price behavior.

Primary Securities Market

The primary capital market (PCM) plays an important role in the overall functioning of securities market. Despite several measures the primary market remained lackluster till recently and the pick up is gradual. According to the SEBI annual report fewer number of issues accessed the primary market during the year and the significantly lower than that of the Previous financial year. Share of the equity issues, in terms of number and amount Mobilized, however, was higher in this financial year compared to the previous one. More than three-fourths of the total amount was occupied second and no resources were in the previous years, banks and financial institutions continued for 84.5% of the resourced mobilized compared to 68.1% in 2001-02. All other industries shared the remaining portion.

Capital Raised During 2002-03

During the financial year 2002-03, primary market witnessed a decrease of 46.0% in the amount raised and also a decrease of 25.7% in the number of issues launched compared to the same period in 2001-02. A total of 26 issues (14 public issues and 12 rights issues) opened during the financial year 2002-03 raising Rs. 4070.29 crore (Rs. 3638.6 crore through public issues and 431.6 crore through rights issues). In 2001-02 a total of 35 issues opened for raising Rs. 7543.0 crore (20 public issues-Rs. 6501.8 crore and 15 rights issues-Rs. 1041.2).

Industry Wise Capital Mobilization

Three industries viz. Banks/Fls, Engineering and Telecommunications accounted for 93.2 per cent of the resourced mobilized in 2001-02. In the current year, the same three industries accounted for 84.7 per cent of the funds raised. With the banks and Fls, increasing their share from 68.3 per cent to 84.5 per cent and companies in the Telecommunications sector and raising any resourced. In 2002-03 the three industries which accounted for 95.3 per cent of the resources where Banking/Fls, Information Technology, Paper and Pulp.

SECONDARY MARKET

During 2002-03, performance of Indian Stock market was, by and large, a lackluster one, S&P CNX NIFTY and BSE Sensex both registered

Duration

In exercise of the powers conferred under Section 5 of The Foreign Trade (Development and Regulation Act), 1992 (No. 22 of 1992), the Central Government hereby notifies the Export and Import Policy for the period 2002-2007. This Policy shall come into force with effect from 1st April, 2002 and shall remain in force upto 31st March, 2007 and will be co-terminus with the Tenth Five Year Plan (2002-2007). However, the Central Government reserves the right in public interest to make any amendments to this Policy in exercise of the powers conferred by Section-5 of the Act. Such amendment shall be made by means of a Notification published in the Gazette of India.

Transitional Arrangements

Any Notifications made or Public Notices issued or anything done under the previous Export/Import policies, and in force immediately before the commencement of this Policy shall, in so far as they are not inconsistent with the provisions of this Policy, continue to be in force and shall be deemed to have been made, issued or done under this Policy. Licence/certificate/ permissions issued before the commencement of this Policy shall continue to be valid for the purpose for which such licence/ certificate/permission was issued unless otherwise stipulated.

In case an export or import that is permitted freely under this Policy is subsequently subjected to any restriction or regulation, such export or import will ordinarily be permitted notwithstanding such restriction or regulation, unless otherwise stipulated, provided that the shipment of the export or import is made within the original validity of the irrevocable letter of credit established before the date of imposition of such restriction

FOREIGN TRADE POLICY

Objectives

Trade is not an end in itself, but a means to economic growth and national development. The primary purpose is not the mere earning of foreign exchange, but the stimulation of greater economic activity. The Foreign Trade Policy is rooted in this belief and built around two major objectives. These are:

(i) To double our percentage share of global merchandise trade within the next five years; and

(ii) To act as an effective instrument of economic growth by giving a thrust to employment generation.

Strategy

These objectives are proposed to be achieved by adopting, among others, the following strategies:

(i) Unshackling of controls and creating an atmosphere of trust and transparency to unleash the innate entrepreneurship of our businessmen, industrialists and traders.

(ii) Simplifying procedures and bringing down transaction costs.

(iii) Neutralizing incidence of all levies and duties on inputs used in export products, based on the fundamental principle that duties and levies should not be exported.

(iv) Facilitating development of India as a global hub for manufacturing, trading and services.

(v) Identifying and nurturing special focus areas which would generate additional employment opportunities, particularly in semi-urban and rural areas, and developing a series of 'Initiatives' for each of these.

(vi) Facilitating technological and infrastructural upgradation of all the sectors of the Indian economy, especially through import of capital goods and equipment, thereby increasing value addition and productivity, while attaining internationally accepted standards of quality.

(vii) Avoiding inverted duty structures and ensuring that our domestic sectors are not disadvantaged in the Free Trade Agreements/Regional Trade Agreements/ Preferential Trade Agreements that we enter into in order to enhance our exports.

(viii) Upgrading our infrastructural network, both physical and virtual, related to the entire Foreign Trade chain, to international standards.

(ix) Revitalising the Board of Trade by redefining its role, giving it due recognition and inducting experts on Trade Policy.

(x) Activating our Embassies as key players in our export strategy and linking our Commercial Wings abroad through an electronic platform for real time trade intelligence and enquiry dissemination.

Partenership

The new Policy envisages merchant exporters and manufacturer exporters, business and industry as partners of Government in the achievement of its stated objectives and goals. Prolonged and unnecessary litigation vitiates the premise of partnership. In order to obviate the need for litigation and nurture a constructive and conducive atmosphere, a suitable Grievance Redressal Mechanism will be established which, it is hoped, would substantially reduce litigation and further a relationship of partnership.

The dynamics of a liberalized trading system sometimes results in injury caused to domestic industry on account of dumping. When this happens, effective measures to redress such injury will be taken.

Roadmap

This Policy is essentially a roadmap for the development of India's foreign trade. It contains the basic principles and points the direction in which we propose to go. By virtue of its very dynamics, a trade policy cannot be fully comprehensive in all its details. It would naturally require modification from time to time. We propose to do this through continuous updation, based on the inevitable changing dynamics of international trade. It is in partnership with business and industry that we propose to erect milestones on this roadmap.

FUNCTIONS OF COMMERCIAL BANKING

A commercial bank is a type of financial intermediary and a type of bank. Commercial bank has two possible meanings:

- Commercial bank is the term used for a normal bank to distinguish it from an investment bank.

  This is what people normally call a "bank". The term "commercial" was used to distinguish it from an investment bank. Since the two types of banks no longer have to be separate companies, some have used the term "commercial bank" to refer to banks which focus mainly on companies. In some English-speaking countries outside North America, the term "trading bank" was and is used to denote a commercial bank. (After the great depression, the U.S. Congress required that banks only engage in banking activities, whereas investment banks were limited to capital markets activities. This separation is no longer mandatory.)

It raises funds by collecting deposits from businesses and consumers via checkable deposits, savings deposits, and time (or term) deposits. It makes loans to businesses and consumers. It also buys corporate bonds and government bonds. Its primary liabilities are deposits and primary assets are loans and bonds.

- Commercial banking can also refer to a bank or a division of a bank that mostly deals with deposits and loans from corporations or large businesses, as opposed to normal individual members of the public (retail banking).

WHAT ARE CENTRAL BANKS?

The central bank has been described as "the lender of last resort", which means that it is responsible for providing its economy with funds when commercial banks cannot cover a supply shortage. In other words, the central bank prevents the country's banking system from failing. However, the primary goal of central banks is to provide their countries' currencies with price stability by controlling inflation. A central bank also acts as the regulatory authority of a country's monetary policy and is the sole provider and printer of notes and coins in circulation. Time has proven that the central bank can best function in these capacities by remaining independent from government fiscal policy and therefore uninfluenced by the political concerns of any regime. The central bank should also be completely divested of any commercial banking interests.

The Rise of the Central Bank

Today the central bank is government owned but separate from the country's ministry of finance. Although the central bank is frequently termed the "government's bank" because it handles the buying and selling of government bonds and other instruments, political decisions should not influence central bank operations. Of course, the nature of the relationship between the central bank and the ruling regime varies from country to country and continues to evolve with time. To ensure the stability of a country's currency, the central bank should be the regulator and authority in the banking and monetary systems. Historically, the role of the central bank has been growing, some may argue, since the establishment of the Bank of England in 1694. It is, however, generally agreed upon that the concept of the modern central bank did not appear until the 20th century as problems developed in the commercial banking system. Thus, the central bank's modern function emerged in response to an already present commercial banking structure.

Between 1870 and 1914, when world currencies were pegged to the gold standard (GS), maintaining price stability was a lot easier because the amount of gold available was limited. Consequently, monetary expansion could not occur simply from a political decision to print more money, so inflation was easier to control. The central bank at that time was primarily responsible for maintaining the convertibility of gold into currency; it issued notes based on a country's reserves of gold.

At the outbreak of WWI, the GS was abandoned, and it came apparent that, in times of crisis, governments, facing budget deficits (because it costs money to wage war) and needing greater resources, will order the printing of more money. As governments did so, they encountered inflation. After WWI, many governments opted to go back to the GS to try to stabilize their economies. With this rose the awareness of the importance of the central bank's independence from the political machine.

During the unsettling times of the Great Depression and the aftermath of WWII, world governments predominantly favored a return to a central bank dependent on the political decision making process. This view emerged mostly from the need to establish control over war-shattered economies; furthermore, countries with newly-acquired independence opted to keep control over all aspects of their countries-a backlash against colonialism.

The rise of managed economies in the Eastern Bloc was also responsible for increased government interference in the macroeconomy. Soon after the effects of WWII, however, the independence of the central bank from the government came back into fashion in Western economies and has prevailed as the optimal way to achieve a liberal and stable economic regime.

HOW THE BANK INFLUENCES AN ECONOMY

A central bank can be said to have two main kinds of functions: (1) macroeconomic when regulating inflation and price stability and (2) microeconomic when functioning as a lender of last resort.

Macroeconomic Influences

As it is responsible for price stability, the central bank must regulate the level of inflation by controlling money supplies by means of monetary policy. The central bank performs open market transactions that either inject the market with liquidity or absorb extra funds, directly affecting the level of inflation. To increase the amount of money in circulation and decrease the interest rate (cost) for borrowing, the central bank can buy government bonds, bills, or other government-issued notes. This buying can, however, also lead to higher inflation. When it needs to absorb money to reduce inflation, the central bank will sell government bonds on the open market, which increases the interest rate and discourages borrowing. Open market operations are the key means by which a central bank controls inflation, money supply, and price stability.

Microeconomic Influences

The establishment of central banks as lender of last resort has pushed the need for their freedom from commercial banking. A commercial bank offers funds to clients on a first come, first serve basis. If the commercial bank does not have enough liquidity to meet its clients' demands (commercial banks typically do not hold reserves equal to the needs of the entire market), the commercial bank can turn to the central bank to borrow additional funds.

This provides the system with stability in an objective way; central banks cannot favor any particular commercial bank. As such, many central banks will hold commercial-bank reserves that are based on a ratio of each commercial bank's deposits. Thus, a central bank may require all commercial banks to keep, for example, a 1:10 reserve/deposit ratio. Enforcing a policy of commercial bank reserves functions as another means to control money supply in the market. Not all central banks, however, require commercial banks to deposit reserves. The United Kingdom, for example, does not have this policy while the United States does.

The rate at which commercial banks and other lending facilities can borrow short-term funds from the central bank is called the discount rate (which is set by the central bank and provides a base rate for interest rates). It has been argued that, for open market transactions to become more efficient, the discount rate should keep the banks from perpetual borrowing, which would disrupt the market's money supply and the central bank's monetary policy. By borrowing too much, the commercial bank will be circulating more money in the system. Use of the discount rate can be restricted by making it unattractive when used repeatedly.

Transitional Economies

Today developing economies are faced with issues such as the transition from managed to free market economies. The main concern is often controlling inflation. This can lead to the creation of an independent central bank but can take some time, given that many developing nations maintain control over their economies in an effort to retain control of their power. But government intervention, whether direct or indirect through fiscal policy, can stunt central bank development.

Unfortunately, many developing nations are faced with civil disorder or war, which can force a government to divert funds away from the development of the economy as a whole. Nonetheless, one factor that seems to be confirmed is that, for a market economy to develop, a stable currency (whether achieved through a fixed or floating exchange rate) is needed. However, the central banks in both industrial and emerging economies are dynamic because there is no guaranteed way to run an economy regardless of its stage of development.

BANKING IN INDIA

Banking in India originated in the first decade of 18th century with The General Bank of India coming into existence in 1786. This was followed by Bank of Hindustan. Both these banks are now defunct.

The oldest bank in existence in India is the State Bank of India being established as "The Bank of Bengal" in Calcutta in June 1806. A couple of decades later, foreign banks like Credit Lyonnais started their Calcutta operations in the 1850s. At that point of time, Calcutta was the most active trading port, mainly due to the trade of the British Empire, and due to which banking activity took roots there and prospered. The first fully Indian owned bank was the Allahabad Bank, which was established in 1865.

By the 1900s, the market expanded with the establishment of banks such as Punjab National Bank, in 1895 in Lahore and Bank of India, in 1906, in Mumbai-both of which were founded under private ownership. The Reserve Bank of India formally took on the responsibility of regulating the Indian banking sector from 1935. After India's independence in 1947, the Reserve Bank was nationalized and given broader powers.

Nationalisation

The next significant milestone in Indian Banking occurred on July 19, 1969 when the then Indira Gandhi government nationalized the 14 largest commercial banks. A second nationalization of 6 more commercial banks followed in 1980. The stated reason for the nationalisation was to give the government more control of credit delivery. After this, until the 1990s, the nationalised banks grew at a leisurely pace of around 4%, closer to the average growth rate of the Indian economy.

Liberalisation

In the early 1990s the then Narasimha Rao government embarked on a policy of liberalisation and gave licences to a small number of private banks, which came to be known as New Generation tech-savvy banks, which included banks such as UTI Bank (the first of such new generation banks to be set up), ICICI Bank and HDFC Bank. This move, along with the rapid growth in the economy of India, kickstarted the banking sector in India, which has seen rapid growth with strong contribution from all the three sectors of banks, namely, government banks, private banks and foreign banks.

The next stage for the Indian banking has been setup with the proposed relaxation in the norms for Foreign Direct Investment, where all Foreign Investors in banks may be given voting rights which could exceed the present cap of 10%.

The new policy shook the Banking sector in India completely. Bankers, till this time, were used to the 4-6-4 method (Borrow at 4%; Lend at 6%; Go home at 4) of functioning. The new wave ushered in a modern outlook and tech-savvy methods of working for traditional banks. All this led to the retail boom in India. People not just demanded more from their banks but also received more.

CURRENT SCENARIO

Public Sector Banks

SBI Group: State Bank of India, with its seven associate banks command the largest banking resources in India. SBI and its associate banks are:

- State Bank of India
- State Bank of Bikaner & Jaipur
- State Bank of Hyderabad
- State Bank of Indore
- State Bank of Mysore
- State Bank of Patiala
- State Bank of Saurashtra
- State Bank of Travancore

After the amalgamation of New Bank of India with Punjab National Bank, currently there are 19 nationalised banks in India:

- Allahabad Bank
- Andhra Bank
- Bank of Baroda
- Bank of India
- Bank of Maharashtra
- Canara Bank

- Central Bank of India
- Corporation Bank
- Dena Bank
- Indian Bank
- Indian Overseas Bank
- Oriental Bank of Commerce
- Punjab & Sind Bank
- Punjab National Bank
- Syndicate Bank
- Union Bank of India
- United Bank of India
- UCO Bank
- Vijaya Bank

Private Sector Banks

- Bank of Rajasthan
- Bharat Overseas Bank
- Catholic Syrian Bank
- Centurion Bank of Punjab
- Dhanalakshmi Bank
- Federal Bank
- HDFC Bank
- ICICI Bank
- IDBI Bank
- IndusInd Bank
- ING Vysya Bank
- Jammu & Kashmir Bank
- Karnataka Bank
- Karur Vysya Bank
- Kotak Mahindra Bank
- SBI Commercial and International Bank
- South Indian Bank
- Tamilnad Mercantile Bank Ltd.
- UTI Bank
- YES Bank

Foreign Banks

- ABN AMRO BANK N.V.
- Abu Dhabi Commercial Bank Ltd
- Bank of Ceylon
- BNP Paribas Bank
- Citibank
- China Trust Commercial Bank
- Deutsche Bank
- HSBC
- JPMorgan Chase Bank
- Standard Chartered Bank
- Scotia Bank
- Taib Bank

Currently (2007), overall, banking in India is considered as fairly mature in terms of supply, product range and reach-even though reach in rural India still remains a challenge for the private sector and foreign banks. Even in terms of quality of assets and capital adequacy, Indian banks are considered to have clean, strong and transparent balance sheets-as compared to other banks in comparable economies in its region. The Reserve Bank of India is an autonomous body, with minimal pressure from the government. The stated policy of the Bank on the Indian Rupee is to manage volatility-without any stated exchange rate-and this has mostly been true.

With the growth in the Indian economy expected to be strong for quite some time-especially in its services sector, the demand for banking services-especially retail banking, mortgages and investment services are expected to be strong. M&As, takeovers, asset sales and much more action (as it is unravelling in China) will happen on this front in India.

In March 2006, the Reserve Bank of India allowed Warburg Pincus to increase its stake in Kotak Mahindra Bank (a private sector bank) to 10%. This is the first time an investor has been allowed to hold more than 5% in a private sector bank since the RBI announced norms in 2005 that any stake exceeding 5% in the private sector banks would need to be vetted by them. Currently, India has 88 scheduled commercial banks (SCBs)-

28 public sector banks (that is with the Government of India holding a stake), 29 private banks (these do not have government stake; they may be publicly listed and traded on stock exchanges) and 31 foreign banks. They have a combined network of over 53,000 branches and 17,000 ATMs. According to a report by ICRA Limited, a rating agency, the public sector banks hold over 75 percent of total assets of the banking industry, with the private and foreign banks holding 18.2% and 6.5% respectively.

DIRECT FINANCE PAYMENT

Definition

Direct Finance Payment refers to payment service where the finance authority issues payment instruction according to fund application by eligible department and ICBC pays the fund directly to the payee account through the treasury's single account system according to the payment instruction.

Products' Target Client

The service mainly serves the finance authorities at each level included in the treasury centralized payment reform and is applicable for the wage expenditure, project procurement, and goods and service procurement of the budgeting units.

Features and Strengths

Large Business Network

ICBC not only has large number of Business Offices in wide distribution, but also possess the largest customer group in the domestic banking sector. It has shaped the banking competitive advantage of highest ratio for efficient fund allocation within system and lowest ratio for cross-bank payment.

Advanced Payment System

All transactions are centralized in one data center for processing. The fund is linked to accounting entries, which effectively prevents the criminal attempts by internal and external personnel taking advantage of time lag between fund activities and accounting entries. The leading "Bank-Finance Link" system in the sector synchronizes the fund flow and information flow. The transaction information is transmitted through encrypted mode. The system achieved the electronic

State treasury fund payment clearing, standardized information transmission, and informationalized reporting system management. The system makes ICBC at the leadership position in China in terms of agency State treasury centralized payment service. Therefore, ICBC is capable to promptly respond to the variety of large batch, inter-region, and inter-bank fund payment requests from the finance authorities and budgeting units.

Diversified Information Feedback Platform

In response to the special requirement by finance authority centralized payment service, ICBC launched automated processing for fund settlement, accounting, information transmission, and reporting. It realized real-time enquiry, collection and sorting, and summary and analysis of information and ensured timely, accurate, and secure feedbacks to the finance authorities and budgeting units at each level. Furthermore, ICBC takes full advantage of its IT and electronic service and makes use of special-line networking, Internet Banking, and other channels to break through the limitation of Business Offices and the business hours. It provides a 24-7 electronic real-time enquiry system for the finance authorities and budgeting units at each level and provides multi-function, convenient and prompt, and safe and reliable electronic enquiry service.

Service Channels

"Bank-Finance Link" system.

Application Condition

The finance authorities at each level that are included in the Treasury centralized payment reform are eligible to apply for direct payment services.

Service Procedure

(I) As per finance authority's notification, ICBC opens the zero-balance account for direct payment and Treasury single account clearing.

(II) The finance authority issues Finance Direct Payment Voucher to ICBC or sends the electronic direct payment instruction to ICBC through special line.

(III) ICBC transfers the fund to the payee or the eligible unit's account on real-time basis through "Bank-Finance Link" system.

(IV) ICBC timely delivers the payment slip to the finance authority and upload the electronic return slip to the finance authority through special line and deliver the Finance Direct Payment Deposit Advice to the budgeting units. It presents the finance direct payment 10-day (monthly) report to the finance authority as per stipulated time and enables the dynamic monitoring service to the finance authority to cover Treasury fund payments.

FINANCE AUTHORIZED PAYMENT

Definition

Finance Authorized Payment is service arrangement where the finance authority allocate the monthly fund limit to the zero-balance account of the budgeting units according to the budget and fund usage plan, whereas the budgeting units make their payments within the allocated fund limit.

Product's Target Client

The service mainly targets to the budgeting units at each level included in the Treasury centralized payment reforms. It is applicable for the procurement payment and random expenditures not yet included in the Finance Direct Payment.

Features and Strengths

Automatic Line Distribution

"Bank-Finance Link" system automatically receives the authorized payment limit transmitted from finance authority to ICBC through special line or other methods and automatically diverts it to the intermediary service platform of each first-tier (direct control) branches and automatically prints the line deposit advice for the budgeting units.

Automatic Line Control

"Bank-Finance Link" system is managed centrally as per first-tier budgeting units for the authorized payment limit. It automatically renew the line after the new line granting or line drawdown; for over-the-limit payment, it automatically stops payment and sends feedback to the budgeting unit; it automatically reinstates the relevant limits when the funds are returned to the Treasury.

Automatic System Resources Retrieval

The teller user only needs to input the few key elements such as receiving account number and is able to retrieve the budgeting unit name, account code, and other voucher data pre-stored in the system, thereby minimizing the data entry volume.

Dynamic Monitoring Service

The system retrieves the finance payment details from the database and retrieves the back office system per minute on real-time basis to generate the real-time monitoring file saved under the designated folder for real-time monitoring by the finance authority.

Automatic Generation of Various Payment Information

The "Bank-Finance Link" system automatically generates electronic return slip and all sorts of reports that are fed back to the finance authority through special line or other means and automatically print the reconciliation breakdown and monthly reconciliation sheet for the budgeting unit.

Service Channels

"Bank-Finance Link" system.

Application Condition

The budgeting units at each level that are included in the Treasury centralized payment reform and who holds approval by the finance authority permitting the unit to open zero-balance account and relevant materials stipulated in Administrative Methods on Bank Account are eligible for Authorized Payment services.

Service Procedure

(I) ICBC opens zero-balance account for the budgeting unit.

(II) The finance authority passes the electronic Detailed Finance Authorized Payment Limit Advice through special line or other means to ICBC's "Bank-Finance Link" system.

(III) "Bank-Finance Link" system automatically breaks down the authorized payment limit and the administering Business Offices enquires and prints Finance Authorized

Payment Line Deposit Advice to be sent to the basic budgeting units.

(IV) The budgeting unit presents the payment application and the administering Business Office generates the authorized payment transaction through "Bank-Finance Link" system. For over-the-limit payments, the system automatically stops payment and provide payment stop feedback to the budgeting unit. For payment within line, the system transfers the fund to the payee account on real-time basis.

(V) "Bank-Finance Link" system automatically generates the Finance Authorized Payment electronic return slip and daily, ten-day, and monthly report to be fed back to Ministry of Finance, the People's Bank of China, and the budgeting units; the system automatically generates monthly reconciliation sheet and detailed reconciliation sheet to be delivered to the budgeting units by administering Business Offices.

NON-TAX REVENUE COLLECTION

Definition

The Non-Tax Revenue Collection refers to service where ICBC opens non-tax revenue special account, fund collection, remittance and transfer clearing, and information feedback for the finance authorities, State authorities, public utilities, and non-government organizations at each level.

Product Target Client

The service is applicable for the collection and payment management for State authorities, public utilities, and non-government organizations at each level including: administrative fee collection, centralized receipts by supervisory department (incl. sector organizations with government function), and other non-tax revenues.

Features and Strengths

Large Business Network

ICBC has a large number and wide distribution of Business Offices. Its Business Office distribution pattern can match with the non-tax income-receiving units' characteristics of wide distribution, highly systematic organization, and wide dispersion of payers. It is capable to provide services for the payers and the receiving units all over China. All its Business Offices accept the finance non-tax fund collection requests and formed powerful network coverage advantage.

Advanced Business System

All transactions are centralized in one data center for processing. The fund is linked to accounting entries, which effectively prevents the criminal attempts by internal and external personnel taking advantage of time lag between fund activities and accounting entries. The leading "Bank-Finance Link" system in the sector synchronizes the fund flow and information flow. The transaction information is transmitted through encrypted mode. The system achieved the electronic State non-tax fund payment clearing, standardized information transmission, and informationalized reporting system management. The system makes ICBC at the leadership position in China in terms of agency State treasury non-tax revenue collection service.

Diversified Information Feedback Platform

In response to the special requirement by finance authority's non-tax revenue information feedback, ICBC launched automated processing for fund settlement, accounting, information transmission, and reporting. It realized real-time enquiry, collection and sorting, and summary and analysis of information and ensured timely, accurate, and secure feedbacks to the finance authorities, supervisory departments, and the receiving units at each level. Furthermore, ICBC takes full advantage of its IT and electronic service and makes use of special-line networking, Internet Banking, and other channels to break through the limitation of Business Offices and the business hours. It provides a 24-7 electronic real-time enquiry system for the finance authorities, supervisory departments, and the receiving units at each level and provide multi-function, convenient and prompt, and safe and reliable electronic enquiry service.

Convenient Service Process

It adopts the leading and revolutionary technology in the sector that optimizes services procedure, shortens the hierarchy of accounting, realizes the flat management, and simplifies the system search and visit procedures to the maximum extent, thereby increasing the speed of service processing. The teller only needs to input the few key elements such as amount and receiving account number, the system can retrieve the corresponding voucher element resources pre-stored in the system for automated data processing, thereby minimizing the data entry volume.

Diversified Fee Payment Platform

ICBC takes the full advantage in Internet Banking to enable customers' fee payment services through Internet Banking. The administering personnel of the supervisory departments or receiving units and the payers may pay fees and enquire relevant information behind the doors. The payer may also enquire fee payment information at any time through Telephone Banking or cell phone SMS.

Service Channels

"Bank-Finance Link" system.

Application Condition

The finance authorities, supervision departments, and receiving units at each level who holds relevant materials stipulated in Administrative Methods on Bank Account are eligible for Non-tax Revenue Collection services.

Service Procedure

Account Opening

ICBC sets up finance special account for the finance authorities as per the finance authority's notice and relevant regulations. ICBC opens the finance remittance and payment special account at ICBC branch institutions for the receiving unit as per the stipulated procedures.

Payment

The payers or the receiving units make payment at ICBC Business office and presents General Non-Tax Revenue Payment Advice ("Payment Advice" hereinafter). ICBC's Business Offices that accept non-tax revenue payment include finance special account bank, finance payment special account bank, and the associate bank (all Business offices other than remittance and payment special account banks).

Fund Remittance and Transfer

ICBC Business Office double-checks the key elements in Payment Advice and input the relevant information into "Bank-Finance Link" system. The system automatically verifies the check code and transfers the non-tax revenue to the finance special account of finance remittance and payment special account on real-time basis through real-time clearing system. It then passes the key information in the Payment Advice to the special account bank on real-time basis through "Bank-Finance Link" system.

Fund Sweeping

By the close of each working day, each finance remittance and payment account sweep the fund deposited in the finance remittance and payment special account to the finance special account through real-time clearing system. It also passes the relevant non-tax revenue collection information to the finance special account bank through "Bank-Finance Link" system. The finance remittance and payment account balance is back to zero after sweeping.

Diversion to Treasury or Fund Allocation

ICBC finance special account bank diverts the fund in finance special account to the Treasury unified account or fund allocation as per instruction of the finance authority.

Feedback

Electronic Feedback: By the end of each day, ICBC "Bank-Finance Link" system pools the non-tax revenue collection information and sends feedback to the finance authority as per stipulated format through data transmission special line or other methods and deliver Non-Tax Revenue Reconciliation Statement to the finance authority upon the next day. The "Bank-Finance Link" system's dynamic monitoring system can also provide the finance authority with ICBC's real-time monitoring and control service for all non-tax revenue collection accounts. The finance authority can enquire the combination information for non-tax revenue collection details, total, and number of payments as per department, account, time period, and other criteria. Meanwhile, ICBC Internet Banking system provides feedback to the supervisory departments for the non-tax revenue collection of its subordinate receiving units and provides feedback to the receiving units for account information of finance remittance and payment special account.

Report Feedback: "Bank-Finance Link" system can automatically generate all sorts of income reports and accounting statements. ICBC finance special account banks double-check the fund data each day and present the finance special account fund collection, payment, balance daily reconciliation statement to the finance authority in the next day and reconcile the finance special account fund account with the finance authority by the next day following the close of the month. Each account bank will print ICBC Ten-Day (Monthly) Statement of Agency Non-Tax Revenue Collection as per stipulated format to the finance authority, supervisory department, and receiving units within 2 days after each ten-day period of the month and within 4 days after each month and reconcile accounts with the finance authority, supervisory department, and receiving units within 4 days after each month

Revenue Refund

As per instruction from the finance authority, ICBC finance special account bank inputs the relevant revenue refund information in "Bank-Finance Link" and process the revenue refund through finance special account. ICBC transfers the fund into the payer's account bank and sends feedback to the finance authority through "Bank-Finance Link" system. The revenue refund is generally completed through account transfer, and there is no cash refund. For refund needing cash, ICBC processes the refund strictly as per relevant regulations by the finance authority.

More Money in Circulation Means more Trade

Many of the mercantilists, some of whom also used the arguments already discussed, wanted more money because they regarded money, not merely as a passive medium of exchange, but as a force acting through its circulation from hand to hand as an active stimulus to trade. An increased amount of money in circulation, they believed, meant (or caused) an increased volume of trade, and since men would produce only what they could sell a quickening of trade meant an increase of production and therefore a wealthier country. Here, it should be noted, money is valued as an instrument or stimulus of trade rather than for its own sake. The writers who stressed "circulation" as the valuable service of money often shifted, however, from the concept of money circulating as a medium of exchange to money passing from the hands of a lender to those of a borrower, and rarely distinguished clearly between them. The underlying reasoning is often presented in the form of analogies, especially with the circulation of the blood, which William Harvey had discovered not long before.

Stress on the importance of an abundance of money in circulation if trade was to flourish is already to be found in very early writers. The most elaborate expositions of the "circulation" argument were made by William Potter and John Law. Potter's argument seems to reduce to this: The wealth of a country is equal to the value of the goods of all sorts therein, money being valuable only as it serves to bring about the production of more goods. The more money men have, the more they spend and the faster they spend it. If men acquire more money and spend it as fast as they receive it, the sales of merchants and manufacturers will increase proportionately. If they sell five times as much in money value, they will produce five times as much, and even more, in physical quantities, since they can afford to charge lower prices on the greater volume of sales.

In reference to a commonwealth, or any society of men, the greater quantity there is amongst them, of money, credit, or that which is taken by them for commodities, the more commodity they sell, that is, the greater is their trade. For whatsoever is taken amongst men for commodity, though it were ten times more than now it is, yet if it be one way or other laid out by each man, as fast as he receives it, it must needs come to pass, that (resting nowhere) it doth occasion a quickness in the revolution of commodity from hand to hand, that is trade, proportionable to the greatness of its quantity.

John Law's argument is essentially the same, although stated more conservatively. The most enthusiastic advocates of the circulation argument, Potter and Law included, were advocates of paper money. But if paper money were accepted as of equal value to metallic money, the great reason for desiring a favorable balance of trade, that it results in an inflow of bullion, should lose its force. Such in fact was the case with some of them, as the following extracts show: For whether a nation have any silver amongst them or no, yet if they can trade as well without it, what need they care? for their estates in vendible commodities (and consequently their credit) is of as real value as if it were in money.

Whatsoever quantity of credit shall be raised in this office, will be as good, and of as much use, as if there were so much money in specie added to the present stock of the nation...'tis more prudent and advantageous to a nation, to have the common standard or medium of their trade within their power, and to arise from their native product, than to be at the mercy of a foreign prince for his gold and silver, which he may at pleasure behold.... Credit can neither be hoarded up, nor transported to the nation's disadvantage; which consequently frees us from the care and necessity of making laws to prevent exportation of bullion or coin, being always able to command a credit of our own,...as useful, and as much as shall be necessary.

The only necessity of a foreign trade for England is because we make a foreign commodity (gold and silver) the standard of all ours, and the only medium of commerce, which (as long as it continues so) if we want, all trades must cease; but if we can find out another and safer medium of exchange (as this credit) appropriated to the place where we live and not subject to such obstruction as the other, why should we not readily embrace it?

And if the proprietors of the bank can circulate their funds of twelve hundred thousand pounds, without having more than two or three hundred thousand pounds lying dead at one time with another, this bank will be in effect, as nine hundred thousand pounds, or a million of fresh money, brought into the nation.

Whether in any one year half a million is brought into a commercial country by trade, or issued out by banks, in notes, upon good security, it will serve for the same purposes.

Some advocates of paper money made little or no reference to the balance of trade or to trade policy in their tracts. This freedom from the prevailing obsession with the state of the balance of trade may have been due to a loss of interest in a policy of securing laboriously through the complicated regulation of trade the increase of money which could be secured more quickly, with greater certainty, and with less effort, by means of the printing press. But some of the advocates of paper money displayed loyalty to the current belief in the importance of a favorable balance of trade, either because of blind acceptance of traditional doctrine, or on the basis of the store of wealth argument or the analogy from personal finance that one should buy less than one sells, and these writers claimed that an increase of paper money would not drive bullion out of the country, but on the contrary would make the balance of trade more favorable through its beneficial effect on production and trade.

THE QUANTITY THEORY OF MONEY

Those mercantilists who sought an increase in the supply of money because they wanted more circulation or more invested capital clearly wanted genuine physical increases in trade or capital and not merely nominal increases in terms of a depreciated monetary unit. Their doctrines, therefore, would seem to come into sharp conflict with any theory of the value of money which makes it vary inversely with its quantity, whether proportionately or not. Only for those mercantilists who wanted an increase of money for use as hoards or stores of wealth would acceptance of a quantity theory of money involve no problem of reconciliation. Many of the mercantilist writers gave no evidence of recognition of the dependence of the value of money upon its quantity. A few of them, in fact, wanted more money as a cure for the evils resulting from high prices. But, although Locke is sometimes credited with the first clear English formulation of the quantity theory, many of the mercantilists, from the beginning of the seventeenth century on, did present, in one connection or another, some simple version of the quantity theory, although in most cases they failed to incorporate it as an integral part of their foreign-trade doctrine and failed also to show any concern about its consistency with the rest of their doctrine. There follow quotations from writings antedating Locke by some forty to ninety years which present some form of quantity theory of the value of money:

Plenty of money maketh generally things dear, and scarcity of money maketh likewise generally things good cheap. Whereas things particularly are also dear or good cheap according to plenty or scarcity of the things themselves, or the use of them. Even as plenty of money maketh things dear, and scarcity of money maketh things good cheap: even so plenty or scarcity of commodities maketh the price thereof to rise and fall according to their use more or less.

It is a common saying, that plenty or scarcity of money makes all things dear or good or cheap.

Gold and silver...in the intrinsic...are commodities, valuing each other according to the plenty or scarcity; and so all other commodities by them; and that is the sole power of trade.

Money through want or plenty raises or diminishes the price of all things.

In those countries where monies are scarce, there the lands and native wares are cheap, so likewise where money doth abound, there the lands and wares are dear.

Several mercantilists faced squarely the apparent conflict between the quantity theory of money and their doctrines and attempted to meet the issue either by arguing that they could be reconciled or by denying the truth of the quantity theory. Apparently the first of these was William Potter, who has not received the attention which he deserves in this connection. Potter, as has been shown, claimed that an increase of money in circulation would result in an even more than proportionate increase in trade and production, or in goods in circulation. In order to refute it, he states a quantity theory of money in its simplest one-sided form:

If then, in opposition to what is thus undertaken to be proved, it should be objected, that an increase of money would occasion an increase in the price of commodities, proportionable to such increase of money, (that is, if the money were twice as much, commodity would be twice as dear) consequently (going never the further in commodity by the increase thereof) would not occasion any increase in the sale of commodity: therefore not any increase of trade; and yet (by causing the price of commodities to rise) incur an inconvenience, contrary to what is before affirmed.

His answer is elaborate and not always intelligible. He assumes the basis of the theory of money he is attacking to be that an increase of money increases prices by increasing the (physical) volume of sales (by increasing the demand for commodities). He replies that if, when money is doubled, the prices of commodities are also doubled, there will be no increase in the (physical) amount of sales. The theory therefore involves a contradiction. He then attempts to meet it by another line of reasoning. Quick trade permits of a small profit, and therefore a lower price. Quick sales enable artisans and others to produce more quickly, and if they sell more they can afford to charge a lower price. The increase in the amount of commodities resulting from the stimulus to trade of an increase in money, instead of raising prices, will therefore lower them. Prices will rise only if the increase in commodities is proportionately less than the increase in money, which is not likely to be the case. But even if prices should rise somewhat, it is better to have an abundance of comforts, though dear, than a smaller amount thereof, though never so cheap.

Another advocate of paper money, John Asgill, denied the truth of the quantity theory of money on different and exceedingly slender grounds: an increase in money would lower the rate of interest and therefore raise land values, but not the prices of commodities in general, because "the price of corn and cattle don't rise and fall with the interest of money." John Law attacked it, partly by arguments closely resembling those of Potter, partly on reasoning peculiarly his own. The stimulus to trade and industry resulting from an increase in money would result in an increase in commodities. Because money would be easier to borrow, merchants would be able to increase the extent of their operations and to sell at lower rates of profit, and therefore the value of the money would not fall, *i.e.*, prices would not rise. Money falls in value only when given to a people in greater quantity than there is demand for; if the money is issued only as there is demand for it, its value will not depreciate, "the quantity and demand increasing and decreasing together. Law concedes that if the quantity of money in any particular country "should increase beyond the proportion that country bears to Europe," prices would rise there, but the rise of prices would spread elsewhere, so that the value of money would become the same, or about the same, everywhere. The country which had acquired the increase of money would profit greatly thereby, "for that country would have the whole benefit of the greater quantity, and only bear a share of the lesser value, according to the proportion its money had to the money of Europe. What would make the prices rise elsewhere, he does not explain.

Another writer, James Hodges, who complained of scarcity of money, wanted plate called in and coined and the monetary value of the English standard coin raised as a remedy for this scarcity. He claimed that these measures would result in higher prices only after they resulted in an increase in the number of coins in circulation. The effect on prices would therefore be gradual, and meanwhile there would be a stimulus to trade. After a short time the value of the coin could be gradually lowered, and the surplus bullion returned to be made into plate again if its owners so desired. His argument is interesting as an anticipation of Hume's doctrine that rising prices are a stimulus to trade, and for its endeavor to find a method of obtaining this stimulus without involving a permanent increase in the price level. The difficulty with the scheme, granting its logic, is, of course, that the period of stimulus would be followed by a period of at least corresponding depression.

Both Potter and Law claimed that an increase of (paper) money would make the balance of trade more favorable and would lead to an inflow of bullion. Potter argued that the beneficial effects of an increased quantity of money would enable England to outsell other countries, for "the greater trade of one country hath a capacity of undermining and eating out the lesser trade of other countries. For reasons not explained, unless it be the fall in English prices alleged to result from an increase in the quantity of money, both foreign and English commodities would fall in price in England, but not abroad. Exports would therefore be paid for with bullion (and presumably imports would be paid for with English commodity exports), and the bullion could be coined into English money without loss. But with unusual consistency Potter admits that when paper money or credit is available as a substitute, metallic money would be of little importance to England. Law showed more concern than did Potter about the state of the balance of trade, but he also claimed that an increased amount of money through the issue of paper money would make the balance favorable: "Most people think scarcity of money is only the consequence of a balance due; but 'tis the cause as well as the consequence, and the effectual way to bring the balance to our side, is to add to the money." More money, by employing more people, would make a surplus of goods available for export, and if sufficient money was issued production would reach a level at which more would be exported than imported. Conversely, if the amount of money was reduced, some of the laborers would be rendered idle, the domestic output would shrink, exports would fall, and an unfavorable balance would result. These results of a change in the quantity of money he would apparently expect not to be transitory but to persist as long as the new quantity of money persisted.

The Mercantilists on Hoards and Plate

Because the mercantilists differed among themselves as to the character of the benefit which resulted from an increase in the amount of bullion in a country, they also differed in their attitudes toward the miser, the collector of gold or silver plate, the usurer, and the spendthrift. Those mercantilists for whom the chief virtue in an increased supply of bullion lay in its stimulus to circulation condemned private hoards as an evil, and also regarded other practices which kept bullion from circulating as money, such as its use in the manufacture of plate, as objectionable. Vaughan condemned hoarding and the use of plate as contributing factors to the scarcity of money, and recommended sumptuary legislation to check the melting of money and its manufacture into plate. An anonymous writer criticized the Established church on the ground that it hoarded riches which should circulate, so that "the money that before ran current in trading, is dammed up in their coffers."

Another pamphlet, written as an answer to this one, condemned the excess of silver plate for the same reason, but claimed that there was no occasion for alarm about hoarding, as there was not much of it, and urged in the defense of the church that it could be charged with responsibility for the prevailing scarcity of money only if the clerics kept "banks of money dead by them, which was not the case. Complaint against the usurer as a hoarder of money was likewise without basis, since "his money walks, though upon other legs, either serving the tradesman or the gentleman, for preparing commodities to export, or to buy what is imported for his expenses.

Manley found fault with the miser, because "money locked up in the miser's coffers is like dung in a heap, it does no good, but being dispersed, and orderly disposed abroad, enricheth the land." An anonymous writer wanted misers' hoards taxed, in order to draw some of their money into circulation, especially in time of war when trade was slack. "I know no difference," he wrote, "betwixt bringing treasure out of an iron chest by a good law, and plowing the seas by long and dangerous voyages" in order to secure bullion through foreign trade.

One of Locke's objections to the reduction of the interest rate by law was that it would result in men keeping their money "dead" by them, instead of lending it, with resultant loss to trade. Petty expressed a preference for money over plate, because it served trade better, as did also Hugh Chamberlain: "Money is living riches, plate but dead; that being capable of turning and improving trade, when this is not."

Hodges's scheme for a forced three-year surrender of plate in return for "raised" money, with prohibition of ownership of plate in the interval, in order for a time to secure relief from the prevailing scarcity of money, and to obtain the stimulus to trade of slowly rising prices, has already been referred to. Another writer urged a similar scheme for raising money 5 per cent, in order to draw hoards of the old, and therefore undervalued, coins into circulation.

One writer made the same sort of contrast between hoarded and circulating money, hoarded credit being the exchequer bills which, because of the high rate of interest they carried, were held instead of being used as money: "...in the frequent passing of credit from hand to hand, consists its great usefulness in trade; for when either money or credit is hoarded up, it may more properly be said to stagnate, than to circulate." Postlethwayt, in a curious argument, claimed that lending of money at interest involved hoarding and therefore on circulation grounds was to be condemned.

If some money is hoarded, the volume of trade will fall. In order to bring the hoarded money back into trade, those in great need of it will offer interest ("profit") for its loan. The result will be that other moneyed men, instead of "circulating their money" in trade, will "lock it up," while awaiting the opportunity to lend it, preferring to get their income by usury instead of by trade. Eventually the money so withdrawn from trade would be lent and would thus return to trade, but bearing an interest charge which would act as a restraint on trade.

Some writers objected, on similar grounds, to the establishment of banks, holding that they monopolized money, and kept it from circulating. Child, for example, maintained that "principally this seeming scarcity of money proceeds from the trade of bankering, which obstructs circulation." Strangely enough, considering his views on the effect of lending at interest on monetary circulation, Postlethwayt made the most effective rejoinder to this argument which I have found:

It may be here requisite to take notice of that erroneous notion entertained by some, that banks and bankers engross the money, hoard it up, and hinder its circulation in trade; but, if such will consider this matter in its true light, they will easily be convinced, that the money lodged in banks, and in the hands of bankers, is the most constantly employed of any; for, though the specie should lie still till called for, yet the notes given out for its value, are continually circulating; whereby is done abundantly more service to trade, than if the same lay dormant in private hands; and yet the necessities of the depositors are effectually answered.

Once hoarding and the use of coin or bullion in the making of plate were attacked, there were few to come to their defense, and the use of gold and silver in the making of thread or in gilding met with almost general condemnation.

Mun, however, opposed restrictions on the melting-down of coin into plate on the ground that gold and silver were more apt to be carried out of the kingdom in payment of purchases of foreign goods if in the form of coin than if kept in the form of plate, and Misselden before him, while conceding that too much plate in the kingdom would cause scarcity of money, nevertheless held that it was better to have bullion kept in the form of plate than to turn it into coin and thus turn it out of the kingdom because of the undervaluation of coin which he alleged then prevailed in England.

A sixteenth-century writer condoned the use of bullion for plate, because it resulted in the formation of a sort of secondary national reserve for emergencies, upon which the king, in case of a great war, could draw "without any grouching of the Commons." The same argument is to be found occasionally in the later literature, and is made by Briscoe to serve as a defense of private hoards. Hoarded treasure, bullion and coin, is part of the "capital stock of national treasure" and can be drawn upon in a national emergency. Private hoarding is as good as having treasure stored by the king.

Toward the end of the seventeenth century there appeared a new doctrine of the existence of a "due proportion" between money and goods, and therefore of the possibility of excess of money as far as trade needs were concerned.

The quantity theory of money also tended to lead to the conclusion that an increase in the amount of money by increasing prices would reduce exports and thus eventually be lost to the country. Writers who on "due proportions of money to trade" or on quantity-theory grounds conceded that there was under any given set of circumstances a maximum amount of money which could be kept in circulation, and who still attached special importance to the precious metals, were likely to approve of turning the money into plate or of its hoarding as a means either of stimulating the further import of bullion or of, checking an outflow.

It was doubtless such reasoning which led John Houghton to the conclusion that "if the King should hoard up much money, it would for the present make it dearer, that dearness would make it be brought in more plentifully, and that would make it more plentiful than it was before." Petty wrote: "For there may be as well too much money in a country, as too little. I mean, as to the best advantage of its trade; only the remedy is very easy, it may be soon turned into the magnificence of gold and silver vessels."

On similar grounds another writer would tolerate the increased use of plate if there was more money than was necessary to carry on trade and "defray the expense of living," and Vanderlint, who accepted the quantity theory and wanted low prices but at the same time wanted a favorable balance of trade payable in specie, recommended as a means of attaining these apparently conflicting objectives that the private hoarding of gold and silver and their use in plate, and even in gold and silver cloth and gilding, be encouraged.

He cited with approval the practice of the East Indians of hoarding the silver they receive, with the result that prices remained low there, exports continued to exceed imports, and the balance was paid in still more silver. Harris presents a similar solution of the same dilemma. If the inflow of bullion resulting from a favorable balance of trade is kept:

> *as a dead stock, either by turning it into plate or by any other method, so as to prevent its getting into trade as money; it may continue to go on increasing in more bullion, which in this case will be a real increase of wealth.... Let an increased stock of bullion get out again into trade, and it will soon turn the balance the other way.*

But gold and silver can be best stored up in the form of plate:

> *But people in general will not hoard up cash; all like to display their wealth, and to lay out their superfluities in some costly things. There seems then no method so effectual for the securing of a dead stock of treasure in any country, as the encouraging the use of plate, by making it fashionable, preferable to more brittle or more perishable commodities. Plate would be a national resource in case of emergency, and not the less so, because the precious metals had not as yet received the shape of coins.*

Hume in 1752 claimed that state hoarding was the only expedient by which a country could raise its supply of the precious metals above the equilibrium level, but commented that this was "a practice which we should all exclaim against as destructive, namely, the gathering of large sums into a public treasure, locking them up, and absolutely preventing their circulation."

Henry Home accepted so whole-heartedly the lesson of the quantity theory of money that he looked upon an export surplus alike with an import surplus as dangerous to the country. The latter meant an outward drain of money, with a consequent fall of prices and stoppage of industry. The former meant an influx of specie, extravagance, rise in prices, and finally a fall in exports, rise in imports, an unfavorable balance again, and a recurrence of the drain of specie. What was to be desired was an even balance.

Therefore, "let the registers of foreign mints be carefully watched, in order that our current coin may not exceed that of our industrious neighbors." But it was not the quantity of gold and silver in a country that determined the price level, but the quantity of money in circulation. Still retaining some traces of the mercantilist attachment for the precious metals, he therefore advocated the conversion of money into plate and even, under favorable circumstances, the formation of a state treasure.

11

Balance of Tradeand Economic Policies

INTRODUCTION

The mercantilist arguments for a favorable balance of trade so far considered all rest upon the desirability of more bullion. But there was one mercantilist argument which was not dependent upon the attachment of superior economic importance to the precious metals than to other commodities of equal exchange value, namely the "employment" argument. Exports were the product of English labor whereas imports, especially if they consisted of finished products and of commodities competitive with home products, displaced English labor. The greater, the exports, and the smaller the imports, the greater, therefore, was the employment of English labor. This argument was not, as is sometimes supposed, of late seventeenth-century origin. It is to be found in the very earliest mercantilist writings, and it persists without break throughout the literature of the seventeenth and eighteenth centuries. It is not even clear that it was more emphasized in the eighteenth-than in the seventeenth-century mercantilist literature, and it could even be argued that the sixteenth-century writers stressed it most of all. Of all the mercantilist reasoning, it withstood criticism most successfully, and persisted into the nineteenth and twentieth centuries as an important element in the protectionist doctrine.

The stress on employment led to an appraisal of exports not merely in terms of their value, or of their value relative to imports, but in terms of the amount of labor they represented. Exports of manufactured articles were rated more highly than exports to the same value of raw materials, because the former embodied a larger proportion of labor. The stress on employment sometimes took the form of measuring the gain from trade by the exports alone, and in a few cases the argument even went to the extreme of recommending production of goods simply to employ labor, even though the product of their labor were burnt upon their completion.

In the case of a few later writers, the employment argument gave rise to a new balance-of-trade concept, in which the amounts weighed against each other were not the values respectively of the exports and the imports, but the respective amounts of labor or employment they represented, i.e., the "balance of labor" or the "balance of employment." Barbon seems to have been the first to come close to this concept. The measure of benefit from different exports is the amount of employment they had given to English labor, and, similarly, the measure of benefit from imports is the amount of employment to which they will give rise in their further manufacture. His employment test leads him at times to liberal conclusions. Imports of raw silk are more profitable than imports of gold and silver, because more hands are employed in the manufacture of the first than in working the latter. If woolen goods are exported for Westphalian bacon and then the import of the latter is prohibited, England would lose even if the consumption of English bacon increased, because woolen cloth employs more hands in its production than does bacon.

Tucker stated the argument somewhat differently. The balance of trade for country A is the excess of the number of laborers working up manufactures for country B in A as compared to the number of laborers working up manufactures for A in B:

When two countries are exchanging their produce or manufactures with each other, that nation which has the greatest number employed in this reciprocal trade, is said to receive a balance from the other; because the price of the overplus labor must be paid in gold and silver.... This is the clearest and justest method of determining the balance between nation and nation: for though a difference in the value of the respective commodities may make some difference in the sum actually paid to balance accounts, yet the general principle, that labor (not money) is the riches of a people, will always prove, that the advantage is on the side of that nation which has most hands employed in labor.

A closely similar doctrine is presented also by Harris, Steuart, and Arthur Young: A nation that pays ultimately upon its trade a balance in bullion, is a loser of so much of its dead stock; and a loser also, if its exports maintained fewer of its own inhabitants, than its imports did of those foreign nations.

In all trade two things are to be considered in the commodity sold. The first is the matter; the second is the labor employed to render this matter useful. The matter exported from a country is what the country loses; the price of the labor exported is what it gains. If the value of the matter imported be greater than the value of what is exported the country gains. If a greater value of labor be imported, than exported, the country loses. Why? Because in the first case, strangers must have paid, in matter, the surplus of labor exported; and in the second case, because the country must have paid to strangers, in matter, the surplus of labor imported. It is therefore a general maxim, to discourage the importation of work, and to encourage the exportation of it.

A balance in our favor is a proof that foreigners take more products and fabrics from us than we do from them, which is an advantage of the highest consequence, because it suggests at least a strong probability that they employ more of our poor than we do of theirs.

These writers apparently would compare the amount of English labor embodied in the exports with the amount of foreign labor represented by the imports in computing the English "balance of labor." On this basis, a given trade balance measured in money would have to be regarded as more favorable the lower the prices at which English exports were sold and the lower the wages earned by English labor engaged in their production, although it is not evident that these writers saw this implication of their doctrine. The objective they had in mind, to the exclusion of other considerations, was employment of English labor, and in the case of Young the assumption is fairly clear that the labor engaged in the production of exported goods would in the absence of such exports remain idle. He states that "whatever is paid to other countries in bullion, as a balance upon the year's trade, is just so much loss to any nation that has unemployed poor or unpurchased commodities," but he concedes to Hume that the loss of the bullion is important only as it is a sign "that we do not export a due quantity of products and labor." The balance-of-labor doctrine is of course absurd and probably even more absurd than the earlier and at the time still dominant balance-of-trade doctrine. It nevertheless can be regarded as a stage of some importance in the evolution toward more sensible doctrine. In the first case, any criticism of or substitution for the dominant balance-of-trade doctrine helped to promote the disintegration of the mercantilist errors, and thus was a service even if it proposed an even less satisfactory alternative doctrine, provided the criticism survived and the proposed substitute did not survive. Secondly, the balance-of-labor doctrine reversed the roles of employment and foreign trade as compared to the conventional balance-of-trade doctrine.

In conventional mercantilism increased population, increased employment, improvement in the arts, in roads, canals, in the energy and skill of labor, were all welcomed because they would make possible increased production of goods for export or in lieu of imports from abroad, and would thus promote a favorable balance of trade. In the balance-of-labor doctrine the end was employment, and the favorable balance was the means, and even if its exponents did not themselves see clearly that income and consumption were in turn the rational ends of employment, and of economic activity in general, they at least made it easy for Adam Smith and later writers to take the next step and thus to bring about a revolutionary change in the orientation of economic thought.

One student of English mercantilism, E. A. Johnson, nothing the indisputable-and undisputed-fact that the mercantilists approved of a large working population, hard work on the part of laborers, the progress of skill in the application of labor, improvements in transportation and industry, and so forth, has concluded that serious injustice has been done to them by accounts such as presumably the present one of their doctrines: All of which should prove that the ultimate concern of the mercantilists was the creation of effective factors of production.

Not ten per cent of English mercantilist literature is devoted to the ill-fated doctrine of the balance of trade. [Let anyone who doubts this assertion turn through the pages of the English mercantilist literature and be convinced!] Their ardent passion for productive efficiency is shown by their advocacy of improvement of lands, mines and fisheries, and by their encouragement of inland communication and canal building. Industry was to be encouraged, idleness to be repressed.

But evidence that the mercantilists desired efficient production, be it piled up mountain high, of itself proves nothing as to their "ultimate concern." They may have desired, and did desire, increased production, because they thought that it would promote a favorable balance of trade, even though they also desired it for other reasons. Such quantitative propositions have an unearned air of precision, but on the basis of my turning of the pages of English mercantilist literature I venture the conclusion that not ten per cent of it was free from concern, expressed or clearly implied, in the state of the balance of trade and in the means whereby it could be improved.

The labor doctrines of the English mercantilists need not be examined at length here, since they have been ably dealt with by other writers. On only one point, it seems to me, is critical comment on their exposition called for. The mercantilists, as they point out, were led by their obsession with the balance of trade and also, perhaps, by unconscious class sympathies, to deal with questions affecting labor as if laborers were a set of somewhat troublesome tools rather than human beings whose own comfort and happiness were a proper and primary object of concern for statesmen. The dominant doctrine, in consequence, advocated low wages, as a means of stimulating the worker to greater effort and of increasing England's competitive strength in foreign trade by lowering the money costs of English products. Sir James Steuart was merely expressing in blunter fashion than was common the position implicit in much of the mercantilist treatment of the labor question when he stated that "the lowest classes of a people, in a country of trade, must be restrained to their physical-necessary."

But Furniss and Gregory fail to do full justice to the size and importance of the dissenting group, who on grounds either of economic analysis or humanitarian sentiment opposed the dominant doctrine that low wages were desirable. Such important writers as Cary, Coke, Davenant, and Defoe belonged to this group, and in the latter part of the eighteenth century the growth of humanitarianism operated to give even stronger challenge to the prevailing views.

Representative of the opposition on humanitarian grounds was the complaint of an anonymous writer: "it is a great pity the laboring poor have not better encouragement, the cries of those unskillful men, who made a clamor of labor being too high, is a doctrine propagated more by theory than practice." Hume conceded that high wages resulted in some disadvantage in foreign trade, but insisted that "as foreign trade is not the most material circumstance, it is not to be put in competition with the happiness of so many millions." Since Hume was an enlightened critic of mercantilism, this is not of great significance, but Wallace, who was a mercantilist, agreed with Hume's doctrine, as "a maxim...suitable to a humane disposition. Agreeably to such a benevolent sentiment, we ought to extend our notions of trade, and consider not only how much money it gains to a nation, but how far it is conducive to the happiness of the people."

International trade allows us to expand our markets for both goods and services that otherwise may not have been available to us. It is the reason why you can pick between a Japanese, German and American car. As a result of international trade, the market contains greater competition and therefore more competitive prices, which bring a cheaper product home to the consumer.

INTERNATIONAL TRADE

International trade is the exchange of goods and services between countries. This type of trade gives rise to a world economy, in which prices, or supply and demand, affect and are affected by global events. Political change in Asia, for example, could result in an increase in the cost of labor, thereby increasing the manufacturing costs for an American sneaker company based in Malaysia, which would then result in an increase in the price that you have to pay to buy the tennis shoes at your local mall. A decrease in the cost of labor, on the other hand, would result in you having to pay less for your new shoes.

Trading globally gives consumers and countries the opportunity to be exposed to goods and services not available in their own countries. Almost every kind of product can be found on the international market: food, clothes, spare parts, oil, jewelry, wine, stocks, currencies and water. Services are also traded: tourism, banking, consulting and transportation. A product that is sold to the global market is an export, and a product that is bought from the global market is an import. Imports and exports are accounted for in a country's current account in the balance of payments.

Increased Efficiency of Trading Globally

Global trade allows wealthy countries to use their resources-whether labor, technology or capital-more efficiently. Because countries are endowed with different assets and natural resources (land, labor, capital and technology), some countries may produce the same good more efficiently and therefore sell it more cheaply than other countries. If a country cannot efficiently produce an item, it can obtain the item by trading with another country that can. This is known as specialization in international trade.

Let's take a simple example. Country A and Country B both produce cotton sweaters and wine. Country A produces 10 sweaters and six bottles of wine a year while Country B produces six sweaters and 10 bottles of wine a year. Both can produce a total of 16 units. Country A, however, takes three hours to produce the 10 sweaters and two hours to produce the six bottles of wine (total of five hours). Country B, on the other hand, takes one hour to produce 10 sweaters and three hours to produce six bottles of wine (total of four hours).

But these two countries realize that they could produce more by focusing on those products with which they have a comparative advantage. Country A then begins to produce only wine and Country B produces only cotton sweaters. Each country can now create a specialized output of 20 units per year and trade equal proportions of both products. As such, each country now has access to 20 units of both products.

We can see then that for both countries, the opportunity cost of producing both products is greater than the cost of specializing. More specifically, for each country, the opportunity cost of producing 16 units of both sweaters and wine is 20 units of both products (after trading). Specialization reduces their opportunity cost and therefore maximizes their efficiency in acquiring the goods they need. With the greater supply, the price of each product would decrease, thus giving an advantage to the end consumer as well.

Note that, in the example above, Country B could produce both wine and cotton more efficiently than Country A (less time). This is called an absolute advantage, and Country B may have it because of a higher level of technology. However, according to international trade theory, even if a country has an absolute advantage over another, it can still benefit from specialization.

Other Possible Benefits of Trading Globally

International trade not only results in increased efficiency but also allows countries to participate in a global economy, encouraging the opportunity of foreign direct investment (FDI), which is the amount of money that individuals invest into foreign companies and other assets. In theory, economies can therefore grow more efficiently and can more easily become competitive economic participants.

For the receiving government, FDI is a means by which foreign currency and expertise can enter the country. These raise employment levels and, theoretically, lead to a growth in the gross domestic product. For the investor, FDI offers company expansion and growth, which means higher revenues.

Free Report: The Five Things That Move the Currency Market. Year after year, key players in the Forex market make a killing by picking the right currencies-now it's your turn. Access industry gurus Boris and Kathy's exclusive FREE report, The Five Things That Move the Currency Market-And How to Profit From Them, right now!

Free Trade vs. Protectionism

As with other theories, there are opposing views. International trade has two contrasting views regarding the level of control placed on trade: free trade and protectionism. Free trade is the simpler of the two theories: a laissez-faire approach, with no restrictions on trade. The main idea is that supply and demand factors, operating on a global scale, will ensure that production happens efficiently. Therefore, nothing needs to be done to protect or promote trade and growth because market forces will do so automatically. In contrast, protectionism holds that regulation of international trade is important to ensure that markets function properly. Advocates of this theory believe that market inefficiencies may hamper the benefits of international trade and they aim to guide the market accordingly. Protectionism exists in many different forms, but the most common are tariffs, subsidies and quotas. These strategies attempt to correct any inefficiency in the international market.

As it opens up the opportunity for specialization and therefore more efficient use of resources, international trade has potential to maximize a country's capacity to produce and acquire goods. Opponents of global free trade have argued, however, that international trade still allows for inefficiencies that leave developing nations compromised. What is certain is that the global economy is in a state of continual change and, as it develops, so too must all of its participants. The world has a long, rich history of international trade among nations that can be traced back to early Assyrian, Babylonian, Egyptian, and Phoenician civilizations. These and other early civilizations recognized that trade can be tied directly to an improved quality of life for the citizens of all the partners. Today, the practice of trade among nations is growing by leaps and bounds. There is hardly a person on earth who has not been influenced in some way by the growing trade among nations.

WHY INTERNATIONAL TRADE?

One of the most logical questions to ask is, why do modern countries trade with one another? There are numerous reasons that countries engage in international trade. Some countries are deficient in critical raw materials, such as lumber or oil. To make up for these various deficiencies, countries must engage in international trade to obtain the resources necessary to produce the goods and/or services desired by their citizens. In addition to trading for raw materials, nations also exchange a wide variety of processed foods and finished products. Each country has its own specialties that are based on its economy and the skills of its citizens. Three common specialty classifications are capital, labor, and land.

Capital-intensive products, such as cars and trucks, heavy construction equipment, and industrial machinery, are produced by nations that have a highly developed industrial base. Japan is an example of a highly developed industrial nation that produces large quantities of high-quality cars for export around the world. Another reason Japan has adapted to producing capital-intensive products is that it is an island nation; there is little land available for land-intensive product production. Labor-intensive commodities, such as clothing, shoes, or other consumer goods, are produced in countries that have relatively low labor costs and relatively modern production facilities. China, Indonesia, and the Philippines are examples of countries that produce many labor-intensive products. Products that require large tracts of land, such as cattle production and wheat farming, are examples of land-intensive commodities. Countries that do not have large tracts of land normally purchase land-intensive products from countries that do have vast amounts of suitable land. The United States, for example, is one of the leading exporters of wheat. The combination of advanced farming technology, skilled farmers, and large tracts of suitable farmland in the Midwest and the Great Plains makes the mass production of wheat possible.

Over time a nation's work force will change, and thus the goods and services that nation produces and exports will change. Nations that train their workers for future roles can minimize the difficulty of making a transition to a new, dominant market. The United States, for example, was the dominant world manufacturer from the end of World War II until the early 1970s. But, beginning in the 1970s, other countries started to produce finished products more cheaply and efficiently than the United States, causing U.S. manufacturing output and exports to drop significantly. However, rapid growth in computer technology began to provide a major export for the United States. Practically speaking, the United States has been slowly transformed from a manufacturing-based economy into a new Information Age-based economy that relies on exporting cutting-edge technology as high tech software and computer companies proliferate.

Political Environment

Each country varies regarding international trade and relocation of foreign plants on its native soil. Some countries openly court foreign companies and encourage them to invest in their country by offering reduced taxes or some other investment incentives. Other countries impose strict regulations that can cause large companies to leave and open a plant in a country that provides more favorable operating conditions. When a company decides to conduct business in another country, it should also consider the political stability of the host country's government. Unstable leadership can create significant problems in recouping profits if the government falls of the host country and/or changes its policy towards foreign trade and investment. Political instability is often caused by severe economic conditions that result in civil unrest.

Another key aspect of international trade is paying for a product in a foreign currency. This practice can create potential problems for a company, since any currency is subject to price fluctuation. A company could lose money if the value of the foreign currency is reduced before it can be exchanged into the desired currency. Another issue regarding currency is that some nations do not have the necessary cash. Instead, they engage in counter trade, which involves the direct or indirect exchange of goods for other goods instead of for cash. Counter trade follows the same principles as bartering, a practice that stretches back into prehistory. A car company might trade new cars to a foreign government in exchange for high-quality steel that would be more costly to buy on the open market. The company can then use the steel to produce new cars for sale.

In a more extreme case, some countries do not want to engage in free trade with other nations, a choice known as self-sufficiency. There are many reasons for this choice, but the most important is the existence of strong political beliefs. For example, the former Soviet Union and its communist allies traded only with each other because the Soviet Union feared that Western countries would attempt to control their governments through trade. Self-sufficiency allowed the Soviet Union and its allies to avoid that possibility. However, these self-imposed trade restrictions created a shortage of products that could not be produced among the group, making the overall quality of life within the Soviet bloc substantially lower than in the West since consumer demand could not be met. When the Berlin Wall came down, trade with the West was resumed, and the shortage of products was reduced or eliminated.

Economic Environment

An important factor influencing international trade is taxes. Of the different taxes that can be applied to imported goods, the most common is a tariff, which is generally defined as an excise tax imposed on imported goods. A country can have several reasons for imposing a tariff. For example, a revenue tariff may be applied to an imported product that is also produced domestically. The primary reason for this type of tariff is to generate revenue that can be used later by the government for a variety of purposes. This tariff is normally set at a low level and is usually not considered a threat to international trade. When domestic manufacturers in a particular industry are at a disadvantage, vis-à-vis imports, the government can impose what is called a protective tariff. This type of tariff is designed to make foreign products more expensive than domestic products and, as a result, protect domestic companies. A protective tariff is normally very popular with the affected domestic companies and their workers because they benefit most directly from it.

In retaliation, a country that is affected by a protective tariff will frequently enact a tariff of its own on a product from the original tariff enacting country. In 1930, for example, the U.S. Congress passed the Smoot-Hawley Tariff Act, which provided the means for placing protective tariffs on imports. The United States imposed this protective tariff on a wide variety of products in an attempt to help protect domestic producers from foreign competition. This legislation was very popular in the United States, because the Great Depression had just begun, and the tariff was seen as helping U.S. workers. However, the tariff caused immediate retaliation by other countries, which immediately imposed protective tariffs of their own on U.S. products. As a result of these protective tariffs, world trade was severely reduced for nearly all countries, causing the wealth of each affected nation to drop, and increasing unemployment in most countries. Realizing that the 1930 tariffs were a mistake, Congress took corrective action by passing the

Reciprocal Trade Agreements Act of 1934, which empowered the president to reduce tariffs by 50 percent on goods from any other country that would agree to similar tariff reductions. The goal was to promote more international trade and help establish more cooperation among exporting countries.

Another form of a trade barrier that a country can employ to protect domestic companies is an import quota, which strictly limits the amount of a particular product that a foreign country can export to the quota-enacting country. For example, the United States had threatened to limit the number of cars imported from Japan. However, Japan agreed to voluntary export quotas, formally known as "voluntary export restrictions," to avoid U.S. imposed import quotas. The power of import quotas has diminished because foreign manufacturers have started building plants in the countries to which they had previously exported in order to avoid such regulations.

A government can also use a no-ntariff barrier to help protect domestic companies. A nontariff barrier usually refers to government requirements for licenses, permits, or significant amounts of paperwork in order to allow imports into its country. This tactic often increases the price of the imported product, slows down delivery, and creates frustration for the exporting country. The end goal is that many foreign companies will not bother to export their products to those markets because of the added cost and aggravation. Japan and several European countries have frequently used this strategy to limit the number of imported products.

Cultural Environment

Before a corporation begins exporting products to other countries, it must first examine the norms, taboos, and values of those countries. This information can be critical to the successful introduction of a product into a particular country and will influence how it is sold and/or marketed. Such information can prevent cultural blunders, such as the one General Motors committed when trying to sell its Chevy Nova in Spanish-speaking countries. Nova, in Spanish, means "doesn't go"-and few people would purchase a car named "doesn't go." This marketing error-resulting simply from ignorance of the Spanish language-cost General Motors millions in initial sales-as well as considerable embarrassment. Business professionals also need to be aware of foreign customs regarding standard business practices. For example, people from some countries like to sit or stand very close when conducting business. In contrast, people from other countries want to maintain a spatial distance between them and the people with whom they are conducting business. Thus, before business-people travel overseas, they must be given training on how to conduct business in the country to which they are traveling.

Business professionals also run into another practice that occurs in some countries-bribery. The practice of bribery is common in several countries and is considered a normal business practice. If the bribe is not paid to a business-person from a country where bribery is expected, a transaction is unlikely to occur. Laws in some countries prohibit businesspeople from paying or accepting bribes. As a result, navigating this legal and cultural thicket must be done very carefully in order to maintain full compliance with the law.

Physical Environment

Other factors that influence international trading activities are related to the physical environment. Natural physical features, such as mountains and rivers, and human-made structures, such as bridges and roads, can have an impact on international trading activities. For example, a large number of potential customers may live in a country where natural physical barriers, such as mountains and rivers, make getting the product to market nearly impossible.

WORLD TRADE ORGANIZATIONS AND AGREEMENTS

After World War II, the world's leading nations wanted to create a permanent organization that would help foster world trade. Such an organization came into being in 1947 when representatives from the United States and twenty-three other nations signed the document creating the General Agreement on Tariffs and Trade (GATT), which now includes more than one hundred countries as signatories. The threefold purpose of GATT was to (1) foster equal, nondiscriminatory treatment for all member nations; (2) promote the reduction of tariffs by multilateral negotiations; and (3) foster the elimination of import quotas. GATT nations meet periodically to review progress toward established objectives and to set new goals that member countries want to achieve. The goals and objectives of GATT vary and change over time as trade issues evolve based on domestic and world economies.

Likewise, representatives from Belgium, Denmark, France, Germany, Greece, Ireland, Italy, Luxembourg, the Netherlands, Portugal, Spain, and the United Kingdom came together to form the European Economic Community (EEC)-sometimes called the Common Market-in 1958. The purpose of the EEC was to create equal and fair tariffs for all of the nations in the organization so that trade could flourish in Europe. The EEC has generally been regarded as successful.

The United States and Canada signed the U.S. Canadian Free Trade Agreement in 1989, which provided for the removal of all trade barriers between the two countries-such as tariffs, quotas, or other trade restrictions-within a ten-year period. This act helped promote even more trade between the two countries, thus further strengthening an already strong trade relationship.

The United States, Canada, and Mexico signed the North American Free Trade Agreement (NAFTA) in 1994 in order to create a free-trade zone among the three countries. Leaders of these three countries realized that a large North American free-trade zone could compete effectively against the EEC and other trading blocs that might develop in the future. This competitive factor was a driving force in the nations' signing of the agreement, each believing that, over the long run, all three would benefit from the agreement. In addition to feeling the impact of trade agreements and trade organizations per se, international trade is affected more indirectly by the financial stability and general economic well-being of all countries in our increasingly interconnected world. Thus two other international organizations ultimately affect the health of world trade.

To further promote trade among countries, the Allied nations of World War II met in 1944 in Bretton Woods, New Hampshire, to help set postwar global financial policies and thereby avoid future financial crises. The International Monetary Fund (IMF) was created as a result of that conference, its mission being to provide loans to countries that are in financial trouble. The

IMF dictates the terms of the loans, which may include cutting domestic subsidies, privatizing government industries, and moderating trade policies. To fund these loans, IMF members make annual contributions, with each country's contribution determined by its size, national income, population, and volume of trade. Larger contributing countries, such as Britain and the United States, have more say as to what countries get loans and the terms of the loan.

The World Bank, with approximately 157 members, is another international organization to which the United States is a major contributor. The World Bank's mission is to help less developed countries achieve economic growth through improved trade. It does so by providing loans and guaranteeing or insuring private loans to nations in need of financial assistance. The World Bank has been characterized as (1) a last-resort lender, (2) a facilitator of development projects so as to encourage the inflow of private banking funds, and (3) a provider of technical assistance for fostering long-term economic growth.

The world has a long history of international trade. In fact, trading among nations can be traced back to the earliest civilizations. Trading activities are directly related to an improved quality of life for the citizens of nations involved in international trade. It is safe to say that nearly every person on earth has benefited from international trading activities.

INTERNATIONAL TRADE COMMISSION

The ITC is a quasi-judicial independent federal agency that provides objective trade expertise to both the legislative and executive branches of government. Tariff information, petitions, complaints, and reports are available here, along with the 1997 Harmonized Tariff Schedule and Federal Investigation Notices. Browse their Recent Petitions & Complaints Filed. Download their Monthly Calendar. They have also recently added a Tariff Database which allows the user to search for trade statistics based upon Tariff number.

Department of Commerce

- *Bureau of Export Administration:* The Bureau of Export Administration (BXA) plays an important role in export controls, guarding the national security, foreign policy and non-proliferation goals of the United States, and balancing them against the need of U.S. firms to be viable and competitive in the world marketplace. The BXA oversees the development, licensing and enforcement of export control laws. Their recently overhauled site now includes access to the Export Administration Regulations (by subscription), the List of Denied Parties, Fact Sheets on obtaining Export Licenses, descriptions of their programs, and office location and contact information.

International Trade Administration

As the DOC's international trade assistance program, the ITA is dedicated to helping U.S. businesses compete in the global marketplace. The site has a number of assistance related work-spaces and information resources, and includes the NAFTA Home Page, the Trade Information Centers, and the very helpful Export Assistance Center. The U.S. & Foreign Commercial Service also prints (along with DOS) the extremely helpful Country Commercial Guides which include worldwide contacts, marketing info, best prospects and more. Their site has also recently added a Trade Compliance Center which helps U.S. exporters receive the fullest benefits from the more than 200 trade agreements the United States has concluded. Also, the OTEA has extensive trade statistics.

Import Administration

The Import Administration (IA) enforces laws and agreements to prevent unfairly traded imports and to safeguard jobs and the competitive strength of American industry. Much information here related to imports including exchange rates, Federal Register notices and policy bulletins, and an extremely comprehensive Import Library with a large number of downloadable files including World Trade Organization Subsidies Notifications and AD and CVD Statistics and Information.

U.S. Census Bureau-International Trade

International trade related statistics, Export Declaration form, AES information and Schedule B, C, D, & K information. Items of special interest include 1997 Schedule B and Correct Way to Fill out a Shipper's Export Declaration, and Country by Commodity Trade Data.

Foreign Trade Zones Board

Foreign-trade zones are designated sites licensed by the Foreign-Trade Zones (FTZ) Board (the Secretary of Commerce is Chairman) at which special Customs procedures may be used. FTZ procedures allow domestic activity involving foreign items to take place as if it were outside U.S. Customs territory, thus offsetting Customs advantages available to overseas producers who export in competition with products made here. Subzones are special-purpose zones, usually at manufacturing plants.

STAT-USA

Daily economic news and statistics sponsored by the Dept. of Commerce. This subscription service also includes trade leads, research reports, country specific economic studies and more.

Patent and Trademark Office, Licensing and Review

Oversees patent filing data sent abroad.

Office of Industry and Trade

The Industry and Trade Office (ITO) is the National Marine Fisheries Services's (NMFS) principal contact for commercial industry issues. Domestic and international issues include, but are not limited to trade (access to markets), standards development and application, inspection of U.S. product imported to other countries, technological barriers to trade, traditional industry development, product utilization, and other issues related to industry competitiveness.

Industry concerns over stakeholder and user conflicts may also be raised through the ITO. Although not up yet, this site promises seafood export opportunities, a basic guide to exporting seafood and more.

Department of the Treasury

- *Customs Service:* As the Nation's principal border agency, the mission of the United States Customs Service is to ensure that all goods entering and exiting the United States do so in accordance with all United States laws and regulations. Their Importing/Exporting section includes extensive resources regarding Quota and Entry information. Also, a very hot topic is their Informed

Compliance information. Check out the Customs Valuation Encyclopedia, or Search CFR 19. Customs has also recently made their excellent Customs Electronic Bulletin Board available over the Web.

- *Bureau of Alcohol Tobacco and Firearms:* The BATF has information concerning the movement of these goods into and throughout the U.S.

ATF Forms

- *Office of Foreign Assets Control:* The Office of Foreign Assets Control of the U.S. Department of the Treasury administers and enforces economic and trade sanctions against targeted foreign countries, terrorism sponsoring organizations and international narcotics traffickers based on U.S. foreign policy and national security goals. FAC documents include "Foreign Assets Control Regulations for Exporters & Importers."
- *International Trade Data System:* ITDS is the National Performance Review (NPR) project A09 consisting of an interagency Board of Directors and a project office residing in the Department of Treasury. We are building a system to facilitate international trade. This system will provide a single entry point for the public to transmit information required by the U. S. government for international trade. The ITDS system is being developed to improve trade procedures, trade promotion, trade policy development, and trade statistics to benefit both the Public and the Government.

Department of State

- *America Desk:* The State Department's repository for commercial information. It includes Country Commercial Guides, business contact information, and security guidelines for Americans overseas.
- *Office of Defense Trade Controls (DTC):* This office controls the export and temporary import of defense articles and services by taking final action on license applications and other requests for approval for defense trade exports and retransfers, and handling matters related to defense trade compliance, enforcement and reporting. This is where you go for export license

information on firearms and the like. Take a look at their Defense Trade News.

Department of Agriculture

- *Foreign Agricultural Service:* The FAS represents the diverse interests of U.S. farmers and the U.S. food and agricultural sector abroad. It also collects, analyzes, and disseminates information about global supply and demand, trade trends, and emerging market opportunities. An excellent international trade site, it provides foreign market research, trade leads, trade data, a wide variety of export assistance programs, detailed reports, foreign buyers lists, and even employment information.
- *Animal and Plant Health Inspection Service (APHIS):* APHIS ensures the health and care of animals and plants in the U.S. They also monitor agricultural products and animals entering the U.S. Their Import/Export Directory has information on plant, animal and biotechnology import and export permits and procedures. Their Export Rules facilitates the movement of agricultural commodities to other countries. Plenty of forms available on their site.

APHIS Forms

- *Food Safety and Inspection Service:* The Food Safety and Inspection Service (FSIS), a public health agency in the U.S. Department of Agriculture, protects consumers by ensuring that meat and poultry products are safe, wholesome, and accurately labeled. FSIS inspects all meat and poultry sold in interstate and foreign commerce, including imported products. Their HAACP Implementation Page provides info and training programs for HAACP. Also valuable is their Export Library which contains information on the extra requirements (labelling, forms, etc.) required by other countries for U.S. agricultural products. The FSIS is also responsible for the U.S. involvement in the Codex Alimentarius Commission via the U.S. Codex Office.
- *Center for Food Safety and Applied Nutrition:* This agency component, the Center for Food Safety and

Applied Nutrition (CFSAN), regulates $240 billion worth of domestic food, $15 billion worth of imported foods, and $15 billion worth of cosmetics sold across state lines. This regulation takes place from the products' point of U.S. entry or processing to their point of sale. Aside from their own HAACP site, CFSAN also has plenty of import and export information, including the very useful Import Alerts and Detentions.

- *The Center for Veterinary Medicine:* The CVM regulates the manufacture and distribution of drugs and feed additives intended for animals. This includes exported drugs and feed additives.
- *Agricultural Marketing Service:* In addition to FAS above, the USDA also runs this service. Although it mainly has information on domestic agricultural marketing, it also has some importer and exporter assistance.
- *Grain Inspection, Packers and Stockyards Administration:* This site includes information and procedures regarding the exports of grain and livestock.
- *USDA Economics and Statistics System:* This library has nearly 300 reports and datasets from the economics agencies of the U.S. Department of Agriculture. These materials cover U.S. and international agriculture and related topics.

Department of Transportation

- *Bureau of Transportation Statistics-BTS:* All types of transportation statistics and information are offered here. The BTS is an excellent jumping off point for packaging, HAZMAT and shipping information.
- *Federal Aviation Administration-FAA:* The FAA site has information and press releases related to airfreight and HAZMAT regulation.
- *Maritime Administration-MARAD:* Promoting the U.S. maritime industry and maintaining the U.S. Merchant Marine, MARAD's web site has all types of international shipping related information.
- *United States Coast Guard-USCG:* The USCG patrols the U.S. waterways. Their web site also has considerable

documentation on vessel containers, hazardous materials and other maritime information.

- *St. Lawrence Seaway Development Corporation-SLSDC:* The St. Lawrence Seaway is a model of cooperation between the United States and Canada and is jointly managed by the U.S. Saint Lawrence Seaway Development Corporation (SLSDC) and the Canadian St. Lawrence Seaway Authority. The current toll schedule and management reports are available on their site.
- *National Highway Traffic Safety Administration:* NHTSA is responsible for reducing deaths, injuries and economic losses resulting from motor vehicle crashes. This is accomplished by setting and enforcing safety performance standards for motor vehicles and items of motor vehicle equipment, and through grants to state and local governments. If you are going to import an automobile, you will need to speak with these people. Especially helpful on their site are the Vehicle Importation Regulations.

Department of Health and Human Services

- *Food and Drug Administration Import Awareness Program:* The FDA Import Awareness Program informs import brokers, wholesalers, retailers and consumers about products that have been detained or would be detained without physical examination when presented for entry into the US via ORA/FDA Import Alerts. The FDA is in charge of monitoring food and drugs in the U.S, and their Office of Regulatory Affairs deals with imports.

Department of Energy

- *Office of Arms Controls and Nonproliferation:* The Export Control Operations Division licenses nuclear technology and technical data for nuclear power and special nuclear materials for export.
- *Office of Fossil Energy:* This office licenses natural gas and electric power for export.

Bibliography

Ariel Buira: *Challenges to the World Bank and IMF: Developing Country Perspectives*, London, Anthem Press, 2003.

Bhagwati, J.: *Trade, Balance of Payments and Growth: Essays in Honor of C. P. Kindleberger*, Amsterdam, North-Holland Publishing Company, 1971.

Bhuleshkar, Vasant: *Indian Economy in the World Setting*, Bombay, Himalaya, 1988.

Bouman, F.J.A.: *Small, Short and Unsecured: Informal Rural Finance in India*, Delhi, Oxford University Press, 1989.

Connolly, M.: *The International Monetary System: Choices for the Future*, New York, Praeger, 1983.

Cooley, Thomas F.: *Frontiers of Business Cycle Research*, Princeton University Press, 1995.

Downs, Anthony: *An Economic Theory of Democracy*, New York, Harper and Row, 1957.

Gerald, K.: *The Less Developed Countries in the International Economy*, Cambridge, Cambridge University Press, 1975.

Greer, Douglas F.: *Industrial Organization and Public Policy*, MacMillan Publishing Company, 1992.

Guhan, S.: *The World Bank's Lending in South Asia*, Washington, Brookings Institution, 1995.

Hauft, Ottomar: *Distribution of Stock of Money*, Effingham, London, 1892.

Hoshii, Iwao: *A Financial History of the New Japan*, Kodansha International Ltd., Lokyo, 1972.

Jha, P.R.: *Agriculture and Economic Development*, New Delhi, Ashish, 1988.

Le Prestre, Philippe: *The World Bank and the Environmental Challenge*, London, Associated University Presses, 1989.

Magliveras, Konstantinos D. *Banks, Fraud and Crime*, Lloyd's of London Press, London, 2000.

McCallum, J. : *Global Disequilibrium*, London, MacMillan, 1992.

Michael Connolly, *The International Monetary System: Choices for the Future*, New York, Praeger, 1983.

Ottomar, H.: *Distribution of Stock of Money*, Effingham, London, 1892.

Paul, Kegan : *Money and the Mechanism of Exchange*, Oxford, London, 1890.

Peet, Richard, Born, Beate: *Unholy Trinity: The IMF, World Bank, and WTO*, New York, Zed Books, 2003.

Polak, J.J. : *The New International Monetary System*, New York, Columbia University Press, 1978.

Raj, K.N.: *New Economic Policy*, Delhi, Oxford University Press, 1986.

Ranade, Sudhanshu: *Rural Banking Adrift*, Bombay, Jaico Publishing House, 1984.

Rao, M.G. and R.J. Chelliah: *Survey of Research in Indian Fiscal Federalism*, National Institute of Public Finance and Policy, New Delhi, 1991.

Robert Z. Aliber: *The International Market for Foreign Exchange*, New York, Praeger, 1969.

Savla, Sandeep: *Money Laundering and Financial Intermediaries*, The Hague and Boston, Kluwer Law International, 2001.

Seligman, E. R. A. : *Currency Inflation and Public Debts*, New York, 1922.

Sinha, R.K.: *Economic Development since Independence*, New Delhi, Deep and Deep, 1988.

Vines, David and Christopher Gilbert: *The IMF and its Critics: Reform of the Global Financial Architecture*, Cambridge, Cambridge University Press, 2004.

Wolfe, J.N.: *Value, Capital and Growth*, Chicago, Edinburgh University Press. 1968.

Index

F

G

I

□□□